All Roads Lead to Rome

All Roads Lead to Rome

Searching for the End of My Father's War

BILL THORNESS

Potomac Books
AN IMPRINT OF THE UNIVERSITY OF NEBRASKA PRESS

© 2024 by Bill Thorness

All rights reserved. Potomac Books is an imprint
of the University of Nebraska Press.
Manufactured in the United States of America.

∞

Library of Congress Cataloging-in-Publication Data

Names: Thorness, Bill, 1960– author.
Title: All roads lead to Rome: searching for the
end of my father's war / Bill Thorness.
Other titles: Searching for the end of my father's war
Description: [Lincoln, Nebraska]: Potomac Books,
an imprint of the University of Nebraska Press,
[2024] | Includes bibliographical references.
Identifiers: LCCN 2024020278
ISBN 9781640126275 (hardcover)
ISBN 9781640126411 (epub)
ISBN 9781640126428 (pdf)
Subjects: LCSH: Thorness, Erick G. (Erick Gabriel), 1912–1969. |
Thorness, Erick G. (Erick Gabriel), 1912–1969—Family. | Thorness,
Bill, 1960—Travel—Italy. | Allied Forces. Special Service Force,
1st—Biography. | Monte La Difensa, Battle of, Italy, 1943. |
World War, 1939–1945—Commando operations—Italy. |
Soldiers—United States—Biography. | Veterans—North
Dakota—Epping—Biography. | Epping (N.D.)—Biography. |
BISAC: BIOGRAPHY & AUTOBIOGRAPHY / Military |
HISTORY / Wars & Conflicts / World War II / General
Classification: LCC D768.153 .T56 2024 |
DDC 940.540092 [B]—dc23/eng/20240814
LC record available at https://lccn.loc.gov/2024020278

Designed and set in Arno Pro by Scribe Inc.

We are now in the midst of a war, not for conquest, not for vengeance, but for a world in which this nation, and all this nation represents, will be safe for our children.
—President Franklin D. Roosevelt, radio broadcast, December 9, 1941

One of the most impressive ways to tell your war story is to refuse to tell it, you know. Civilians would then have to imagine all kinds of derring-do. . . . Of course another reason not to talk about war is that it's unspeakable.
—Kurt Vonnegut, *A Man without a Country*

CONTENTS

List of Illustrations   ix

Author's Note   xiii

Part 1. Difensa   1

Part 2. From Helena to the Winter Line   37

Part 3. Anzio   87

Part 4. Postwar   225

Further Reading   255

ILLUSTRATIONS

Maps

1. Anzio to Rome   x
2. Monte la Difensa to Cassino   xi

Photographs following part 2

1. Soldiers in Anzio
2. Artena plaque
3. Hiking the Anzio plains
4. Interview with Eugenio di Giacomo
5. Susie Thorness and Karen Leisy
6. Monte la Difensa cliffs
7. Anzio cemetery
8. Ruins of San Pietro Infine
9. Erick Thorness at parachute training
10. Rome's Ponte Sisto
11. Rome parade
12. Portrait of Erick Thorness
13. Interview with Euginio Loreti

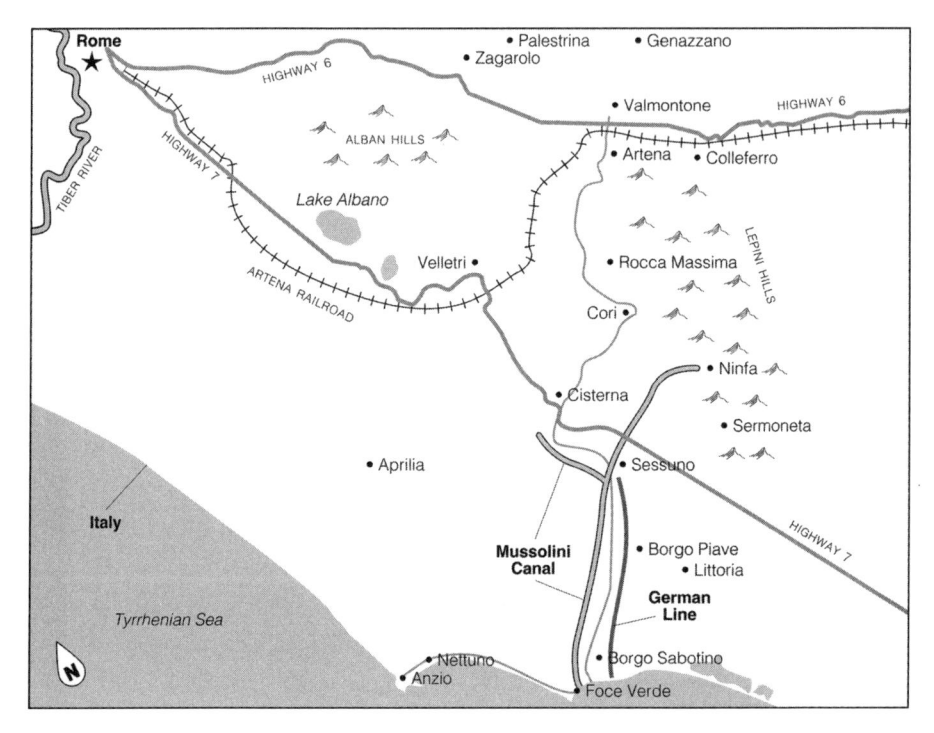

Map 1. Anzio to Rome. Created by Stevie VanBronkhorst.

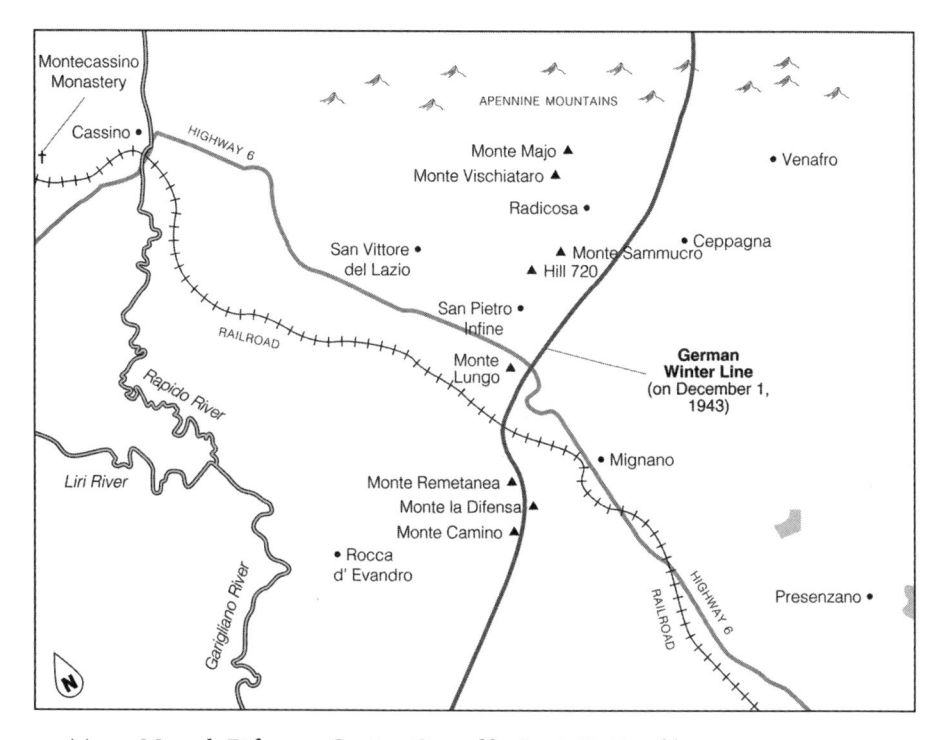

Map 2. Monte la Difensa to Cassino. Created by Stevie VanBronkhorst.

AUTHOR'S NOTE

The story of my father's U.S. Army unit has been told many times, and I am indebted to the education gained from the books, personal accounts, documentary films, and fictionalized movies that enabled me to retell those scenes of battle.

My first exposure to the Force story came from *The First Special Service Force*, a book published in 1947 by Lieutenant Colonel Robert D. Burhans, the FSSF's communications officer, who relied on his own and other Force soldiers' firsthand experiences. His book is referenced numerous times in these pages, and I am grateful for being able to see history through his eyes. That book and other referenced works are listed in the "Further Reading" chapter.

My research was enhanced by sessions at the National Archives in Washington DC, where one can pore over original daily reports from the battlefields and official records of each unit. Research at the Seattle Public Library, North Dakota Historical Museum, and the Library of Congress contributed as well. A visit to the Montana Military Museum at Fort Harrison in Helena was crucial to understanding how the Force was trained. Visits with Forcemen and their families at conventions of the FSSFA—and a pivotal Italian meetup with a FSSFA tour—brought the facts of history to life. The Force's Italian guide and historian, Gianni Blasi, greatly aided that effort. Thank you also to Erik Brun, John Hart, Lori Miller, Jackie Ostrowski, Susan Strange, and Bill Woon for research assistance. Although informed by those many sources, the interpretation and retelling of history are filtered through my own comprehension of it all, and any misstatements or historical errors are entirely my own.

AUTHOR'S NOTE

Visits to the sites of my father's battles, from Naples to Monte la Difensa to the Anzio plains and the hill towns like Artena, allowed an even closer understanding of the Force's challenges. For the sake of brevity and continuity, my story combines elements of multiple visits in a few instances.

Interviews with Italian elders and townspeople I met on my trips to Italy resulted from the assistance of local people who offered their aid, most notably Virginia Agnoni and Ivano Bruno. *Grazie mille.* My recordings and transcriptions from their translations are presented as directly quoted from the interviewees. Thank you also to Stefano Palermo in Rome and to Andreas, Camilla, and Valerio Borghese in Lazio.

Family, friends, and colleagues have been instrumental in the development of this book. Thank you to my sisters, Maggie Kalb, Karen Leisy, Sherri Nelson, and Bev Solseng; and my brothers, Steve, Rick, and the late Marv and Mike Thorness. Thanks also to the family genealogist David Nelson, the family poet laureate Laurence Snydal, and my many extended family members for their support and encouragement.

Reading a work in progress can be a tortuous and tedious task, but it was willingly undertaken by the good-hearted and perceptive Kit Bakke, Craig Kenworthy, Erik Larson, and Jim Thomas. I am also eternally grateful for the crucial expert guidance of the editor and writing coach Susan V. Meyers. Thank you, too, to Taylor Gilreath from the University of Nebraska Press for enthusiastic support.

For camaraderie and encouragement, thank you to Erica Bauermeister, Doug Canfield, Paola del Sol, Connie Fisher, Ted Fry, Beth Jusino, Janet Kimball, Kris Fulsaas, the late Nicoletta Machiavelli, the late Tim Olson, Kate Rogers, Jennie Shortridge, Emily White, Randy Woods, and Joeth Zucco.

And especially and always, my first reader, Susie Thorness. Always ready to embark with me down another trail, Susie continues to be my inspiring companion. Thank you, my love.

This book is dedicated to the next generations of my family. I hope this helps you understand our shared history.

All Roads Lead to Rome

PART 1

Difensa

Chapter 1

May 2009

I stood on the beachfront of my father's last campaign, looking out at the slate-gray sea where the commandos had come ashore. "He never got to tell me about this place and what he went through," I said to my wife, Susie. "Didn't make it long enough to be there when I was ready to hear about it."

"He wouldn't have talked about it anyway," Susie said, "according to . . . everybody." Undeniably true. And yet, that was what I wanted. Maybe I could have forced it from him, looked into his eyes and gotten through to the soldier inside, and agonized with him over the indelible results of his battles. Taken some of the pain away. But I would have to have been an adult to do that, and I'd have needed to catch him on his own turf.

A grainy picture swam into view. My dad, Erick, leaning on a bar rail, two fingers holding the neck of a beer bottle, not quite a smile on his face. The photo had been taken at his main watering hole, in the one-street town of Springbrook, North Dakota. That dusty country bar would be where he might have given up a story, his tongue loosened by a drink. But as a child, I wouldn't have heard it, even though sometimes I was only fifty yards away. On occasion, when a couple of us kids would hop into the back seat of the car for a trip to town with him, the errand would end with the old Chevy nosing into place in front of the tavern and him disappearing through the dark doorway. If the stop went on very long, we might be visited by the bartender, who'd step out to the car with bottles of pop and bags of chips. Forbidden from leaving our seats, we would wait for Dad through the hot afternoon.

"Guess I'm just feeling sorry for myself," I said. "And for him." Susie and I turned to walk up the boardwalk, stepping over a scree of gravel on the crumbling sidewalk. She laid one hand lightly on my back. Could the clues in this old war landscape redeem his memory and help me understand his struggles?

There are moments when the lens spins into focus and unexamined connections become exposed, a flash defining before and after. I had never much studied war or imagined how battles half a world away would shape my life. But illumination began to dawn in me, as real as the seasons, on the occasion of a death. Standing on the beachfront on my first visit to Italy, my thoughts went back to the family gathering that launched me on this quest.

Seldom had the table been so crowded as when the letters came out. Unfolded from a slim box, the simple stack sat shorter than a coffee cup, envelopes yellow against the expanse of polished wood. I exchanged glances with my younger sister Karen, removed from knowing Dad by three additional years, and then scanned the oval table that filled the dining room of my eldest sister, Maggie. Most of my eight brothers and sisters, some spouses, and a smattering of their many children looked on in anticipation.

With knotted fingers, Maggie pried out the first letter, an act that sent a pang of grief through my mind. She, most of all of us, had inherited my mother's arthritic hands. On that day of the funeral of my mother, Shirley, in late summer 2007, the letters Mom had kept near her Bible in her bedroom were being uncovered, having been spared the dustbin but allowed to be read only after her death.

My father's words had not been heard in thirty-nine years. And I, only a boy at the time of his death and now nearing fifty, could not recall the timbre of his voice any more than I might the rare touch of his hand. The old farmer loomed, but he was mute, stoic as his Norwegian forefathers. He was about to become unquiet.

As Maggie prepared to read, I leaned over, and there, in orderly script with sharp corners on every cursive word, were my father's thoughts—sent to his new love back home, who would become my mother—from a hospital bed three states away. He had returned from fighting Hitler's forces in Italy with immobilizing battle wounds, and as he healed, he discovered her. His treks home to the northern prairie broke up the surgeries and months of convalescence, which also were referenced in his letters, but it was clear that his anticipation of her spurred his recovery. He signed off with "All my love, Erick."

As the correspondence unfolded into the air, and the young lives of our parents-to-be took shape in his words, Shirley and Erick became alive again in the imagination of their youngest son, me. Was I holding my breath? My mother's death five days previous had settled a cloud over my mind, which the words cut through. Air seeped back into my lungs, relaxing my muscles. The dining room's glow cast youth back onto the faces of my family gathered two deep at the memory pool. I had not known the letters existed, but my disbelief was edged out by awe at the treasure of ink on paper, folded away for a lifetime.

And I began to consider the mystery of a man so important to my mother, who was the most cherished person in my life up until the time of my own marriage. Dad's absence at my wedding was barely noted, he had been gone so long, but the love and pride in my mother's eyes had completed the day for me. Shirley had lived four decades beyond him, but his memory had lingered in her heart, and the letters were a part of him still there for comfort. When they met, he was thirty-two, she was twenty-one, and it may have been the first love of his life and of hers. I wondered if the travel and the battles and the worldliness that came with wartime service made him more open to love, more bold in it. He pined for her deeply as soon as each furlough ended.

When I read your letters, it seems as though you are talking to me and I surely wish it was so, as I can't think of anything I would enjoy more.

His words on paper conjured his voice, echoing as rare pieces of instruction but also as an overheard murmur of his nightmares or an angry shout at a family dynamic fueled by his frustration at life and pain in his body, amplified by alcohol. Looking back from adulthood, I recognized that throughout his too-short existence, he battled physical and emotional demons, suffering that may have soured his expectation of the future and twisted his enjoyment of postwar family life into endurance. Perhaps he lived in withdrawal, choosing to fight his battles alone and stoically shielding his family from the misery he had endured on the battlefields of Italy. But the tenor of the letters did not foreshadow those problems.

My siblings and I stayed up late with coffee and talk, grateful for this glimpse of family history. The war still held power to affect us all, including Susie and other family present, and it was clear that the letters would trigger more exploration. As I finally set myself off to bed and drifted into sleep, my mother's absence softened slightly into images of a young couple planning a postwar life.

Memories of the whole family together, though, remained grainy and distant. A dust cloud blew through the sparse trees that barely had shielded our clapboard farmhouse. I felt the need to make the landscape come back to life. Erick's writings brought hope that an image could again emerge with him in it, as a husband, a father, a son, a decorated soldier, and a man who left the earth with a devoted wife and nine children on it. I didn't possess that picture yet, but the letters sparked kindling. He could come into view, if I looked.

It was hot and windy when we laid Shirley to rest next to Erick at the back of the little-used cemetery on a rise west of Epping, the North Dakota village closest to our family farm. I thought about the endurance of place and the devastation of time, two immutable facts of existence. You had to live somewhere, and hopefully you made the best of it, in a life of meaning, joy, community, family. You affected others in ways you'd never know. As the days passed, you built up memories, which augmented and sometimes replaced reality. Finally, you became the memory. My thoughts were jumbled about death and anything that might come after, but standing graveside, I held on to an idea that the two of them would be closer than they had been in many years. I realized that I was joining them together in my mind, possibly for the first time, and I became even more grateful for the gift that came from my father writing those letters and my mother keeping them.

Once I returned home to Seattle after we laid my mother to rest, the autumn days whirled by. My first book, a travel guide on regional bicycling, was about to be released, launching me into a new aspect of my writing career. I spent the rest of the year regaling audiences with pictures and stories and advice about experiencing our world from the seat of a bike. Travel, for me, had become an exercise in exploration that I could share with others.

The holidays arrived with an unexpected treasure. Some family members had assembled Dad's letters and arranged them into a spiral-bound book, enlivened with historical photos. Images of the letters filled the tan paper, and I could again marvel at the thoughts and endearments he had sent to his "Dearest Shirley," all in the sharp, flowing cursive of my father's pen. I savored them. And as I reread his mentions of the war and his army service, I became more and more curious about that early chapter in his life. Certainly it was a turning point, in a way that my first published book would be for me. Army service provided a direction for the second-in-line farmer's son who had become a man in the destitute Depression years and had cast about for a way to contribute, to lessen the hardships for himself and his family. What had it felt like, I wondered, to emerge from the disastrous decade of the 1930s only to see the planet inflamed with a calamitous world war? The letters offered bits of evidence about his path out of the war, but how did he get into it? Who was he when he signed on as a private in the U.S. Army, and what did it make of him? It was then, reading between the lines of those postwar letters, that the germ of an idea came into my head. Could he be rediscovered through that pivotal time in his life? Could I regain the father that had been lost to me for decades? How would knowing who he was affect my understanding of myself?

Chapter 2

December 1943

The winter sky flamed with exploding artillery, but that could not warm the stiff joints of the commandos as they coiled for the attack. Crouched on narrow ledges nearly three thousand feet above the valley floor, the soldiers of the First Special Service Force (FSSF) were counting on diversion and surprise to shove the defenders off Monte la Difensa's coveted high ground. They needed to crest the ridge and land a crushing blow before daybreak—and before the Nazis could respond.

Difensa, a craggy peak hunched over the crucial highway that led to Rome, bristled with German weapons, which were also in place on nearby Monte Remetenea. The two peaks—also called by U.S. Army mapmakers Hill 960 (Difensa) and Hill 907 (Remetenea), as that was their height in meters—were connected by a shallow saddle. A third, Monte Camino (Hill 963), loomed to Difensa's south, separated by a significant ravine. On all three peaks, German soldiers manned artillery pillboxes and machine-gun nests, while snipers and forward scouts were concealed throughout. Routes up and down the mountains were sown with mines and booby traps and, at the slightest rustle of leaves, were swept by gunfire.

The lead Force platoons waited in the clammy darkness on Difensa's flank because leaders had decided that the best way to surmount this well-defended aerie, whose own name seemed to throw down a dare, was by shinnying up its north side, the mountain's most difficult approach. That face frowned on the attempt, its slate-gray cheeks presenting a vertical granite slab looming over the valley. The rocky visage held little but crevices and cliffs above its thousand-foot tree line. The terrain was exposed to the enemy's view but often cloaked in swirling fog or storms. Scant relief was provided by flinty ledges near the top, perhaps seeming to the soldiers like hooded eyes squinting down at their efforts. But those cracks in the mountain's armor looked also like opportunity.

And the interlopers weren't alone, as evidenced by a hailstorm of Allied ordnance that assaulted the granite grimace in the night. Two in the morning on December 3, 1943, marked the explosive moment that triggered the Force's action. The incessant bombardment to free this crucial Nazi-defended pass also laid a cover of smoke across the hills, useful for the raiders. Already, scouts from the Force's Second Regiment had scaled the cliff above the ledges and discovered a saucer-shaped area just below the peak and hidden by a ridge from German outposts within the bowl. Another team set ropes that would allow the Second's soldiers to climb the last two hundred feet, a nearly vertical rise, to the peak's rocky rim. The Germans clearly sensed an assault was imminent as they sprayed heavy fire on the hill's other trails, where three weeks of failed Allied attempts had originated. But Nazi weaponry was facing the wrong direction for the coming onslaught.

Staff Sergeant Erick Thorness scrambled to his feet, strapping a loaded pack onto his back and shaking off the soreness from the long wait. The thirty-one-year-old soldier—"Pops" to his troops and the man who would be Dad to me—joined his squad as, man after man, they grasped the ropes and began the final climb, leaning backward over the abyss and setting their feet flat on the giant's jowls, their eyes turned to the sky.

The first Forcemen to crest the mountain let go of the ropes and slithered into positions around the edges of the bowl. They felt the blasts from the concealed German artillery and machine-gun emplacements that were still firing down the other approaches. They were so close they could smell the cooking coming from the German mess. They were given an order to fix bayonets and use only blades as long as they were undetected.

Two Force platoons had surmounted the wall, setting dozens of men in place, before a crumbling rockfall got a German sentry's attention and triggered the battle. "All hell broke loose!" recalled one soldier, according to the history *The First Special Service Force* penned by unit communications officer Lieutenant Colonel Robert D. Burhans. The Germans exposed the American attackers by firing flares over the bowl, then frantically swiveled their mounted machine guns from within six fortified barriers and began to shoot. Mortars whistled and the rocks atop the mountain erupted. Pinned down, the leading Force company dispatched nine commandos to silence the closest guns and clear the way for an advance. The bewildered Germans were quickly flushed out, and Forcemen rushed in to overtake their gun batteries and even their armored headquarters. There they seized a German officer, who exclaimed, "You can't be here. It's impossible to come up those rocks."

Chapter 3

May 2009

At the University of North Dakota in the late 1970s, I didn't think about Dad very charitably. He had been gone since 1969, most of my cognizant years. Paradoxically, as I piloted my old car across the state, books and clothes as traveling companions on my first time away from home, Dad was much more distant to me than he would later become. My mother, siblings, friends, and hometown would fill my thoughts as I studied accounting practices, storytelling techniques, and how to socialize with the opposite sex. When I settled on English coursework to study writing, the stories of my own family hardships were buried so deeply that they did not enter into my composition essays. I was so out of touch that I didn't even try to dig in and consider him.

Dad existed mostly in hazy memories claimed by me and my siblings. Whenever one would try to tell a family story, another would inevitably say they didn't remember much about growing up. We sincerely believed that—a thought that caused me to shake my head. I wished we had been courageous and pushed through those defenses. Mom went along with it, and nobody pushed her. She'd been through so much. What was in our minds was too much of the late Dad, the hurting, damaged one, and not enough of the early Dad, the powerful, courageous soldier. The World War II fighter who survived, at least, when so many around him didn't. We owed him more. We owed Mom more too.

But having decided to travel to Italy, I was focusing on Dad and his journey. En route with Susie to his battlegrounds near Anzio and the inland campaigns undertaken by the Allies as they pushed the Germans out of Rome, I had him on my mind constantly. Not what I knew. Not my memories. I was thinking about what I didn't know, about him or about myself.

And a worry tightened the muscles at the base of my neck that no airplane pillow would soften: What if I didn't like what I found? Or worse ... what if it didn't matter?

In planning the trip, it had been clear to me that I would be treading unexplored territory, and not just on the ground. I could not square my father's war heroism with his heavy alcohol use and ensuing rage that combined to push memories out of our heads. I wanted to be a kid again, lying on my stomach on the living room rug; flipping through the pages of the treasured history book written entirely, incredibly, about my father's unit; and then hearing from him about how that history got written. Carefully I would turn to the picture that showed him in a training situation, or another that might have been him parachuting through the Montana air. But that scenario would get shoved into a corner of my mind by remembered flashes of a violent kitchen scene with chairs skittering and an older brother crying, caused by my dad's red-faced anger over a minor slight like an unfinished meal or a defiant retort. What did he go through that turned him into that man?

The choppy bay was the color of a navy destroyer. Waves peaked like emerging shell casings. Beneath my feet, water rushed up the khaki sand like an invading force and exploded into foam along the rock jetty. Gazing at the expanse of the sea from Anzio's shore, home had never seemed more distant. Down the crescent beach, a row of piers held the reins of a handful of boats. Behind me rose the Italian town that hosted a small fishing industry and tourist transportation to nearby islands. *Anzio* had been an exotic word when I was a kid. It didn't mean "town" or "port"; it meant the place where Dad fought. It meant the battle, which he was evidently still enduring.

I turned back to our rental Fiat, parked askew with Susie leaning on the door, her long legs crossed at the ankle. My wife's chestnut hair, cut short for travel, swished behind her ear as she scanned the row of hotels across the road.

"We could have stayed at one of these."

"Yeah, but they're as sad as the beach," I said. "Nobody's around." Low walls enclosed oceanfront patios, but the metal chairs and tables were crowded up against the buildings as though fearful of being washed away.

Anzio was the beach town made famous by the Allies choosing to land there on a campaign to kick the Nazis out of Rome. My dad was among the eighty thousand soldiers who sailed in or waded ashore in early 1944. Before that, the place existed as a summer escape for wealthy Romans. And many centuries earlier, the area had birthed a man named Nero, destined to become the fifth ruler of the Roman Empire and the leader when, in July of 64 AD, fire consumed nearly three-quarters of the city of Rome. Nero was not in the city but rather in the seaside town of Antium, later to be known as Anzio, his hometown. Already hated by many for his despotic rule, Nero became known as the man who "fiddled while Rome burned," thought to be a colloquial statement of his ineffective leadership. The fire did, however, cause him to enact strict building codes in the city.

Anzio's port, hotels, and shopping streets offered scant clues to its history. There were few cobblestone streets and no marbled, columned temples. The war's devastation had stripped it of its past. The plate glass of its paneled storefronts reflected sea and sky and did not invite our browsing. On a windblown spring weekday, few people were on the streets or on the water. Crumbling patches in the cement sidewalk next to our car reminded me that the salt air that stung my sinuses also cut relentlessly into its surroundings. Even the air, it seemed, wanted Anzio to fade away.

A fishing boat, peeling paint obscuring its name, motored toward the docks, its net in a heap on the deck. Its black smoke echoed my thoughts. As I stood staring at the harbor, color washed from the scene as I conjured photographic images of the wartime landing: clouds of black diesel billowing from hulking docked ships, blocky landing craft hauled up on the beach in a long line, smoke rising from craters made by enemy bombs, and lines of men digging their heels into the sand as they strained to cross the beach to the relative safety of the rubble that had been waterfront property.

This was where my father's last campaign began. I considered my family's next generation, who had never met their grandfather and were even more removed than me from the stories and struggles of his massive war.

At Museo Dello Sbarco di Anzio, the Anzio Beachhead Museum, glass cases had been shoehorned into a warren of basement rooms in the town's crumbling city hall. Peering through a layer of dust, I was shocked by a familiar sight. On the shoulder of an olive-drab uniform draped over a mannequin, a red arrowhead lay stitched onto the fabric. In white lettering within the patch were "USA" horizontally near the tip and "Canada" vertically below. I stepped back to get a better angle through the glass. It was the first time I had seen my father's FSSF uniform outside of his bedroom closet. The mannequin was kitted out by the tools of the commando's trade, most prominently a blue-barreled rifle and a dagger in a leather scabbard. Above the display hung the movie poster for *The Devil's Brigade*, lettered in Italian with a Technicolor battle depiction of the Force's ascension to history at Monte la Difensa.

I looked to Susie and guided her through the artifacts of my father's unit and the Hollywood story told of their escapades. But as we examined more of the battle history in case after case, words disappeared into the dust. We left the museum with its cobbled-together mementos and drove out of Anzio to the American military cemetery a few miles inland.

Crushed gravel echoed under our feet on the long walk from the entrance, past a parade lawn and reflecting pool, to the memorial building at the center of the cemetery. Arcing through an expanse of green grass on each side of the path were white crosses in precise rows, broken up by mature trees, also marching in line. I found myself taking deeper breaths as I looked out across three thousand crosses in their green setting under the blue sky. Manicured trees, their lower limbs pruned away so only the high canopy remained, sheltered the graves and framed the long vista.

Walking up the white marble steps of the memorial building, I heard a sound behind me and turned to look. I decided the man stepping out of the golf cart must be the facility's director, whom I had asked to see.

"Buon giorno," I offered politely but was surprised with the return.

"Hello, what can I do for ya?" That most American greeting was delivered in a loud, clipped New Jersey accent.

I walked down the steps to shake hands with the burly man in the golf shirt, squinting a bit at the sun reflecting off the marble.

"My father fought at Anzio," I said. "Of course, he didn't die in Italy, so he isn't buried here"—I gestured to the crosses—"or I wouldn't be here."

The director nodded.

"I hoped to gather some more information about where he fought."

"There were so many battles here," said the director. "Which unit was your father in?"

"The First Special Service Force."

The director's head performed a move I had only seen in movies, the "double take," swiveling twice quickly to look at me. I knew Dad's unit had been famous. There was the movie. I knew of a couple of books. But history books teased out even the most obscure details of World War II, and popular culture still brought its stories to page, stage, and screen. And I wasn't really a history buff. I knew the Force was specialized and had been decorated, but I was surprised at his recognition. He seemed surprised by my naivete.

"When you're done here," he pointed to the memorial building, "come back to the office. I'll pull out some things to show you."

I climbed the wide steps and passed under six fluted pillars into a courtyard at the heart of the memorial where Susie was pondering a map that commanded a wall. My eyes calmed down under the shade of the open-sided building. The mural cut into the marble wall flanked by two pillars showed—in bas relief that highlighted the topography bordering the farming plains of Anzio—all the Allied battle routes of the nearly half-year campaign in early 1944. It was labeled the Rome-Arno campaign, and lower on the map were the snaking lines showing the Naples-Foggia campaign that preceded it, beginning on the island of Sicily. I stood in silence, tracking intersecting arrows that bled over the blue rivers and green hills. All pointed north, toward Rome.

We stepped into the cemetery office building, American flags and military insignia bringing color and stature to the small reception area. The cemetery's history and significance spoke to the effort of those lying under the crosses. That land was deeded in perpetuity to the United States after the war in gratitude from the Italian people. A British cemetery, created in the same way, sat a few miles north. They were places where soldiers' bodies could rest in the land where they fought, and families could visit the ones who were not able to be returned home. Due to the extensive loss of life from the drawn-out campaign, the Sicily-Rome American Cemetery and Memorial became

America's second largest of its kind; the only one bigger would be created on the banks of the English Channel at Normandy, the site of the D-Day invasion, the decisive turning point for World War II in Europe.

The director ushered us into his office, walls plated with photos of visiting dignitaries. He spoke casually across a clean desk as we relaxed into our chairs. We focused on maps he laid out that showed the location of various army units arrayed against the German front lines. In one area along a winding waterway, a series of boxed arrows were labeled "FSS." That, he said, was the Force. The map's lines, rows of Xs, and cryptic writing swam before my sight. I waited while he tried, first with a computer database and then with record books, to look up details of my father's service. He found nothing, so I told him the bits of family lore that were the basis of my curiosity.

"Dad fought on the Anzio plains, but his biggest battle happened right before the Allies broke through the German defenses and liberated Rome," I recited. He was injured in a battle in a tiny mountainous village, where he was cut down in the town square. The townspeople—after the fighting had moved on—were rescuing injured soldiers, and they got him to the military hospital triage area. "They brought him out on the back of a mule," I said.

"That must be at Artena," said the director.

I sat stunned. Immediately, he could identify the location.

"That's how the local people there did the transfers of wounded soldiers," he said. "The streets are so narrow, the mules were the only way goods could be transported up into town. They've been doing it for centuries.

"They still use the mules," he said. "You can go see them."

What's more, he knew the town well. "They really like the Force up there." The locals credited the commandos with liberating the town, he explained, and a plaque on the town plaza commemorates the Force's efforts. And every year the townspeople held a memorial dinner. "I've been up to the dinners. Now I always send flowers."

My stomach fluttered with the news. On the first day of my exploration, which I was only beginning to think of as a search and was not even sure of what I was seeking, the cemetery director had matter-of-factly pointed me at my objective, and even pointed it out on a map. I wanted to hop right back into the Fiat and double-clutch it to that tiny mountain town east of the Anzio plains.

Chapter 4

May 2009

Standing before the ancient rocks that had been shaped into Artena homes whetted my imagination about Dad's battles. But the heights of Artena were as forbidding as the unexamined history of my own family. We had ventured up into the town square, seeking evidence of war but finding modern life swirling around the base of cobbled lanes that rose steeply into the stone. There were historic plaques, and there were mules. But the history was silent. I looked out over the valley below, with its wide motorway thick with traffic, and couldn't find the way into the war. It seemed relegated to the museum and the cemetery.

Artena was unfortunately the end of our brief foray onto Anzio's battlefields, as our return trip home was looming. And I realized the task of looking deeply into Dad's world would be its own stone-strewn hill to climb. As I piloted the Fiat into the stream of cars heading for the city, I decided I should start over. Rather than looking for the spot where his war ended, I needed to picture him on the journey to becoming that man who would go halfway across the world and tackle near-impossible feats.

The brief vacation in Italy would trigger a reminder tour to North Dakota. One year later, my Connecticut-born wife beside me in the borrowed boat of a family Buick, I aimed toward the tiny town of Epping once again. When there for my mother's funeral, I hadn't taken Susie to see the town—or rather, the museum that now comprised the town, since a handful of restored pioneer-era buildings were about the only things left in the village. I wanted her to understand why those letters, that glimpse into my father's early life, had felt so extraordinary. But as I'd begun to do many times in my thoughts, I also wanted to plumb through Dad's world for connections, to tie the equation of his beginnings to my own and how his life had steered my development. If I could just pry open the door to *that* museum and blow the dust off those artifacts...

Erick's early life was, as mine, spent between the farmstead on the hill and the town four miles east. Large farm families ensured many hands for the chores after school and during summers, providing the labor for efforts like "picking rocks" from the fields that had been heaved out of the ground by winter frost or the plow. But a boy had entertainment, too, like fishing and hunting. That active outdoor life was to qualify him for a unique opportunity in army service.

As we dipped into the farming valley that led to Epping, where I went for my first four years of school, I described to Susie the map that hung on our classroom wall: "The state of North Dakota was a tan blob of dirt in the middle of the North American continent." We were clearly far from the center of anything. But grounded in that rural home, my father's life—as well as my own, as it was turning out—would be influenced by venturing out in unexpected directions.

Idling onto Main Street, I pointed at the whitewashed museum buildings, then stopped the car at an angle on the gravel street. There were no other vehicles in sight. Dust devils hit us hard in the face as we stepped out to walk the two blocks that had been restored to depict the town's former glory. "It must have been something," I said, using a term I heard so much growing up, which now made me shake my head with its banality. "Ellingson's was the general store, and C. F. Carpenter sold horse-drawn buggies," I said, pointing at the blocky black lettering restored on the false fronts of buildings that faced each other. There was a newspaper, the Epping *Bulletin*. "And there were two banks!"

Two years before Erick was born, the town celebrated the opening of a new school, foursquare and lined with red brick, that would educate two generations of Thornesses. But what had been a bustling farm town sadly became memorized history, and the only reason to "go to town" now was to visit the museum. "Today," I told Susie wryly, "they say you need to call ahead if you want to eat at the café, just to make sure she's got something on the stove."

After poking at the past through the dusty museum windows, I aimed the car north toward "our valley," the Buick floating over the scree of crumbling asphalt filled with gravel. This old road, which had been the area's main highway in my youth, had long since been replaced by a wider road a few miles north, and now they were letting this one return to gravel, as it had been in my father's day.

Just two dozen miles farther sat Fort Union, the state's first trading outpost, where the idea of settlement took root. The Dakota land had come into U.S. possession in the Louisiana Purchase of 1803, and people began trekking into the seventy thousand square miles that would become the state in the 1830s, and in earnest after the U.S. Congress recognized the Dakota Territory in 1861. It was the same year the government established the Homestead Act. That had triggered a land rush, and the first European settlers to the northern plains surely must have been amazed. The American buffalo—hulking brown bison with shaggy manes like a lion and humped backs like a grizzly bear—roamed in herds, eating the prairie grass and trampling what they left behind. The nomadic and settled First Peoples, numerous tribes the settlers called American Indians, were treated by the newcomers and the government like hostile foreigners. The wide prairie sky loomed over a harsh, violent environment.

"It must have felt so remote when people first started homesteading here," Susie said, her eyes on the horizon.

"Unlike now?" I joked, gesturing toward the rolling grassland stretching in all directions.

The road to the farm paralleled railroad tracks, which had been the means to achieve widespread settlement. Perhaps the only feature of the land more common than the farmsteads surrounded by prairie were the rail lines. Most of them had disappeared into weedy paths or wheat fields, but in the nineteenth century they spurred a settler's revolution. In North Dakota, they ran straight and level across the bottom third of the state but also spread like fingers northwest from Fargo, like greedy hands seeking to grab and hold the land.

The railroads sought to populate the areas around their tracks to generate further income from both land sales and transportation fees. In the mid-1880s, Northern Pacific and other rail companies had established offices in Scandinavia and other northern European countries to entice people to make the trek, sometimes with exaggerated or misleading claims. Immigrants were promised cheap land from the railroads' land grants, and "reception centers" were provided where families could live until jobs were found and living quarters obtained. The U.S. Army charged about, pushing the Native Americans out of the way of "progress." But settlers didn't focus on the politics. The New World meant survival.

How could Norwegians handle this dry, flat land? It was a question I'd been trying to satisfy by digging into history. One answer was a population crisis that swept Scandinavia. In Norway, the population doubled between 1750 and 1850 and again by 1928.

And they just had too many mouths to feed. On the fjords of Norway, only one person, usually the eldest son, could take over the family farm and make a living. That would happen on the North Dakota prairie too, but coming to America, they would see an opportunity for the family to spread out, and they dared to imagine prosperity.

Sitting on a rise with exposure to the south and east, the family homestead could be seen from a distance. When Erick finally set foot on that Italian mountaintop in his first army battle, he could not have been farther from his upbringing. On the farm, the only climbing had been up a ladder to the barn's hayloft, and the only use of ropes was to handle a draft horse. There was no granite, but Erick had built his muscles picking rocks in the field and completing the endless farming chores. The Italian air dense with mountain fog held little in common with the prairie's stinging winter wind.

I paced a well-worn path between the farmhouse and the barn, describing the homestead's development to help Susie get a feel for the old place. The "quarter" of rural real estate, 160 acres of tall grass homesteaded by my grandparents Mikkel and Ragnhild in 1910, epitomized the inhospitable land. Although a few trees sheltered the home now, old photos showed nothing to slow the wind. "Their first task would have been to erect this rickety cabin," I said as we stood in front of the weathered, boarded-up shack that slumped behind the farm's two-story house. The cabin door and its one small window faced north. A freestanding "outhouse"—a toilet over a pit, enclosed in a wooden shed—had sat nearby, I explained, drawing shapes in the air from remembered photos. A cramped, drafty barn had been built to the south of the cabin, with a proper barn with multiple horse stalls and a hayloft planned for a spot north of the new home. From the cabin's window, the well was twenty paces north, and water was brought from the ground by vigorously pumping an iron handle attached to the well pipe. Later, the well would gain a spidery angled-steel tower topped by a windmill to harness the wind for drawing water. We walked past the rusty windmill and circled the weed-covered drive to our car parked by the barn.

In their second spring on the farm, planting was upstaged by another event that made the *Bulletin* on April 4, 1912: "Mr. and Mrs. Mikkel Thornes are rejoicing over the arrival of an infant son at their home on Saturday." My deep dive into Dakota history had revealed that, on March 30, my father and future soldier Erick Gabriel Thorness joined his brother Ed and sister Cora under the roof of the clapboard cabin.

Erick would be the first Thorness (with a second *s* added to the family name) to be born on that western land and would join his siblings in an upbringing as different to his parents' as was prairie sod to mountain fjord. As all farm kids, Erick worked on the homestead throughout his youth alongside his older siblings, and later he helped corral five younger siblings. The family expanded with one more boy, Melvin, and four more girls: Inga, Ruth, Hazel, and Helen, the youngest born in 1926. Eight children packed with their parents into a modest two-story house was not unusual in that era, and in fact Erick would come to replicate such a situation when marrying my mother, Shirley, and fathering nine children in a home just down the valley.

As my father reached adulthood, the Dust Bowl hit, and prairie farming became nearly pointless. The large family, including a young cousin who'd come over from his folks' place because that family was even more desperate, tried to subsist on drought-ravaged crops. Erick sought to relieve the pressure by looking for work and life elsewhere, traveling to Fergus Falls, Minnesota, where the drought had not been as devastating, to work on Uncle Tom's farm. His older brother Ed would help their father manage the farm.

Erick would have sat at Aunt Tillie's kitchen table to read his letters from home. One from Ed arrived as the 1933 harvest was concluding.

"We got all the corn stacked," Ed wrote on October 9, "and potatoes dug, only 15 pounds."

Those spuds won't last long, Erick no doubt thought, *and I know the wheat turned in nothing again. Of course, he wouldn't mention that.*

"We had to buy a new back tire for the truck," Ed admitted, "before we could get the coal home." They had hauled in twenty tons to last the winter.

A cruel expense, but damn necessary, must have been Erick's reaction.

A few men they knew got work at the lumberyard, but Ed reported that another fellow was selling out and yet another was heading off to "some eastern state," no doubt in search of work.

Ed had folded thin news clippings into the letter. Andrew Anderson had lost his wife and was now alone. Another fellow they knew had been shot. A friend's father had died. *Things are grim all over*, Erick would have thought.

"The Moster boys came back a week ago," said Ed's letter. "They drove about 4,000 miles without finding anything suitable."

The Thorness boys endured as the situation eased toward the end of the Dirty Thirties. Erick traveled to nearby states, always finding a bit of work, and returned to the farm as younger siblings graduated from school and, one by one, moved from the farm into town jobs or married life. Erick helped Ed with the crops but also found work off the farm. Just as prosperity began to return, the country faced another dire circumstance: a war in Europe that threatened the existence of cherished democratic allies.

As Susie and I sat by the barn for a picnic, the weathervane creaking in the constant wind, I tried to imagine my father's attitude coming out of those unbelievable times. Living through the Dust Bowl must have felt like surmounting the most difficult possible task, but surviving into the 1940s would be for him just a precursor to a life-changing, debilitating endeavor.

Chapter 5
December 1943

When the fog at dawn drifted in and then rippled back across the mountainous Italian landscape like a billowing curtain, the features of Difensa's crest were revealed. Erick's glimpses of the open field beyond his position among the perimeter of boulders would have got him thinking defensively. *We'll need to set covering fire for anybody to get across this battleground*, I imagined him thinking, *and they will need to stay low to survive.* Man after man in his squad would belly crawl from the boulder line under the staccato flashes from the German pillbox. Gripping his rifle with both hands and slipping between rocks during a dark moment, Erick would lean heavily on his elbows while creeping forward, knees and boots propelling first one side of his body, then the other. Before him, barely visible below his helmet brim, was the rising ridge. He would need the bayonet fixed to the muzzle of his rifle—and maybe even the commando's best friend, his V-42 double-sided stiletto knife strapped to his leg—when he reached the next promontory.

The battle was the culmination of more than a year of training and transport to bring Erick's unit into its first engagement with the German enemy. The trip to this mountaintop began with an order on November 22 that placed the FSSF under the command of the U.S. Fifth Army, which attached the Force to the Texas Division, the Thirty-Sixth Infantry. "You will fight for the Mignano Gap," they were told. "You will punch through Germany's Winter Line fortifications."

Nazi infantrymen were sequestered among the granite hilltops all across the Camino hill mass, which included the Mignano objective. Their defenses shielded the network of trails that allowed them to move about undetected. But it was the gap below Monte la Difensa that fueled the efforts of both sides. Briefings with maps and aerial photographs had educated the Force from its safe bivouac near Naples. As long as the Germans could control the high ground of Difensa, Force fighters were shown, the Allies would be prevented from passage along Highway 6, which shot through the Mignano Gap and bisected the Liri Valley on its way to Rome. If—when—the gap was breached, the path to the Eternal City took the Allies through the second line of German defenses, drawn in arcs across the topographical map laid out by the intelligence corps. More hill fighting would be necessary all along the foothills that edged the highway, but only at Mignano was there such an impervious obstacle. Any Allied advance would encounter a deadly hailstorm from armaments on Difensa.

A Force scouting team had been sent forward to observe the fighting already underway on Difensa, as the commandos were being injected into the midst of Operation Raincoat. Previous attempts, most recently a twelve-day campaign that had just ground to a halt due to punishing Allied casualties, had merely earned the fighters positions at the base of the mass of Difensa and its two adjoining peaks, Remetenea and Camino, and at great cost. Force scouts reported that dead American soldiers lay along Difensa's trails, unrecoverable due to persistent enemy fire. Some army brass opined that Difensa could be taken, but it would be a three-day battle. Others called it a suicide mission. But the Force's plan was to use their mountain-climbing training to scale Difensa's north side. They would move under the cover of darkness and a barrage of artillery cover, while other elements of the Texas Division and British troops would rush the adjoining peaks. A coordinated effort was essential, as one hill could not be sustained without the others. D-Day for Raincoat was to be a blur of soldiers and armaments blistering the hills that shadowed the crucial highway.

Erick's Second Regiment had drawn the lead card for the operation. The First Regiment would tackle resupply, first aid, and evacuation, with the Third Regiment held in reserve so that fresh soldiers could maintain the high ground once the initial forces had attained it. The Force consisted of three regiments of about six hundred men each and a service and headquarters battalion equal in size. That brought the total Force manpower to 2,400, which was barely the size of an official army regiment. Naming the small battalions as regiments was a ruse to belie the unit's size. But as would be dramatized in Hollywood, the Force's strike capability would carry the effectiveness of a much larger unit. When word came that the Second was to lead, regiment commander Colonel D. D. Williamson took a team on reconnaissance to work out the plan of attack. They maneuvered to within one thousand feet of their objective and got a view of the task. "It is very high and rugged and promises real difficulties of getting up even without German opposition," came their report. But Force leader Colonel Robert T. Frederick had reasoned that the Germans had left that side undefended because they viewed it as a "back door" escape route if necessary. "If they could come down," he said, "our men can go up."

The Force spent the last week of November preparing, but the weather thwarted the Raincoat launch . . . with rain. Downpours swamped transportation. Artillery needed to be moved into position, and clear skies were necessary for air support. Ready and waiting and scanning the sky, the Force scrambled when the German Luftwaffe staged an air raid on Naples. The Force's headquarters at Santa Maria Capua was right in the flight path. Formations of Nazi planes droned past, and men jumped into their slit trenches outside the barracks, but no bombs fell. Forcemen were then sent to protect a bridge at nearby Capua that would be vital to the Allied assault and was considered a sabotage target. Two companies guarded the bridge for two nights but encountered no enemy approach.

Finally, on December 1, the green light clicked on, and the Force mobilized. Under a glowing dawn sky, a dusting of snow was visible on the mountainous spine to the east, the Apennines. The strike was to take place in forty-eight hours, at dawn on December 3. By early afternoon, the Second Regiment was loaded into their cargo trucks and chugging up the muddy route, with the other regiments following. Erick would jostle shoulders with his squad and see the artillery support arrayed along their path. The army's mounted guns were dug into the fields adjoining the road, barrels aimed skyward. Blasts shook the ground and assaulted eardrums as missiles flared toward their target at a cadence suitable for marching. One soldier later dubbed Difensa "the Million Dollar Mountain" due to the volume and cost of armaments thrown at the hill that day. The barrage blasted for more than four hours.

But though the day had turned clear, Force transports could not deliver the troops all the way to the base of the mountain. Terrain combined with swampy conditions would force the men out onto their feet for the final approach. The first trucks arrived at a debarkation point near the village of Presenzano at 9 p.m. as gathering clouds signaled that more rain was on the way. Company after company began the march toward the hills, still ten miles distant. The poncho-draped soldiers, their loaded packs appearing as square humps beneath the canvas, continually wrenched their booted feet from the mud along the road.

Erick and his squad slogged along into the night. Allied artillery cut the air open and lit the hillsides to engage and distract the enemy and allow the safe movement of the commandos. As the trail opened into a clearing and the outline of Difensa filled the horizon ahead, one fellow observed, "The whole mountain is on fire." Purple blooms of exploding ordnance grazed the upper ridges, and some billowed into mushrooms of flames. Erick's unit chugged forward, the silence broken only by the warning of a hazard or the grunt or curse triggered by the trail conditions. Halfway through the night, they crossed the lowest point in the valley. With their ascent in sight, they splashed through a creek hidden in dense underbrush. A line of Force squads followed, packing in supplies, ammunition, and aid-station gear and marshaling litter bearers and reinforcements. They hiked deep into the night, and by 3 a.m. they had reached the ridges on Difensa's southeast side to begin a switchback climb along the slopes. Their ascent would bring them to an area at the top of the tree line sheltered by scrub pine, which they attained just before the break of dawn. "Doff your packs and get low," they were told. They would spread out under the tree canopy for cover and wait for nightfall to make their final advance.

The day cleared and warmed, allowing the soldiers to dry their clothes and gear. Erick sat with his platoon on the woodland understory, their backs against slender tree trunks. They ate K rations, cleaned their rifles, and passed a honing stone among themselves to sharpen their specially made two-sided daggers pulled from their leather leg scabbards, which some strapped to their calves rather than attaching them to their belts. An attitude of patient waiting emanated from their matter-of-fact commander and continued through Frederick's officers, so it was mirrored by the men down to their newest recruit. No matter the rank, Frederick saw in each man his equal and expected performance that would meet up to his own effort. Nobody would slack, and no one would be left behind. Every man thus expected this attitude of professionalism among the rest, and it created camaraderie that ran deep. The Force was well trained—mentally and physically. Trust and confidence vanquished the battlefield conditions and squelched doubt about the difficulty of their undertaking.

As darkness returned to cover their movements, they began the final climb. Frederick took the lead, turning to his second-in-command Colonel Paul Adams, who would manage the continual advance from their position, and saying casually, "Look after things, Paul." Soldiers stepped into a line, geared up from camouflaged helmets to high-laced parachute boots. Each shouldered a load of weapons, extra ammunition, and the bedrolls, half tents, wool clothes, and rations that were intended to allow them to remain in place and defend the hilltop once it had been conquered until reinforcements could relieve them. They knew the plan was audacious. *Allied fighters have been assaulting this hill for weeks from all other approaches*, Erick must have thought. *We have only this one shot to make this work.* Angling up the ridges to the mountain's north side, the men hugged a steep trail, using handholds along with ropes preset by scouts to steady their loads and remain in position. The last one thousand feet to a set of destination ledges beneath Difensa's crown was all rope work, with the men leaning their bodies away from the sixty-to-seventy-degree slope. Hand over hand, feet braced against the stone, and fingers stiffening in another freezing rain, the first companies advanced to the narrow ledges by midnight, where they wedged themselves into resting spots to wait for the battle signal.

At 2 a.m. the cacophony of Allied artillery shattered the night and gave the Forcemen their wake-up call. The first men began their final ascent. Erick's platoon waited for the signal. He would be in the second wave, going up with Frederick's command group. One after another, they gripped the ropes and began the climb. A barrage of Allied bombs cratered the hilltop beyond the basin where the first Force soldiers had assembled to deploy across an open field beneath the peak. Once alerted to the presence of a foe that had come up the mountain's "impossible" side, the Germans peppered the Force zone with their own artillery, which steadily grew more accurate. But subject to relentless Force raids and grenades, they began to abandon their pillboxes, retreating into caves and dugouts. When the Force attacked those positions, the Germans pulled back to adjoining Remetenea. A radio message from the Force at 4:40 a.m. on December 3 reported that the peak had been taken, but perhaps that was aspirational thinking. Intense fighting was still underway. The Force had commandeered the German field headquarters, a tightly concealed bunker, and turned it into a first aid outpost. They continued to exchange fire with snipers and the now more distant enemy forces. Mortar fire rained in from Remetenea. Wanting to break out of the exposed saucer that was the focus of the Nazi response, Force leadership sent the Second Regiment's First Company across the saddle to charge the next objective, but they were repelled and forced to dig in defensively in the no-man's-land between the peaks.

The first wave of Forcemen had command of Difensa by sunrise but was spread thinly across the mountaintop, with only rocks and shrubby ground cover to conceal the men's locations. Erick's unit and the rest of the Second had crested the wall by dawn and set a defensive line facing the saddle between the two peaks.

"By the time I had gone over the top," recalled Erick's Sixth Company mate Sergeant L. J. "Jack" Martin of Calgary, Alberta, the first companies had "pretty well secured the top, and our job was to hold it against any counterattack. Our section was assigned an area looking right across from a lower area with a ravine between us and the Germans, Hill 701 or 704, and within range of their mortars and machine guns. Fortunately there were a lot of shell craters we could use as cover."

The company settled along the north edge of the peak facing Remetenea. This was to be the defensive line from which they would mount the operation's next phase. As light came over the battlefield and rain again began to fall, Erick's trench shovel would have come out. He'd gaze through fog that rolled in and out among the crags and, on orders, begin to dig in. It would have been an impossible task on that flinty crust. But temperatures hovered barely above freezing, and at least the effort would warm him. Skirmishes continued through the day, as snipers were flushed and prisoners were marched across the mountaintop. But when night fell, the Germans resumed mortar attacks on Force positions. Erick, bunkered in a line with close compatriots, would feel the earth shake when each mortar hit, craters appearing in the low field in front of him as shell after shell bombarded the ground. Shrapnel flew, slicing through anything in its path and flinting off the rocks. Suddenly, Erick's platoon mate on one side was jolted by a mortar's direct hit. It must have seemed like only a desperate moment before the man on his other side fell victim as well. In the course of this first fight, atop the peak where the commandos would earn a fierce reputation, Erick must have lain stunned by the quick violence that took the lives of two of his Force comrades. Flanked by death, he held his position through the night.

As Force casualties mounted, the support regiment buzzed, evacuating the injured and hauling the deceased, all while resupplying the frontline troops. From valley floor to ridge required a six-hour climb, each man heaving under a brutal supply load roped to their square plywood packboards, and the work went on nonstop. Ammunition, water, blankets, rations, and litters to carry out the wounded were all packed up the trail. Along the line, Forcemen wielded their shovels to create a slit trench that might offer some shelter against the shrapnel. Erick would see Frederick fighting along the line, as covered in mud as a private, leading in word and deed. Combat raged under recurrent rain and fog so dense that visibility was sometimes twenty feet or less. The Germans engaged with snipers and machine guns from Remetenea and Camino. Artillery strikes turned the terrain to rubble, and the casualty rate spiked. Wounded men in many cases had to fend for themselves until they could be discovered and evacuated. "Their groans were agonizing to hear," recalled one captain. "The shells now came so fast that there was a continual outcry all the time." The Force would inch forward during a lull in the shelling, trying to move the front line away from the wounded, who were at the mercy of shrapnel when the sky again and again rained bombs. An injured Forceman discovered one of the many shallow caves in the hillside. With a leg wound that prevented escape from the front lines, he went to ground, holing up in the hillside's opening, its entrance just wide enough for a man to wiggle through. Other nearby wounded dragged their way to his hideout as well. Shielded from the bombardment, they survived through the worst of the brawl. Discovered, they were evacuated and taken down the mountain to safety via the ropes, some being strapped to stretchers, others bandaged and sent hobbling down the precarious trail.

Casualties had been brutal, but the energy of the Forcemen holding the peak was bolstered by their feat: in a battle lasting just over two predawn hours, the commandos had accomplished what had been an impossible task for the Allies in weeks of fighting. The Germans had been deposed from their Difensa castle above the crucial road. Over the course of the first day of holding their achievement, mortar and artillery fire would continually harass the troops snaking up their assault route. It would not be until dusk on December 3, about 5 p.m. on that early winter day, that Erick and his remaining Sixth Company would see reinforcements pouring in to back them up. Dug in against the continuous shelling, Force leadership decided to hold off on advancing to Remetenea as they continued to navigate men and matériel up and down Difensa's path. The effort caused all to suffer. It took eight men ten hours to get a wounded man down the mountain and along the sodden road to a jeep for evacuation. Famed journalist Ernie Pyle witnessed the assault and wrote in his 1944 book *Brave Men* that "the trail was too steep even for mules." Over the course of the second night, as they held the mountaintop, the artillery barrage raining onto the open ground continued to devastate the Force companies. But it was not until the next dawn that litter bearers and medics could rejoin the climb and retrieve more dead or wounded comrades. "That night I was put on outpost duty," Erick's mate Jack Martin in the Sixth Company of the Second Regiment—which the Force shorthanded to 6-2—recalled. "It was so cold and wet so I was all covered up in my poncho cape." Finally relieved at 4 a.m., Jack got a bit of sleep.

On December 4, the battle bloodied the reinforcements under continuing miserable weather. Across the peak, soldiers, finding they could not burrow an inch into the ground, began to pile rocks into defensive barriers. Unfortunately, those could be pulverized into flying shrapnel when hit by a German mortar. And as night again fell, and with it another icy downpour, Forcemen were faced with a new threat, the Nebelwerfer. Those electrified rockets, which the Germans could fire in fast succession from a six-tube launcher, came to be known as "screaming meemies" due to the screech made by the shell as it flew toward its target. Pyle called it "a long, drawn-out moaning sound that was bloodcurdling."

Martin recalled that, as he performed a second sentry shift to guard against attacks by "Jerries," a derogatory nickname for German troops that came from a British term for a chamber pot, 6-2's Lieutenant Walker tagged him and a handful of others, including noncommissioned officers who he named Vetleiner and Sneider (most likely C. F. Veitenheimer and J. R. Schneider, both members of 6-2), to advance on a patrol. He warned the men "not to touch any of [their] own or German dead as they could be booby trapped." Martin recalled,

> A firefight broke out. Jerry had ambushed us and we were yelled at to get out. The mortars started to roll in. We started discharging grenades in Jerry's direction, which just brought more mortars. Vets and I were both hit several times. I had a chunk torn out of my right arm, several pieces in the feet and a small piece just above my left eye. Thankfully the fog started to roll in and we decided to make a dash for it. About 50 yards away the machine pistols started up but we kept moving and soon came upon Sneider lying on some rocks with several holes in his back but still alive. Just then a rescue team from the company came along and gave us fire cover to get back to safety. I could feel the blood building up in one of my jump boots but we made it over the bank and down to the aid station.

Southwest of Difensa, battle also raged on Mount Camino as a British contingent attempted to displace the Germans from that hilltop. Forcemen were sent to scout the saddle between the two mountains to reveal the German defenses, which would hopefully aid the British advance. The scouting party came under fire and was forced to retreat, but their account of the assault's location was enough to direct an artillery barrage, and later intelligence revealed that the action had prevented a planned German counterattack against the Force on Difensa.

Putting further operations on hold until reinforcements and a higher-probability attack could be formed, Frederick placed an unusual request for supplies to his weary Forcemen wedged into the mountain's crags. He ordered "several dozen grosses of condoms and at least ten or twelve cases of whiskey," according to the account by Force intelligence officer Colonel Kenneth G. Wickham. In disbelief over the intention or sense of the request, rearguard supply commanders nonetheless fulfilled the order, breaking into the medicinal stores for the alcohol. As the crates were heaved onto the mountaintop and cracked open, soldiers spread the bourbon through their ranks. Each received only a slight dram, but the spirits lifted spirits, and they were heartened by the gesture. As to the condoms, they were inflated and pulled over gun muzzles to keep the weapons clean of rain and debris and used to contain personal items to keep them out of the muck. Wry smiles no doubt spread across the faces of Erick and his companions as they took a moment in their battle-weariness to make use of the unusual requisitions.

After the battle to take Difensa, Frederick was determined to marshal fresh troops and firepower atop the hill before pushing on. On December 5, he sent many of the Second Regiment down onto the mountain's warmer southern slope to recuperate. Throughout the day, fog rolled across the battlefield, and close skirmishes ensued. Patrols went out to clear snipers and ascertain German positions and strength. The remaining Second, with support from a company from the Third, readied for another push toward Remetenea.

Appealing to command for fresh troops on the morning of December 6, Frederick provided details of the situation to back up his request: "Men are getting in bad shape from fatigue, exposure and cold. Much sickness from a bad batch of K-rations . . . German snipers are giving us hell and it is extremely difficult to catch them. They are hidden all through the area and shoot bursts at any target. Please press relief of troops from this position as every additional day here will mean two more days necessary for recuperation before next mission. They are willing and eager, but becoming exhausted." However, Frederick was determined to finally take the adjoining hills, and he ordered a full-frontal attack across the open saddle in a head-to-head battle. Force companies surged forward through machine-gun and mortar fire that came from several directions in the adjoining hills. With an overwhelming momentum that was given voice in a battle cry bellowed by Forcemen on the attack that one soldier recalled "scared the hell out of the Kraut," the Force pushed the Germans into retreat and clambered onto the peak. By late morning, they had begun to clear the many trails from the hilltops and had achieved secure movement across the adjoining mountaintops.

The British finally succeeded in pushing the German forces off Camino, the third peak in the hill mass, and finally establishing their own defenses atop that crucial outpost on December 7. They joined ranks with the Force in the valley between the peaks, then worked forward down the slopes to the village of Rocca d'Evandro.

By December 9, the Force began to be relieved of duty on Difensa by the 142nd Infantry. Colonel Williamson clambered down the well-trod path with the last company just after midnight on December 10. Seven days had passed. The weary Forcemen returned to their base at Santa Maria, where their barracks had been cleared of rubble and made more comfortable and weatherproof. The Force had taken brutal casualties. Half of the Second Regiment men were injured or killed. To fight again, they would need replacements. But they now could assess how they had fared in their first major engagement. Soldiers spoke of "the spirit and determination of the men on the attack and their superiority, man to man, over the Germans."

After the costly fight for Difensa they had just been through, the Force needed to shake off the weariness and loss. Orders came for R&R, rest and relaxation. They ate hot rations and took showers in the spruced-up barracks. They were visited by USO entertainers like Joe E. Brown, a popular film actor and comedian known for his expansive, rubbery smile. Light training kept the Forcemen limber, but passes were issued for visiting Naples, and daily excursions were set up to local sights.

In the wake of the battle, army leadership commended the Force's action. General Mark Clark, commander of the Fifth Army, wrote of the difficult conditions, heavy shelling, and counterattacks and concluded, "The fact that you have acquitted yourself well in your first action under enemy fire is a tribute to fine leadership and a splendid reward for time spent in arduous training." Major General Geoffrey Keyes, in command of II Corps, wrote, "I am fully cognizant of the stubbornness of the enemy and the difficulties of weather and terrain encountered in the seizure of Mt. Difensa and Hill 907, and of the bravery, fortitude, and resourcefulness with which your command overcame them. It is with genuine anticipation that I look forward to your next assignment under my command."

The Force's actions also caught the attention of General Dwight D. Eisenhower, who commanded the Allies' entire European theater. He later commented on their "remarkable exhibition of mountain climbing." He continued, "With the aid of ropes, a few of them climbed steep cliffs of great heights. I have never understood how, encumbered by their equipment, they were able to do it."

On December 12, the Force gathered for a memorial service honoring their brothers lost in the Difensa fight. General Clark stood with the fighters. Seventy-three Forcemen had died, including many officers who were at the forefront of the battles.

Erick took his place alongside his comrades at the memorial. Afterward, he sat down to write a rare letter to his parents back in North Dakota:

December 12, 1943

From: Sgt. Erick G. Thorness, 6th Co., 2nd Rgmt., 1st Sp. Sv. Force
To: Mr. & Mrs. M. O. Thorness, Epping, N. Dak.

Dear Folks,

It is soon Christmastime again. There is nothing I would like better than to be home and spend an old-fashioned Christmas like we used to. But that is something I can only hope for in the future, possibly next year. This year I thank God that my folks are all living in a country where they can be free from fear, free from want and free to worship as they desire. After what I have just been through I am convinced that there is a higher power than any power here on earth that is controlling the destinies of our lives. And with this thought in mind I have often wondered, lately, are we stopping often enough in the daily routine of life to give thanks to God for all the blessings and protection which we receive from Him day after day throughout the year. At any rate it is a thought that should be uppermost in our minds especially during the holidays.

I want to wish you the very best during Christmas and the coming New Year.

Love,

Erick G. Thorness

PART 2

From Helena to the Winter Line

Chapter 6

October 2010

Italy continued to beckon, as I felt the unfinished business of briefly visiting the Anzio battlegrounds. But with a full life in Seattle, I was only considering Italy from afar. In the fall of 2010, Susie and I joined a boisterous crowd for the opening of the Italian Film Festival, a weeklong event put on by our Seattle cinema organization. Sinking into theater seats, I noticed that the woman next to me was speaking Italian. She pulled back her volume of auburn hair as she chatted with those around her, gesturing and laughing as she said something that I'd need subtitles to understand. Curiosity grabbed me, and when she stopped talking, I introduced myself to her and asked where she was from. Smiling, she admitted to living in a nearby suburb. Offering her name and her hand, Nicoletta Machiavelli explained that she was surrounded by her students, to whom she was teaching Italian. Just repeating her name back to her felt like speaking the language, and saying my own name felt inadequate, not enough syllables to make an impression. However, my mind reeled with the coincidence. Here was a teacher, just as I was contemplating another excursion to Italy. My first trip had scratched the surface, but my travel guide sense told me that more meaningful connections would be enhanced with deeper preparation, especially if I wanted to tell my story and learn from others.

The Italian for Travelers classroom filled up fast. People shrugged out of their winter coats and into the half-moon of chairs facing Nicoletta. Posters enlivened the tan cinder-block walls of the chilly basement room below a retail travel store.

In the year since our first visit to Italy, I was yearning to look more deeply. Reading about the war through Rick Atkinson's retelling of history in *The*

Day of Battle and the less skilled but compelling firsthand accounts by soldiers from my father's army unit had laid open details of ancient towns being turned to rubble and of men experiencing more hardship and horror than they'd thought possible. To go back and learn directly from people in those towns would be incredible.

But flipping through the blue folder of language lessons, I realized that I had no concept of sentence structure or conversation, even after trying to learn a bit for my first trip. *Ciao* and *grazie* were familiar to me from a Pimsleur Language audio course. I tried to respond verbally to a question from Nicoletta when her gaze rested on me, but I froze when she uttered a string of words that my ears just couldn't keep up with. "Non capice!" stumbled out. "Mi scuze!" I felt my face redden as she mercifully turned to the next student but directed a comment back at me that "non capisco" was indeed my state, but "grazie mille" for trying. Her smile said it would be okay. The first day of school was the same as it ever had been.

Each week I bumbled a bit closer to sentences. Parts of speech began to announce themselves. The logic of building a statement became clearer as I visualized myself on a train platform asking for directions, inviting a person to have coffee with me, telling someone they had a beautiful garden. Or asking an Anzio local about their family's experiences with the war. I faced reality. I did not imagine that I would be able to hold a conversation with any elders who had lived through those pivotal years. Indeed, I worried that I would not even meet anyone of that age. But if a son or daughter of Italians who had suffered through the war could be persuaded to share some insight from the family memories—if perhaps their older generation spoke about it, unlike mine—then I wanted to be able to follow along, ask an occasional question, and thank them for the conversation. I would need a translator if I wanted to conduct real interviews and build a story in the journalistic methods I practiced, but the value of connecting through a bit of language effort, I suspected, would make people much more talkative.

"Why are you going there?" Nicoletta asked when I inquired after class one day if she knew anyone in the Lazio region south of Rome.

"I'm going back to the battlefields," I said, "to see where my father fought in the liberation of Rome." I didn't know her well enough to say that what

I really sought was a key to myself through this distant man. But the lock was rusty, the image hazy. I felt my path was defined by something I didn't understand, and I wondered how many more in my generation, from my family to the millions of strangers with dads in the war, felt incomplete from this hole in our history.

I knew that Lazio didn't seem like a region for tourists. There were very few towns of any size, only a smattering of seaside resorts strung out like beach glass washed up along the edge of the ocean. I intended to venture inland from the port of Anzio, I told her, and I wanted to stay a number of nights so that I could really get a sense of the land and a feel for the people. The idea echoed my guidebook writing, where I'd previously preached from the pages about the intimate connection gained when slowly making your way through a landscape. Already, I knew from experience how clarifying close proximity could be. "Maybe I'll walk from place to place." As I said it, the plan emerged in my mind like an itinerary presented by a travel agent. Day 1, survey the beachfront assault. Day 2 and beyond, move as my father did, pack upon my back, through the landscape of the war. Could my boots on the ground put me in his shoes?

Perhaps Nicoletta saw the gears working behind my eyes, because she stood up from her improvised teacher's desk and widened her eyes, spreading her hands as though sending me off. "That sounds like a wonderful idea!" she said. "But there they will think you are crazy. This is not like the Cinque Terre"—those five linked seaside villages up north between which hiked a constant stream of tourists. "I don't think there are places to walk." She promised to give it some thought, and I drove home with my mind buzzing. My travel planning was about to begin.

The day of the last language class approached as my vision came into focus. Cold winter weather had been keeping me holed up at home, researching and planning for our second trip, which I hoped to take in the coming spring. As I compared modern maps to those of the war history books, I began to find the route that could approximate the movement of my father's unit. Their mountainous battle sites could be visited, as could the Anzio beach where they joined the invasion and fought for months in a stalemate along the canals. Some of the historic locations could be seen in the current topography. I shared my ideas with Susie, who was enthusiastic, as always, about engaging in active tourism and having a purpose. It wouldn't be the first time we'd hoisted backpacks together.

But Nicoletta's admonishment echoed in my mind. Anzio would be a hike along the roadside, from one tiny town to the next, in an area that attracted so few visitors even the guidebooks gave it scarcely a page. But in one spot I found a *locanda*, the most basic of accommodations, and in another a farm stay at an *agriturismo*, which for all I knew might be just a bed in a barn's hayloft. It was such an overlooked area that most local proprietors had not thought to provide websites for their services, much less translate their occasional bare-bones sites into English. I need an introduction, I thought, something beyond my bumbling Italian travel phrases, to describe why I was there, give evidence of a purpose and an understandable reason for being the only tourist they might ever meet, and, what's more, one hoofing it around the countryside. I approached my teacher for some help. Would she translate a basic message for me, something that would sound reasonable and make sense to the people of Lazio?

On the last day of class, after many emailed discussions, Nicoletta handed me a printed note and asked me to read it out: "Sto camminando sulla via di Roma in memoria di mio padre. Ha combattuto qui nella seconda guerra mondiale. E 'stato ferito prima della liberazione di Roma. Sto finendo il viaggio per lui." (I am walking the route to Rome in memory of my father. He fought here in World War II. He was injured before the liberation of Rome. I am finishing the journey for him.)

Chapter 7

May 1942

Dad might have felt at home there, I thought as I studied images of Anzio's rural countryside in preparation for my second trip to the battleground. Or at least he could see the comparisons to his farming life on the northern prairie. My research preparing for the visit—where some of my family members would join Susie and me as we tagged along for a bit with a group tour of the larger Force "family"—had provided context for Dad's entry into the Force. North Dakota's contributions to the war effort were, chiefly, the efforts of thousands of young men. But I couldn't imagine that fighting in Italy (or serving in the Force) would have been Erick's expected path when the draft board sent him an Order to Report for Induction on May 4, 1942, two years after he had been issued his draft number. He was to report for duty at a Minnesota recruiting station. Many area men, including his younger brother Melvin, would ship out to the islands of the Pacific theater and battle the Japanese, and initially, his service assignment pointed in the same direction.

He stepped off the train in late May 1942 and found his way to Fort Snelling in the Twin Cities, at the confluence of the Mississippi and Minnesota Rivers. Erick would have walked into the fort's buzzing induction center, one that would process three hundred thousand men and women for service in World War II, moving up to eight hundred new soldiers a day through its system at its peak in 1942. After being sworn into the military, he would have gotten the required medical examinations and vaccinations, then assigned to a training unit and handed a pile of clothes and gear. Per instruction from the Selective Service board, he would be carrying only socks, underwear, a toothbrush, a comb, and two towels.

Private E. G. Thorness—age thirty, a single, white U.S. citizen with a high school education whose occupation as a farmer was classified 3-06.10—was recorded at 176 pounds and six feet tall, with brown hair and blue eyes. Although his enlisted record did not mention it, Erick's ability to speak Norwegian and to ski would have been facts of note, as the fort also organized and trained specialized units, including the Ninety-Ninth Infantry Battalion Separate, which prized those Scandinavian qualities. The Ninety-Ninth was part of the army's plan to train units that could operate more easily in Axis-occupied countries, along with Filipino, Japanese, Austrian, and Greek units.

I pictured my dad standing before a uniformed clerk who reviewed the papers that were to send the new soldier into the fray. Perhaps the clerk had just skimmed the notes on Erick's file, or maybe that day there was an urgent call for recruits to do different duties. He was slotted into not the Ninety-Ninth but rather a coastal artillery unit that did basic training in the San Francisco Bay Area. He was to make his way to Vallejo, California, and join the 211th Coast Artillery Regiment (211th C.A.) for training in antiaircraft defense of the cities and military installations in the Bay Area.

As Erick was learning the army's ways in Vallejo, the search began for volunteers to join a commando group that would be known as the First Special Service Force, or FSSF. The army's adjutant general's office was asked to canvass all training camps in the Southwest and along the Pacific seaboard for men with specialized abilities. The request, wrote Major Scott R. McMichael in his 1987 research survey "A Historical Perspective on Light Infantry" for the U.S. Army Command and General Staff College, tasked commanders with recommending from their ranks "single men between ages 21 and 35 who had completed three years or more of grammar school within the occupational range of Lumberjacks, Forest Rangers, Hunters, Northwoodsmen, Game Wardens, Prospectors and Explorers." Somehow a North Dakota farmer—who was listed as "Rancher" in the prospect list submitted by the 211th C.A.—fit the description. Perhaps his Scandinavian qualifications also entered into his recruitment, as early plans for the Force would prioritize a ski-based operation in Norway.

Force organizers toured the camps and interviewed the men whose names had been submitted to those lists, seeking to fill their unusual requirements so they could be ready to fight in the campaign code-named Operation Plough. One of the three elements of Plough was to attack the industrial power-generating facilities in Norway, which was occupied by the Germans. The attacking force would land high in the mountains and proceed down to the ports by a just-invented snow-amphibious vehicle called the Weasel and by skis, setting explosives to cripple the power plants and thus deny Hitler the massive generating power being stolen to fuel his war machine.

The Force recruitment team administered intelligence tests and graded their applicants. Their one-page questionnaire asked for occupations and hobbies but also, in sixteen questions, dove deeper into the attitudes and abilities of the recruits. They asked simple things such as, "What did you think of school?" "Do you like working with people?" "How much time have you spent outdoors, in what part of the country and under what conditions?" And perhaps the most telling questions: "Does your present assignment in the army give you what you want?" "If you could write your own ticket, what would you do?" When interviewers gained responses like "More action!" and "Fight the Axis powers" and "I would want a front line position in the midst of the fighting," their pen would hover over the "Recommended" line. One final question sealed the deal: "Are you willing to take parachute training?" An answer of no sent the recruit back to his unit.

"I've got a good notion to join an outfit of special forces," Erick wrote in a letter to his buddy Rueben, "with the Canadians."

Rueben was mystified. "For a guy who was scared of heights—he wouldn't go up a six-foot ladder—he got in the 'Air Force'!"

On that recruiting day in Vallejo, Private Thorness's questionnaire ended with a check mark in the right place, and in early August 1942, he packed up his gear and went on his way to Helena, Montana, and Fort William Henry Harrison, the base being constructed for the Force.

Rueben once hopped a train out to Helena to visit Erick during his initial Force training, where the dreaded jumps separated the men from the boys.

"I went up in the plane," Erick told him, "and you know, it's funny, when I got up there, I just did it."

Getting from San Francisco to central Montana in 1942 involved some arduous treks by train, and the trip was by no means taken in a straight line.

The leadership of the FSSF, who had been on-site in Helena for months overseeing the build-out of the base, intended to have the entire 2,400-man force in camp to begin training by August 3. Erick missed that date, arriving at the base on August 14.

For weeks, soldiers had streamed into Helena from all directions of North America. As this was to be a joint American-Canadian force—the first of its kind—the Canadian contingent was reporting to two marshaling centers in Canada and then traveling en masse to Montana. Erick would have arrived in a swirl of fellow soldiers, each handed fresh coveralls and jump boots as their names were checked off, each assigned to a cot in one of the newly built barracks. Erick was assigned to 6-2, which was populated with other farmers and relatable men, like one who ran a laundry in Florida and another who served as the postmaster of Roseau, Minnesota.

Their unique cross-border collaboration and the unit's orientation in the West informed their attitude and were evident in their insignias. They chose the crossed-arrow design of the frontier army Indian Scout unit that had recently been decommissioned and an upright spearhead that was so much a part of Native American lore for their shoulder patch. A suggested name for the unit was the Braves, presumably in line with the famous Rangers, and though it wasn't chosen, the term stuck as a nickname that the men of the Force called one another. It carried the twin connotations of the fierce fighting warriors of the West's Native tribes along with the expected mental condition of the men who wore the red arrowhead cryptically labeled "USA Canada."

Driving the unit development, base construction, and accelerated training program was Colonel Robert T. Frederick, the son of a San Francisco doctor. Frederick also started his military career in the Coast Artillery in California but had moved to the general staff at the War Department. He had initially been tasked by his boss, General Dwight D. Eisenhower, with evaluating the British plans for Operation Plough. He recommended against it. But when army brass decided to proceed with the idea anyway, reasoning that it would build camaraderie with the British, Ike handed the job over to Frederick. Trim and a youthful thirty-six years old, with wavy hair and a clipped mustache that telegraphed his discipline, Frederick was to prove himself an inspiring leader, one who would stand in battle with his men, endure their hardships, and always have their best interests at heart. Those traits would fuel loyalty just as his techniques would build camaraderie among the troops.

The Braves bunked in barracks being constructed just in time for use, as were other facilities at the base, a mothballed National Guard facility. The wood-frame, eight-man barracks were covered in tar paper, roof and walls, with a grid of slender wood strips securing the siding materials against the Montana wind. Mess halls, latrines, classrooms, and a theater were constructed. Engineers plowed the prairie flat for an airfield, and various training facilities such as firing ranges and obstacle courses were constructed. The building frenzy sent dust clouds into the hot summer that must have reminded all the Western men of the insufferable previous decade. The air settled a haze onto the Force's new home.

I pictured my father breathless and sweating through a hot August day. First thing out of bed, boots hastily laced, his company fell into a line that marched toward the distant, dun-colored hills. "Double time!" would come from the sergeant as he loped alongside the rows of men, dust rising with the slap of boot leather against the dirt path. Before they could break for lunch, they were back from fifteen miles at a fast trot, their rifles remaining cradled in both hands and teeth gritted by the end of the march. Beans and bread on a tin tray, then back into the sun to lie prone in the dirt, lines of men creating a cacophony of cracks as bullets whizzed toward paper targets pinned to upright hay bales. And then suiting up, full coveralls in the heat, for brief stints of parachute training to get them ready to deploy from the sky. Erick would barely have had a thought for family or wheat harvest as the day slipped toward the evening meal, which might be followed by sitting cross-legged on the dusty grass, listening to a man describe the inner workings of a Norwegian power-generating turbine.

The goal was to create an elite fighting force in just four months and be ready to deploy to the Norway campaign by December. To that end, wrote McMichael, the Force followed "a training program that, in terms of intensity, difficulty, variety, and scope, far surpassed that experienced by any other regiment or division in the U.S. Army during the war."

Such a program, though, did not escape the notice of army leaders at the time, who expressed high hopes for the unit's effectiveness and were impatient at the time that even the accelerated training would take. Later, the unique group would attract the attention of Hollywood as well, who would depict the effort as the epitome of the competence and determination of Allied forces. Recognizable in a genre of filmmaking intended to chart the nobility of the war, the 1968 movie *The Devil's Brigade* chronicled the exploits of the Force. Frederick, played by A-list star William Holden, dialogues with the British foreign secretary Lord Mountbatten about the formation of the unit to undertake a daring escapade in Scandinavia: "You propose in a period of four months to recruit a unit, half American, half Canadian, and drop them in Norway in the middle of winter. You have a new snow machine. But what kind of officers and men will you recruit and how will they be trained, organized and equipped? . . . But the most important thing: how will you get them out? Your plan doesn't say."

When the recruits arrive, the characters playing the soldiers are rough and rowdy just getting off the train in Helena. Fights erupt, and one recruit even tries to escape. An officer says, "One summer I worked in a fish cannery. We threw away better material than this." Many of the soldiers had black marks on their records or reputations as troublemakers. Frederick is, perhaps accurately, portrayed as unconcerned with potential discipline problems. In his first talk to the new recruits in the film, he spells out his expectations for the Force: "I want men who are tough, fight to win, and would rather die than give in." Later, he defends the exhausting training regimen, saying, "They can rest after the war is over."

Chapter 8

August 1943

Erick was not bred for battle on a mountain like Difensa. Is any man? His farm-boy upbringing surely included unpleasant situations, and he was used to hard work, but penning and feeding the livestock during a blizzard holds little in common with drill-sergeant training that led to mountaintop firefights, even if North Dakota storms did meet you horizontally through a forty-mile-an-hour gale.

Before he and his compatriots would be ready for warfare, though, they would need to be hardened from civilians into soldiers in the army's time-honored way: relentless training. The drills and mock battles and regimented living would hone their spirits as well as their bodies, making them ready to fight as a team and grit out even the toughest day.

For the "Braves," a key challenge began with a bravery test: parachute training. Erick would have looked skeptically at the gear for that task. Instead of a pack filled with battle gear, onto his back would be strapped a canvas pillowcase stuffed with the silk chute, cinched tight over the gray coveralls that served as his jumpsuit. But that load was offset by a smaller, if more uncomfortable, pack strapped to his chest—the backup chute. Dangling from it was a tab to be released if a pull on the back chute didn't result in the whooshing deployment of the silk that jerked you from a downward plunge like a slingshot back into the sky. The getup's straps looped across the ribs, and the combined tightness caused Erick to lean forward at the waist. A skull-tight leather helmet and suction-cup goggles gripped his head, and high leather jump boots stiffened his ankles. He got in line to walk tautly to the Dakota, the Douglas C-47 transport that was to take his group skyward for their first plunge.

Well, at least I prepared by jumping out of the hayloft, he might have thought wryly. Every farm kid had taken mighty leaps from the upper level of the barn that would no doubt exceed the pre-jump training the Force had been given. The day before their first jump, the soldiers gathered around a hammered-together wooden scaffold that would look to some like it was ready for a noose and an executioner. From its platform eight feet off the ground, they'd been told to jump and shown how to hit the ground and roll to protect their bodies from broken bones. *You break your leg,* he would remember them hollering, *and you're out!* He had arrived at Fort Harrison just two weeks earlier. *No way is this going to make me leave Montana,* he would have vowed. So he climbed the steps, walked to the edge of the platform, and launched himself toward the ground like making a quick exit through the hayloft door. The ankles and legs held. At another dummy jump station, he was shown, while standing on the ground with a chute harness suspended above, how to pull this way or that to direct his fall. An instructor issued him the pair of parachutes and demonstrated the cinching. Thus "trained," he was ready for his first jump, scheduled for the next day, followed in twenty-four hours by a second one, which would badge him as a qualified paratrooper. *The brass spared no expense to make us experts.*

As it happened, the training made a significant impact on the unit. Some men would master the platform jumping, but when they got to the door of that transport plane three thousand feet in the air, they would freeze, their fear preventing them from stepping out into space. Still others, whether the training didn't take or just through bad luck, would hit the ground wrong and feel the sickening snap of a bone (initial casualty rate: 25 percent). Either situation would send the soldier home or off to another base; both scenarios saw them washed out of the Force. The only men moving on showed backbone and the ability to learn from the brief training.

Erick stepped closer to the hulking gray plane, then walked up the metal gangway into the cargo hold with the rest of the platoon, a slow, clattering march into darkness. Finally stepping inside an airplane, Erick may have felt cheated by his first experience in this new way that people were being whisked about from city to city, even to foreign lands across oceans. *We won't even get out of this valley,* he might have thought. *They'll toss us right back to where we started*. The flight trainer barked out one last command as the plane lumbered into the sky, wind whistling from its open doorway. "From the jump elevation, it will be forty-five seconds to the ground," the soldiers were warned, "so get yourself quickly oriented for landing. If the main chute doesn't open, don't waste any time, just yank on that backup one." They stood, they lined up, and they shuffled toward the door, hands steadying themselves from the pitch and yaw of the craft. Erick and his fellow jumpers would have muttered to themselves the mantra that had been drilled in: "Stand up. Hook up. Check equipment. Stand to door." And the final command: "Go!" Then, blue sky blazing through the opening, one by one they would disappear, crazy whoops and hollers ("Powder River!") escaping as their muscles clenched with the shudder of free fall, then again when the reversing jerk of the open chute pulled them skyward. Then, "you virtually chinned yourself up by pulling down on the shroud lines to slow you down," recalled Erick's platoon mate Jack Martin, "and as your feet hit the ground you rolled forward to break the shock." Years later, my father would look at a photo in the Force history book of parachuting soldiers floating like scattered clouds in a clear Montana sky and inscribe a small check mark over one man high in the air, indicating himself. He conquered the parachute challenge and moved on.

August and September were earmarked for parachute training, but that was merely one task within an intense period of effort designed to bring the men to the peak of physical fitness. The daily workout began at 0430 and continued until 1700 hours. The men attended nightly lectures but were given Saturday night and all day Sunday off. The regime instilled both mental discipline and physical toughness.

In that twelve-hour workday, Force soldiers would train in subjects such as weapons, demolitions, stealth fighting, and small-unit tactics. Calisthenics built strength, flexibility, and endurance. They worked to a precision schedule, always twenty ticks faster than the standard army cadence, punctuality obsessively required. The relentlessness instilled pride. Obstacle courses and long marches were taken "on the double" into the nearby Scratch Gravel Hills, and the men were regularly sent on full-tilt runs up the steep rocky mound west of camp known as Muscle Mountain. Fifty-mile hikes with full packs were common, with competition between companies for the fastest completion time. Some were overnight marches. "It was kind of tough going because there was blood running out of your shoes, that sort of thing," recalls Larry Story of Newcastle, British Columbia, a Third Regiment lieutenant, in the 2007 documentary *Stories from the Northwest: WWII—The Black Devils* by Seattle public television station KCTS-9. "Some of [the guys] had passed out and the stronger guys just picked them up." Training in hand-to-hand combat was led by a legendary Irishman, Dermot Michael O'Neill, on loan from the Office of Strategic Services (OSS), the nation's short-lived first intelligence agency, which deployed secret agents to sabotage enemy efforts. Prior to the OSS, O'Neill had been in service in Asia, and he taught the men a lethal "kick and poke" attack that was based on karate, jujitsu, and trick fighting.

The men were to qualify on all manner of weapons, from pistols and bayonets to submachine guns and hand grenades, light mortars, and flamethrowers. In the fall the camp received a shipment of the Johnson light machine gun and a new shouldered weapon called an antitank rocket launcher, otherwise known as the "bazooka." Each Forceman was to carry a slender, double-edged knife with a cross guard, called the Case V-42 Stiletto, and was trained in effective use for quick lethality. Time from stabbing to death was three seconds if you hit the heart, they learned, but many more seconds or up to minutes for various arteries. Unique to the Force, they also trained on captured German weaponry. In Erick's copy of the Force history book, another check mark went over a photo that shows him kneeling with three other soldiers behind a gun identified as a German 28-20 Gerlich-principle AT rifle. The antitank gun's long, slender barrel rested on two flipped-down legs under the front of the stock. Erick and his compatriots—dressed in leather bomber jackets and billed caps, tar-papered barracks in the background—were studying the foreign weapon. The Gerlich design made it able to pierce tank armor because the gun's tapered bore compressed the bullets when fired, sending them at a higher velocity and flatter arc toward their target. Capturing such a weapon in battle was one thing, but advance experience with enemy weapons was a practice unheard of in most American military outfits.

They drilled intensively on many tactics, such as camouflage, scouting, map reading, and patrolling, which were tailored to the Force's expected service in mountain terrain and raiding. They learned to set demolitions in darkness—a practice that would serve as a key advantage in many battlefield operations to come. Smearing their exposed cheeks black, night raiders faced off against compadres serving as enemy squads.

Such training lit a flame of camaraderie among the Force soldiers and confidence in their unique abilities as a unit. Military historian McMichael noted "an attitude of recklessness, daring and aggressiveness" and concluded that the shared sense of cohesion and "derring-do" helped the Force gel into "an effective elite unit." The soldiers had a swagger and brashness that would be noted by many who encountered them in operations throughout their campaigns, and the tone was set by the intensity at the Montana camp. In tactic after tactic, instructors noted how fast the Forcemen picked up the training and how skilled they were becoming. "In six months," recalled Forceman Charles Mann in the 2014 documentary film *Victory Remembered*, "we had been viciously trained to do the job."

Ah, that smells like home, Erick might have thought when sucking in a draught of the cool air that came to the northern prairie on autumn evenings. Saturday nights were becoming legendary times to blow off steam and put aside the hammer blows of daily training, and he would head to downtown Helena with hundreds of his fellow Forcemen. *Last Chance Gulch, here we come.* Perhaps he'd stop at the Gold Bar, the Main Street watering hole for the enlisted men to holler into the din and speculate about "what the hell this outfit aims to do," recalled Force communications specialist Lieutenant Colonel Robert D. Burhans, writing the company history. The Montana Club was the officers' chosen escape hatch. Last Chance Gulch, also known by its prosaic civilian name, Main Street, appeared as a curving canyon walled by two- or three-story sandstone, brick, and clapboard storefronts. The domed Montana State Capitol presided over the city on an eastern rise, while in the other direction, snub-nosed Mount Helena loomed above the valley. Each weekend the soldiers could look over an array of dance halls, restaurants, and "houses of ill repute," as noted by Martin. The locals met the challenge, he said, in "a city filled with the most hospitable people you could ever meet." They welcomed the Force with park picnics and outings. They bought war bonds in quantity to support the troops. When hunting season opened in the fall, local men invited soldiers to join them in a deer hunt. Many engagements were announced with the local girls, and occasionally a Forceman had to hike or catch a late ride back to the camp, sometimes sneaking back in after hours to avoid being caught AWOL—absent without leave.

But as steam was blown off and wild oats were sowed in anticipation of being shipped off to war in Scandinavia, plans for the fate of the Force were evolving. War strategists had been studying the scheme to engage the Germans in Norway and concluded that it likely would be ineffective and, worse, probably a suicide mission. Accelerated training was producing a unit that could become a first-class cadre of fighters, and there were many Allied commanders itching to put their talents to use. The significant investment was not to be squandered. So the Force trained at Helena through the winter, deepening their skills and camaraderie.

As winter brought snow to the mountains, the men began a monthlong course of ski training. Trucked to a remote railway pass in the Rocky Mountains near Blossburg, Montana, the troops billeted in boxcars as they learned to maneuver down slopes deep with snow on slender skis clipped to their boots, balanced by long poles tipped with wheel baskets. This was the style of skiing practiced in the Nordic countries and would be familiar to children of immigrant families who'd come from those mountainous northern lands. The soldiers called their tutors "ski-wegians": Norwegian army ski instructors, commanded by Captain Einer S. Kiil. They skied with full packs and a rifle slung across their backs. Cold weather endurance and climbing were taught by Second Lieutenant Lincoln Washburn, a famed National Geographic mountaineer. On Mount Helena, they learned rock climbing, navigation in mountainous terrain, rope techniques, and survival in extreme conditions. On the Continental Divide slopes, where temperatures frequently dropped to 45 degrees Fahrenheit below zero overnight during the ski exercises, they had a chance to practice their fortitude.

By early spring 1943, Erick had been promoted to Technician Fifth Grade (between Private First Class and Corporal), and the Force was being considered for an assault on the Japanese troops holding Kiska Island in the Aleutians off the Alaska coast. They also were being requested for operations in North Africa and Sicily. They would soon be tasked with putting that intensive training into practice.

However, armies were deployed by ship to join a campaign, so the Force needed training on amphibious assaults, and they prepared to depart Montana for the coast. They had grown so fond of their prairie home base that the departure ceremony turned emotional. On April 6 the Force, 2,300 men strong, paraded through the Helena business district, and the unit put its armaments and equipment on display at the Civic Center. Townspeople lined the streets and thronged the event. Then on April 11, packing five passenger trains and one freight, the outfit departed Helena, heading east. They arrived for amphibious training at Camp Bradford near Norfolk, Virginia, on April 15. Their efforts in climbing ship-deployed rope ladders and maneuvering landing crafts in simulated combat landings showed off the peak fitness of the unit, which at one point bested a record set by U.S. Marine Corps soldiers in night loading with full combat gear onto boats (thirty-three seconds per team, as opposed to the previous best, the marines' fifty-two seconds). They ended their training weeks ahead of schedule.

But battle preparations were not quite complete. Plans shifted, and they were told they'd deploy from Boston's harbor, so in May they were moved to Fort Ethan Allen outside Burlington, Vermont. In the Green Mountains, the men continued their mountaineering training and additional parachute work, as well as scouting and intelligence procedures. Local Lake Champlain yachtsmen and the Burlington Coast Guard Auxiliary offered their boats for the Force to continue to hone amphibious landing techniques.

Deployment to Europe or North Africa was to be sidetracked, however, as fighting in the Aleutians intensified, culminating in a battle at Attu, an island 1,500 miles from Anchorage and so far into the ocean as to be on a longitudinal line with New Zealand. The Force would steam off in that direction and soon enough be putting their mountaineering and cold-weather training into practice on rugged island terrain.

Force leaders were given the unit's marching orders, even if Erick and his compatriots were still in the dark. On June 26, the Force again filled five trains. Soldiers thought they were headed for Boston so they could deploy to battle the Germans. But as the trains with their blacked-out windows turned west, they realized their destination would be thousands of miles in the other direction and against an enemy who threatened North America from across the Pacific. *The last time I was on the West Coast was in basic training,* Erick perhaps realized, *and I expected I'd be facing the Japanese. Turns out it's going to happen.*

It was a slog across the United States on the rails, with the entire complement initially sitting up in day coaches. Slowly they were transferred to more comfortable Pullmans with sleeping compartments: one trainload at Buffalo, more at Chicago, and the final group—which cruelly had been the first to depart—at Kansas City. By the time the Force arrived in San Francisco on July 3, the eight-day journey had left many of them aching and antsy. They transferred to the Angel Island ferry on the city's sparkling waterfront and, before embarking to Alaska, would spend a week at Fort McDowell on that island, renewing their training to work the kinks out of their bodies, strategizing, and looking out at the bay and into the unknown.

Erick must have found the inactivity to be tiring. They had trained for so long and achieved such cohesiveness that the delayed engagement would have made many of them grind their teeth. Battle reports topped the daily news, yet there they were, marching in circles on a California island, waiting for the go signal. Finally, the order came: sail to Alaska and engage. They steamed northward from the San Francisco harbor, soldiers billeted in hanging bunks eight deep that filled the converted freighters' holds. Their first journey into battle would prove to be eleven challenging days. "It was something to pass under the Golden Gate Bridge," Jack Martin recalled, "but when we hit the open water the seas became terribly rough. It was so rough for the first three days that we lost all our deck cargo, everyone was sick, including the merchant seamen." Men would climb to the deck to escape the close quarters below. Few visited the galley. The seas finally began to calm, and the soldiers attained their sea legs and regained their appetites.

As they headed north, news came that American warships were shelling Kiska Island in preparation for a landing of Allied troops. Their destination and battle plan were thus no longer secret. Ever since Pearl Harbor, the Japanese had been engaging the Allied military in the Pacific and sailing ever closer to North American soil. Battles such as the brutal Midway Island fight in June 1942 showed the determination of the approaching Japanese.

The Aleutians were an area little known to most Americans. The islands hopscotch out into the Bering Sea from the sharp point of the Alaska Peninsula that people would recognize on the maps, its long comma shape stretching southwest off the mainland from Anchorage. Dozens of islands form an arc that signaled the ring of a volcanic chain known as the Pacific Ring of Fire. Attu, at the tip of the archipelago, sits close to Japan and the coast of what was then known as the USSR (now Russia), and a group of the chain's smaller islands belonged to the Soviet empire. The second significant island east of Attu was Kiska, and the next was Amchitka, followed by Adak. The Force was slated to land on Adak, along with many other infantry units being deployed in the operation, but commanders insisted they push on to Amchitka, where the airstrips were located. On Amchitka, the Force would be just forty miles from occupied Kiska.

Erick shouldered his pack with the rest of his platoon and stepped onto Kiska's wooden pier on July 24. Just four days earlier, he had gotten his sergeant stripes in a memo from the FSSF headquarters issued not from Helena but from Seattle. Their hike to camp would turn out to be five miles up the island's sole road, but there were no complaints. *Terra firma never felt so good.* They would end up camping amid the mossy, treeless landscape for a month. They resumed training—this time in real-world conditions—using the landing crafts and rubber boats that would ferry them from the ship to the battlefront shore. They stormed the rocky, kelp-lined beaches of Amchitka and got baptized into the frigid North Pacific seawater. Long marches were taken through steady drizzle. They studied the attack plan and maps of the target island until each Forceman could sketch Kiska from memory. A cold fog shrouded the island for most of their stay, although the northern latitude at midsummer meant it was light from 4 a.m. to 10 p.m.

D-Day was set for August 15. Erick heard the news with the rest of his unit as they were finally briefed on how the attack would proceed. The main force would be on ships stationed off the northwest side of Kiska, with a smaller force stationed off the island's east side, where a submarine base had been detected. The landings were to be directly across from each other in the island's narrow-waisted center. But Erick learned his regiment would be split in half, and his unit was to go in with the second wave, which was tasked with a different approach. While the first wave was to attack from the sea and secure the beachhead, Erick and the remaining Second Regiment would load onto C-47s at the recently built steel-planked airstrip on Amchitka and parachute into the fray.

The first Forcemen were to land under the cover of darkness. As high tide approached in a night described as "inky blackness," navy ships lowered their rope nets, and the soldiers clambered over the sides and into inflatable rubber boats. They each shouldered over ninety pounds of gear and ammunition. American troops hit the beach running and swarmed across the island. "However, they found no Japanese," Jack Martin recalled. "They had left in the night." Forcemen discovered caves with evidence of recent use and uncovered stores of Japanese military supplies and equipment, including two submarines. Meanwhile, Erick and Jack and the Sixth Company platoon sat, burdened by their parachutes, by the Dakotas on the tarmac, fog shrouding the airfield. It would be a long day of waiting. Finally, on August 16 they received a coded message from Colonel Frederick—"Baby needs a new pair of shoes"—that instructed them to stand down. The second wave would not be parachuting in or seeing action on the island, a source of frustration that was only tempered by the fact that their compatriots had not faced an enemy either.

Over the next few days, some Force units would patrol Kiska while the others would break camp, and on August 22, they "marched to the shore and onto a destroyer and headed back to San Francisco," Jack recalled. Erick's unit sailed south on August 24. They steamed into San Francisco Bay on September 1, then boarded smaller boats and sailed up the Sacramento River to Camp Stoneman.

Heading back to the farm, Erick might have told his mates as he joined a contingent who gathered their gear and boarded trains on a furlough. His orders were issued on September 2: "The brass said to report for duty at Fort Ethan Allen by September 15. That should give me a few days with the family." After enduring the cross-country trip to get to the West Coast, not to mention the tedious sailing to and from Alaska, he surely was not looking forward to more days on his duff, rocking with the rails. But he would console himself with the break that would come halfway across his journey, when he could again set his feet on the Dakota prairie.

The Force returned to Vermont for another month of training, which played out vigorously, fueled by the desire to shake off all that travel and the inevitability that it would lead to deployment in the other direction, finally engaging the enemy. The orders came through: proceed on October 19 to Hampton Roads Port of Embarkation. For the third time, five trains were filled, and again they rumbled out of Vermont, headed south toward Virginia. Hampton Roads was the number one embarkation point for the European theater. Their travel already had taken them back and forth across America; by heading across the Atlantic, they would journey a third of the way around the globe before seeing action. *This long trip of waiting ends here*, Erick perhaps realized as the trains clattered to a stop at the Virginia port. *It's past time to put our training to use in a real battle.*

Chapter 9

May 2011

My long-planned return to Italy, to mine the shores of my father's war, arrived in the spring of 2011. Two years after our scouting trip, Susie and I were heading back, this time to walk the battlefields of Anzio. And this time, at least briefly, we were to be accompanied by two of my siblings and their spouses. My quest had piqued their interest, and they were going to explore the area with us before we headed off on our walk.

To say that my travel was on a different scale of luxury than Dad's would be an extreme understatement. I adjusted the inflatable pillow behind my neck and the headphone buds in my ears. Six hours into the ten-hour flight from Seattle to Rome, my eyes were getting heavy. The cabin lights had just been dimmed, so only a blue glow emanated from the edges of the overhead luggage bins along the Boeing airplane's curved outer wall. The seat was adjusted as far back as I could manage without my knees getting crushed into the cracks between the seats in front. I was too big for comfort in an airplane seat, but it was a small quibble over being able to jet halfway around the world in little more time than it would have taken to drive home from college in North Dakota. Cabin staff had come by and cleared away the food and drink, which also contributed to my lethargy. I was tethered to the seat-back entertainment system (what would Dad have made of that?), and on screen and in my ears was a retrospective R.E.M. concert showcasing the rock band's many BBC appearances. How small the world has become, I thought, that I am connected to my college days by a British broadcaster's recording while surrounded by a jet filled with international travelers high above the Middle Atlantic. And for the thousandth time, what would Dad think!

In the video, one of the R.E.M. musicians said that the soundtrack of college is exploratory, and singer Michael Stipe added that at some point the band had grown up and the music had changed. His compelling, inscrutable singing style and their melodies had been inescapable on my campus. Their records had been in perennial rotation on my turntable. But, Stipe said, it was always his job as a lyricist to hear the music as a landscape and to populate that landscape with characters. His statement seemed so relevant, even profound.

"Did you never call?" came lyrics over a fast guitar riff. "I waited for your call." Talk about off-the-charts appropriate to my mood! I closed my eyes and succumbed to the chorus. "I'm sorry," came Stipe's high tenor. "Sorry!" How could I have been so shallow as to think that my missing father was not still in my life? Or so callous as to not care, even enough to have just one serious, adult conversation about him with my mother, the person who knew him best? I had squandered that opportunity to learn about him right there in our own home. Looking back, there were years of missed chances. And now I had the temerity to think that I could discover him half a world away. Was this quest just another deflection? *Sorry* never seemed like a less adequate word.

Strapped into my seat with a sheaf of maps folded into my carry-on, I was picturing the Italian landscape I was about to hike, and I wanted to populate it with characters. I intended to walk the route of my father's war and seek context for the building of his character. Maybe later I'd walk the farmsteads of North Dakota again and try to repopulate them, too, with family, neighbors, and friends. I realized that, in taking the journey, I was desperate to rehabilitate my father's memory, but perhaps what I needed to do was to atone.

College was an exploration of so many things, including my own relationship with alcohol. That had begun in high school, when we'd drive across the North Dakota border into Montana, where the drinking age was eighteen, and buy cheap beer to take back home and consume around bonfires by the river on warm weekend nights. I had little thought of my father's addiction then, just a sense of the disapproval of my mother, who would never touch alcohol until late in her life when she'd accept a glass of wine on a special occasion. I'd find her waiting up for me on those weekend nights, making sure I got home safely.

In college, partying took a back seat to my studies and a social life stunted by my low self-esteem of being a very overweight young man. Gradually I found my place with other writers, and by my senior year I was the arts editor of our student paper and enjoying socializing and classes in equal measure. After graduation, I wasn't ready for a regular job and just couldn't see myself behind a desk. I kept a position that had been part-time in college, tending bar at a popular steakhouse and nightlife spot. I'd end up spending three years in a white shirt and red polyester vest enjoying the party from behind the bar, but on my days off I was often with my work buddies on the other side. It took some sober conversations about the future with a friend and a burning desire for a lasting romantic relationship to cause me to doff the vest and pack my car for a trip west that landed me in Seattle to pursue a writing career. And to meet Susie, when both of us were volunteering in support of a live theater company. Our first outing together almost fifteen years prior to our Italy trip was, coincidentally, a hike, although one on a very different scale than we were about to undertake.

In the weeks before the trip, I had told Dad's story and talked about my travel plans to so many people that the expedition seemed essential. I also felt the fear of the unknown. I could see the shape of the journey, but the path was behind an opaque curtain. As I related my plan, everyone who heard it seemed to have a World War II story from their own family history. At first their stories triggered impatience, a feeling that people were too quickly pivoting away from my story and minimizing the importance of my quest. But I began to realize what their stories meant: war affected everyone. Clearly, people needed to talk through their history, display it, and reveal its lessons. They were walking their own paths through the past, and my story was a catalyst. If I could do that while chatting in person, hopefully my writing could trigger more connections for others.

A month previous, as I told my plan to an editor friend in front of tall condo windows at a downtown Seattle cocktail party, she advised, "Let life do it." I smiled at her and nodded as though I understood. Perhaps I did. The setting sun had turned the Olympic Mountains into a jagged silhouette, and the Space Needle's curved white lines glowed in the photographer's magic hour. In that moment, those four words seemed profound. Just go and search, and the world will deliver it to me, I thought. So simple. I hoped so.

"You have to tell this story," urged a pastry chef in San Francisco a week later, gripping my arm as she talked. I was on a visit to the city to research another book and talk at a conference, and I'd made a pilgrimage to her café. We stood in the back of the sun-filled shop, Mission Pie, after I had finished devouring a stew of organic vegetables slipped between flaky crusts.

"I want to be half as good at telling those stories as you are at feeding the world," I told her.

"It's so important," she said, "because we are losing them, our ancestors."

"That is true. We let them slip away without making our history real for us," I said. "And then, long after most of the witnesses have been lost to us, when our memories are only reliable into the recent past, then we get interested." But was it too late? I told her I hoped a clearer view would help me become the person I wanted to be.

Now, finally on the journey, I felt the presence of those friends and so many others like warm hands on my shoulders supporting me but also pushing me forward, propelling me onto the continent like my father was thrust by the army into the most challenging, destructive period of his life.

The whine of the landing gear penetrated my earbuds and signaled the approach to Rome. As I brought my seat back up and shook myself awake, history suddenly became immediate. I was about to delve into the landscape, try to bring decades-old events to life, and pry up clues about my father through his war. It had been the pivotal point in his life, and I wondered if this would be the same for me. He went into the war as a single man, an untraveled farmer, a survivor of the Depression era, an older-than-average soldier. He emerged from his battles a very different man, changed irrevocably by what he had seen and done, and yet he started over, married, fathered a large family, and sought out a new life. I had never—yet, anyway—experienced such an arc of life and thought it was unlikely to happen to me. But I was eager to get on the ground; into the trenches, metaphorically; and back to that Anzio beachhead. From there, I would seek the world through the eyes of my father.

Chapter 10

October 1943

On October 21, 1943, the Force arrived at Camp Patrick Henry, near the port city of Hampton Roads, Virginia, for transport to Europe.

As a farm boy in landlocked North Dakota, Erick had never spent any time in a boat, much less tackled water transfers to a ship, but his service was full of new experiences. He would have grabbed the rope ladder like he was climbing onto a tractor to start plowing and hauled himself up onto the deck of a ship as though launching into the bed of a farm truck. Swimming had been limited to the wide spot of a lazy river, but the rigors of cold, salty seawater would have just woken him to the serious purpose they were undertaking. A man would grab his arm if he faltered in that unfamiliar terrain, and he would do the same for the next. That was the Force way, drilled into them from Helena and back. He knew it was why the Force could break those time records. But the teamwork and closeness soon would be challenged as they headed for battle. The confident soldiers also would need to steel themselves for the pain of loss. Not all the men would be on the ships home.

There was little time to ponder their situation. From a temporary camp, the Force moved to an embarkation area at the Hampton Roads port, where the *Empress of Scotland* loomed over the army pier. Marshaling on the dock on the morning of Tuesday, October 26, Erick and his mates would need to crane their necks to take in the grand vessel. Approaching the pier, they could see the massive rigging that cut the sky apart. Masts both fore and aft spiderwebbed among three towering smokestacks. Along much of its six-hundred-foot hull—painted a dull gray to disappear into an ocean mist—rows of portals revealed many of the eight stacked decks. As the soldiers crowded toward the gangplank, equipment was shoved up ramps through yawning cargo doors and lowered from overhead cranes into the hold. Erick set his feet onto the ramp that would feed him and his mates into the center of the ship. They tramped through passageways lined with paneling and polished wood. Meant for passengers in evening dress, they were narrow for soldiers shouldering full packs and weapons.

The ocean liner was to transport a broad assemblage into the fray. Along with the entire cadre of Forcemen were three thousand replacements for other units, known as "casuals," and two companies of WACs, the Women's Army Corps. Only months earlier had the WACs been converted to active duty from status as "auxiliary" units, so now they would be serving alongside male soldiers, although not in battle. Enlisted men were sent to the lower decks, with the WACs and officers directed to the upper decks. Men of the Force were not just any passengers, though. They were on active duty during the crossing—the Force Maintenance Company would man the multiple deck-mounted antiaircraft guns around the clock—so the unit was assigned an upper deck.

What time is dinner with the captain? Erick might have quipped to his mates. For its era, the passenger ship *Empress of Scotland* was the ultimate in comfortable sea travel and much more luxurious than their Kiska transports. By the time the Force loaded aboard, the *Empress* already held a storied career. The ship was the pride of the Canadian Pacific Railway Company and one of the fastest and most luxurious liners ever built. Sailing between Vancouver, British Columbia, and Asian ports, the *Empress* had set speed records through the Pacific, steaming at just over twenty-one knots. When war was declared between Britain and Japan, the ship was in Shanghai and was called back to Canada. She was retrofitted with defensive guns on the decks, her blazing white hull dulled for camouflage, and she began wartime service ferrying soldiers and equipment to and from Australia and New Zealand to the Middle East. She moved into service in the Atlantic in late 1940, steaming in a convoy that included the Cunard Line's *Queen Mary* and two of the other *Empress* liners, *Britain* and *Canada*. The *Empress of Scotland* had begun troop transports from Hampton Roads earlier in 1943; Erick and the Force would be on her fourth round-trip to Africa's most northwesterly port.

Keeping with the tradition of a sea voyage, Erick joined his mates and most other passengers on the top deck for departure. "The band played and the hawsers fell free just before noon on the 27th," recalled Force historian Burhans. The soldiers settled in for the five-day crossing to Casablanca. The ship would steam at top speed for nearly four thousand miles from North America to North Africa. It was accompanied by two navy destroyers along the coast but saw no engagement from enemy forces. Once, off Bermuda, a distant ship fired a "halting round" and flashed its searchlights on the giant troop transport. From the deck, the Force sent a brief burst of rounds at the ship, and the *Empress* did not slow. Nothing more came of the encounter. The destroyers turned away as she headed out to sea, as the *Empress* really didn't need a convoy; in open water, her speed was tough to match.

As they proceeded across the Atlantic, the weather became increasingly warm. Three days out of Morocco, men wrote in their journals that it was summer again. The ship sailed in sight of the Madeira Islands off Morocco on the morning of November 5 and began careful navigation through a minefield to approach the mainland. Their destination was the first of Casablanca's two long city piers.

From the deck, a dense jumble of buildings loomed on the point of land to the ship's starboard side. After days of seeing nothing but open water and slate gray waves, the city's landscape along the shore would have been as welcome as it was exotic. Soldiers looked over the rooflines that blended into the city's medina, or ancient quarter, where the modern version of Casablanca, Spanish for "white house," began in the late 1700s. It was aptly named, as the two- and three-story homes and businesses filling the flatland beyond the bay were almost all shades of white, thanks to the color of the primary building material, a local sandstone.

The harbor cast a very different scene. Troop transports and cargo ships crowded the docks, with the port's cranes busy pulling crates and trucks and all manner of military supplies out of the holds, while soldiers massed along the planked-wood piers and streamed into the city. After so many days at sea, the *Empress*'s passengers eagerly lined up to set foot on land. As the ship passed the breakwater and headed for a long, cleared spot along the nearest pier, a look back out to sea would reveal—beyond the rows of round, linked floats that signified a sunken antisubmarine curtain—a line of Allied destroyers prowling the coast to ensure the harbor's safety.

The piers were forested with warehouses, two rows deep, and down the middle of each pier ran sets of railroad tracks. People swarmed over every square foot of the industrial scene, loading gear into the warehouses or stacking it onto the trains and trucks. The air was thick with black diesel smoke belching from all those vehicles and clouds of dust rising from the dry streets that fanned out into the city.

Beyond the docks, Casablanca came into clearer view. Government buildings and market shops lined the streets. The facades of the grander buildings featured pillars holding rows of arched doorways, their curves rising to a point reminiscent of the draping of a tent. Behind squat waterfront buildings rose slender towers. Most were square, and two of the closest featured large clockfaces. Some were topped with rounded spires intricate with colored tile work and scrolled open archways. These were the towers of the mosques, the religious buildings of the Muslims, and a man would climb the stairs of those towers five times a day to stand in the archway and sing a call to prayer.

Past the sights of guarded ships being unloaded and goods being hauled aboard the idling line of trucks, bearded men in linen-wrapped heads and face-covered women in dust-colored robes shouldered through the brick-paved streets and crowded the tables selling goods in the souks, or open-air marketplaces. There were plenty of civilians in Western dress as well, men in crumpled suits standing in small groups smoking cigarettes and intently watching the military activity.

The *Empress* docked at 10 a.m., and by noon unloading was well underway. Armies landing there were to depart in thundering caravans to travel through Morocco, Algeria, and Tunisia, a hard-won route that had been clear since that May, as the Germans and Italians had been driven back in two years of fighting to the coastal cities of Tunisia and then shoved by force from North Africa.

Initially, the Force encamped at Camp Don B. Passage, a tented outpost near the city, ringed in concertina wire, surrounded by desert. They would embark by train on their trek to another port, Oran, Algeria, where they would sail across the western Mediterranean and through the Tyrrhenian Sea before finally reaching the Italian front.

On November 6 they boarded clattering, narrow-gauge trains that were powered by coal (or even wood, when coal got scarce), pulling boxcars stenciled with their capacity: "quarante hommes, huit cheval" (forty men, eight horses). The route went north along the coast to Rabat, then inland to Fez, over the Atlas Mountains, and into Algeria to Sidi Bel Abbes before returning to the coast at Oran. The tedious journey ended as they passed through the last foothills onto the Algerian coast on the afternoon of November 8.

The Force again bivouacked while waiting for the next and final leg of their journey to the front. Men and equipment were staged at the military base in Oran, where a fleet of 110 new 6×6 cargo trucks waited for loading with the mountain of gear. The green trucks, sitting on a chassis high above stout tires on three powered axles, could hold twenty men standing in their slat-sided cargo beds or a five-thousand-pound load of material. Six navy transports formed a convoy for all the gear and the assembled units. Traveling with the Force were armored and railway battalions, army postal units, military bands, communications companies, and more casuals.

Erick would have been reminded of their Aleutian trip as he marched with his platoon aboard the USS *Barnett*, as other companies formed up to march onto two sister ships, the USS *Jefferson* and the USS *Dickman*. Although the *Dickman* and the *Jefferson* steamed seaward, Erick's ship was not as purposeful. Just four hours into the sailing, it experienced engine trouble and was forced to turn around and return to Oran. They waited in port through the day for the repairs to get underway, then waited half of the next day before finally again setting sail on the afternoon of November 16. Nearly two days behind the other transports, Erick's ship did not dock until November 19.

This endless voyage is finally over, Erick might have thought, his landlubber legs yearning for solid ground under his feet. *We didn't start this fight*, he might have thought through a clenched jaw, *but by God the time for talking and planning is done.* Like all men facing a perilous unknown, he might have wondered if there was a future for him, way back across a vast ocean. *Maybe I will someday walk with my own sons on the farm, if all goes well and we have a little luck on our side.* The waving wheat fields of North Dakota might have floated briefly back into view. *This war business sure makes it tough to predict the future*, he could have thought as he stepped off the ship onto a wrecked Naples dock, *but a man surely knows what's going to happen tomorrow.*

Chapter 11

May 2011

We navigated the rural land south of Anzio on a grid of two-lane roads, exploring the area first by rental car. Distant hills gleamed with V-shaped clusters of towns that hung in the creases of the hills like commandos on a mountain ledge. "This is where they fought!" I said to Susie, who returned a headshake at my practice of stating the obvious. But I was struck by the plains where farming had replaced swampland and where battle had obliterated a short history of inhabitation. In this sparse land, that violence seemed now to be visible only in the war cemetery's white crosses on green grass. The countryside was as silent as those tombs.

We came upon a crossroads that held a bit of commerce, passing a combined service station and market that had attracted a cluster of cars, angled in as though their metal grills had been drawn to a magnetized building. The scattered village beyond sprouted utilitarian architecture. To someone looking for history, that setting—boxy buildings, a cement thoroughfare, and a marching row of silver steel streetlights—was entirely useless.

We took hours exploring the Anzio countryside before heading for our destination, the town of Cassino, where we were to meet a tour group from the First Special Service Force Association (FSSFA).

We had brushed off the dust from our day of driving and were gathering for a FSSFA dinner, my first, at the Cassino hotel where our new Force family was staying. Edging into the group that stood in front of the lobby windows, I had immediately, surprisingly, been made to feel at home by the welcomes of members. As I began to meet people and compare my father's service with that of others assembled for this tour, I realized that the military connection had relaxed my social reticence.

"My uncle was the only Norwegian in the Force!" proclaimed Jan, sitting across from me at the long dinner table we'd settled into in the hotel's banquet room. "You've heard of him," he said with a familiar lilt in his English. "His name was Finn Roll." My father was of Norwegian heritage, as I'm sure were many others of his Force comrades, but I was sitting at dinner with a nephew of the only man in the unit who came directly from Norway on an unlikely path to serve in the U.S. military.

Finn was certainly one of the more famous Force characters in a phalanx of them. Jan, a finance manager from Oslo whose name was pronounced "Yan," tall and slender with a shaved head, offered a big smile with the introduction.

"Of course, I've heard of him," I said and introduced myself and Susie. "Amazing to meet you!" I began to tell Susie who Finn Roll was, before realizing that the story would be more accurate and entertaining from Jan.

"Finn didn't tell anyone, but he and a friend prepared to leave their home," Jan related, eyes gleaming and eyebrows raised. "They had just a few belongings in a small boat." The pair sailed along the coast down from Oslo to the southern tip of Norway, then across the North Sea to England, a perilous and long journey in such a small craft, he said.

"But that was just the beginning," Jan said. "He got himself to America and traveled to Oakland, California, where he had a relative. Then he enlisted and joined up with the Force." I pictured this young Norwegian in the Bay Area's army facilities at the same time as my father and even imagined they'd met, discovered a shared heritage, and had an exchange in the old language. Surely the Force recruiters would have jumped at the opportunity to add this asset to their ranks as they contemplated Operation Plough.

"My father was in the same area for basic training," I told Jan, "and that's where the Force recruited him. I wonder if they met each other then. Maybe even traveled together to Montana!" The coincidence would have been too unreal. Jan just beamed at me from across the table.

Finn Roll did indeed become an integral member of the Force, rising to captain and serving in the headquarters detachment as an intelligence officer. He performed with distinction throughout the war and remained in the U.S. Army for a long career. In his native land, "he was honored as a hero," Jan said proudly. "His exploits were legendary!"

I looked to my left, fully expecting another revelation from the next table mates we were to meet. Although it didn't quite materialize, we engaged in conversation with a gracious couple from Ontario, Murray and Maureen. They were the epitome of Canadian politeness. Murray's father was a radio operator in the headquarters detachment and, as such, no doubt worked closely with Finn. As we talked, he was handed a sheaf of papers from another member of the FSSFA, who evidently had done research on his behalf. Glancing at his photocopies of army records and unit reports, I realized there was a long path of discovery in front of me.

The villages around Cassino appeared heavily influenced by the nearby, and legendary, Montecassino Monastery, which itself had a tragic war story, being bombed by the Allies nearly into oblivion and then commandeered by the Germans as a defensive post. With names like San Nicola, Sant'Angelo, Pieta, and Santa Lucia, the towns echoed their Catholic history, and after dinner we rumbled out of the hotel parking lot in a tour bus, heading for a nearby village to experience another religious activity: a festival honoring the patron saint of the town. Architectural archways of spidery steel were erected over the village street and densely wrapped in lights that cast a gold glow onto the pedestrian scene. The narrow motorway was closed to traffic and filled with people performing the Italian evening ritual of *passeggiata*, a stroll after dinner, often with a gelato in hand and an arm wrapped around a loved one's waist.

We joined the parade through the streets, gelato or *birra* in hand, flanked by a younger contingent that I learned were current Canadian special forces soldiers on special duty for the Memorial Day weekend with the Force families, perhaps making some positive memories that would outlast any active duty that could inflict pain on their psyche as it had my father's.

Chapter 12

November 1943

The Force soldiers, after sailing from the United States via North Africa to finally enter the war in Italy, disembarked from their days at sea into a somber battle zone. The Allies had only recently descended on the devastated city of Naples, freeing it from the German forces on October 1, 1943. Entering the harbor, the troop transports navigated around a graveyard of vessels that were destroyed or half underwater. On shore, buildings lay in rubble, while those still standing showed their bones. Few contained windows with intact panes of glass. A major dock and the blocks surrounding it had been destroyed by the explosion of a German ammunition ship that lay at anchor. Beyond, the beleaguered city suffered from a drained and destroyed water supply; sabotage to its trains, trams, and bridges; and the aftermath of an occupation that starved the populace. At the battered docks, ship after ship disgorged the Allied armies for their trek to the Italian campaign. The Force "was expected with particular relish," related historian Martin Blumenson in his 1969 book *U.S. Army in World War II*, "for the men had been specially trained for mountain warfare," and the craggy heights of southern Italy were in the Allied gunsights. It had been raining steadily for months, and November clouds hung low and dispatched more rain to turn the streets slick and the people miserable in the short, cold days.

After a temporary bivouac in the city, the Force assembled on November 20 to join the Fifth Army moving north up the peninsula. The clouds parted, and their departure was greeted by patches of sunlight illuminating green hills. They were headed for a station at the Italian Artillery School barracks, approximately a half mile west of the town of Santa Maria Capua, a few miles from Naples. Most traffic headed north with them, clogging the road. The army rolled past a steady stream of civilians, who left Naples with whatever they could carry, pulled in a cart or balanced atop a bicycle. Enemy fighter planes twice strafed the Force convoy. Two drivers were hit, but it was much worse for the civilians, who had no protection and thus took the brunt of the attacks.

The artillery school compound was impressive in size, but it too had been roughly treated. Multiple concrete buildings, two or three stories tall, stood boxy and plain beyond a circular drive with an entry plaza of the same unadorned style. Many of the buildings were camouflaged, with the likeness of a forest covering the exterior walls. As at the Naples harbor, nearly all the windows were blown out. The complex had been commandeered by the Germans and had housed the Hermann Goering Panzer and Parachute Division, which had fought the Allies ferociously on Sicily, before the Nazis were pushed out of the area. As those forces escaped, they sought to make the buildings unusable. Plumbing was destroyed, the roofs were gone, and the living quarters were filled with rubble. The Force set about to make the compound livable. Debris cleanup began, and tent material was stretched over the buildings to shed the rain. Regiments were assigned to their own buildings, and the Forcemen were to bed down in their mountain sleeping bags on the tile floors. As the first day at Santa Maria Capua waned, some soldiers gathered in the cellar of their new barracks, where a fire was being stoked to heat up their army rations. Another American unit had left behind a stash of rations when they moved on, and the Forcemen chowed those down as well.

For days, the equipment and supplies trickled in from the African transports. The units got organized, uncrating weapons and getting them in shape for use. Erick and his mates attended mine school, where engineers gave lectures on the various types of German mines and booby traps. The noncommissioned officers of the Texas Division, battle hardened, arranged a multiday course to steel the Force for action, returning them to fighting condition after the long travel period that included little physical activity. They shook out their stiff muscles with long cross-country marches, packs across their shoulders, and sharpened their aim with firing range practice. The commandos slowly returned to form.

The FSSF was about to make a name for itself and earn the reputation that it had been building during its training period. The front line at Monte la Difensa and the other peaks a few dozen miles north would soon become familiar territory. It would test their strength, determination, and cohesiveness—and their storied actions would reveal few deficiencies.

Chapter 13

May 2011

The May morning was already beginning to get hot when my family and I met the group of Force tourists to visit Monte la Difensa. Our visit to Difensa was to hike one of the German trails, a winding route that would thankfully require no climbing or rope work. Previewing the approach from the west, I saw mountain slopes that rose gently and were smothered in green.

We drove southeast on the Autostrada del Sole (the A-1), exiting the motorway at a roundabout filled with commercial services that gave way to countryside. My brother Steve and his wife, Anne, along with my sister Karen and her husband, Jeff, had come for the hike and a Memorial Day weekend stay with us at Anzio, a capstone to their Italian vacation spent mostly in Tuscany. They filled one rental car, and Susie and I were in ours. We trailed the Force tour bus.

Farmhouses lined the road, which wound along the edge of the hills. At Rocca d'Evandro, we angled into the town and swiftly out again, not needing to slow for the village, whose homes and shops held little of historical interest. Perhaps it had been in the line of fire, with its ancient buildings decimated in the battles. As I was to discover, that was the story in many villages. We turned onto a narrow lane that abruptly headed up into the hills, vegetation towering over our windows wherever we passed a flat spot large enough to support a farm. As forest rose along the road, I clutched into first gear. We were at the base of Monte Camino, the hill to the south of Difensa that contained another monastery, not as storied as Montecassino, but one whose aerie also had provided a threat as a German defensive position. Craning to look at the steep incline through the car's sunroof, I pictured the sweat and blood shed by the British troops who were tasked with silencing those guns. While the

Force was knocking the Nazis off Difensa, their Allied counterparts surged toward the same result on Camino. Hard to imagine the cacophony in our gentle spring morning, whose silence was only shattered by the growl and smoke from the tour bus downshifting up the terrain.

A guardrail appeared along the downhill edge of the road, and suddenly we spied vistas to the valley below. The vegetation thinned, with a scalp of whitish stone showing beneath a scruff of spreading low bushes. At a wide circle, we pulled off the edge of the road and parked across from a rural grocery. Gathering in a farm driveway, we began the hike, eager to see if the real Difensa could bring the battle to life.

As soon as the buildings were out of sight around the first bend, we passed through a double gate fashioned from tree limbs and barbed wire and onto a rocky path. A pair of wheel tracks led out of sight around another turn; between them, a swath of green weeds gave evidence of the road's scant use. We soon rose above the tree line and could see west to a town with tall cement agricultural silos. Fields of rock defined the hillsides, boulders strewn about a scrubby backdrop. In areas that would catch some shade and moisture, white and pink flowers bloomed from spreading, waist-high tangles. A three-inch green lizard sunning itself on a rock disappeared, activated by our approach.

From points along the trail, we peered downward, reviewing other approaches that could be traversed to join our position. We were walking the main route the Germans had used to occupy and hold Monte la Difensa and Monte Remetenea. Multiple side trails split off our path, which had been a cattle trail for generations of ranchers who summered their livestock in the hills.

I scanned one of the side paths, but my gaze couldn't follow it far because overgrown brush made it impassable just yards from the main trail. Had this last been trod by Nazi boots, its brushy edges concealing snipers? Did the ground under my feet hold the blood of American troops that fell in the first Allied attempts to knock the invaders off their perch? That thought stopped me, and I had to take a few breaths to shake off the sadness that must have resulted from the violence that had occurred on those trails. I stooped and reached down, intending to scoop up a bit of soil or palm a rock, but stopped myself as my hand neared the ground. To someone, probably many, this was sacred land where a loved one had perished. It should be left for others to capture its essence.

The first sign of battle history appeared. We passed half circles of stacked rock three feet high that had been German gun emplacements, which would have been covered with heavy timbers for concealment and overhead protection. We looked over ravines where Allied troops had tried to get a foothold on the German positions but were repeatedly rebuffed. Across the Liri Valley below, the slopes were covered with trees, with only the red tile roofs of groups of buildings visible. A band of vegetation marked the winding path of the Garigliano River, and more forested hills rose at intervals out of the river bottomland. A patchwork of green and brown squares signified farms. In the midmorning sun, a haze obscured the horizon.

We crested one hilltop and looked across at a ridge. We were standing on the edge of Remetenea, and before us was Difensa. Hiking next to Steve, I heard his sharp inhale as we looked up simultaneously when we heard our guide name the mountain. We both stopped hiking and straightened. The sight of our destination disappeared as we plunged forward and down into underbrush, traversing through the saddle toward Difensa under the cover of rangy trees. The heat brought sweat to my brow whenever I stepped out from beneath the scant cover. On a downhill slope in a heavier stand of trees, our Italian guides waded into the brush and cut a number of walking sticks for our hiking group, reappearing to prune off the twigs and hand the stakes out to the elders in the group. Rising out of the ravine, slowing as we climbed, we began our final ascent. Although the easy approach, we were about to summit Difensa.

Hiking to a gentle, final slope, we sidestepped rocks protruding from the grass across a wide-open hillside. Our group moved in a staggered, halting line. One of the guides, dressed for the occasion in a Force uniform reconstruction complete with the infantry's bowl-shaped helmet and a standard-issue rifle, topped the ridge ahead of us and stopped. His silhouette against the sky plunged me into the story of the bloody battle. I wanted to yell "Take cover!" but of course the sunny day in no way resembled the actual field conditions I'd read about. Posing for pictures, the Force's red arrowhead shoulder patch glowing on his khaki jacket, he was safe from everything except a bit of sunburn if he doffed the helmet to reveal his bald head.

In a few more steps Difensa's "top" was revealed, as recounted in the history books, to be a shallow bowl rimmed on two sides by outcroppings of rock. Cresting the hill was to simply stride into this bowl, about the size of an American football field, one hundred yards long and a third as wide. The ridge still loomed on the far side, perhaps twenty feet above the open bowl, and I felt exposed to whatever would lurk beyond that edge. Clearly the world could come crashing down on us, and we would have scant time to react and nowhere to go. The bowl, as the hillside below, contained a field of small boulders, few large enough to even sit on, much less to use as cover if someone was shooting at you. I skirted the bowl counterclockwise and found a steep edge—the north face—where the commandos had risen from the insurmountable wall. Stepping close to the edge of a cliff has never been easy for me, and this one dropped from a field of loose scree along the perimeter. I baby-stepped on the rough stone and peered over the edge to the smooth wall of rock below. It glared in the midday sun, lines of red and tan revealing veins and crevasses in the face, like it had been forever bloodied and scarred. Two hundred feet down began the tree line, starting with lone trees hanging on to small ledges along cracks in the face and finally gathering into a forest canopy that obscured the slopes below. I felt my leg muscles tense to try to root my feet to the ground. There it was, the overnight cover, the last-stop ledges, a ridiculously steep and smooth climb that looked like an invitation to death. Dad came up right here, making history, becoming part of the legend.

Beyond the trees, a cluster of buildings that must have been the village of Mignano occupied a narrow valley, and a steady stream of movement clued the location of the highway cutting through the gap. That was what they had been fighting for. Across a hazy stretch of sky, forested hills stepped up in the east. The Apennines, Italy's spinal range, sat sentry behind a cloud bank that shielded their peaks from view.

We broke ranks to rest, pull out our water bottles, and consider our achievement of summiting Difensa. Even though just a two-hour walk from a parking place high on the slopes, the effort deserved handshakes and smiles. I stood there—where my father had climbed and scrambled and shot and probably killed—along with other family members doubtless raking through similar thoughts. The Forcemen had fought to exhaustion, straining under extreme conditions: cold, fog, and rain, the winter gloom lit with muzzle flashes and cratering rockets. Our hardship: squinting at the sun's glare, exuding a bit of sweat.

As we explored the surroundings, there before us in the hillside was a flat gash of blackness, an opening beneath the rocks. The story of a survival tactic taken by Erick's comrades had become part of the day's legend, and on our visit so many decades later, my siblings and I approached the still visible shallow cave that had shielded a few injured Forcemen. Nearly obscured by the overgrowth, it nonetheless was preserved, its entrance memorialized by a weathered wooden sign on a post. We took our turn bending to peer into the darkness and then to surround the sign for a commemorative photo. Painted on the signboard was a wry title, named after the First Regiment's second-in-command Major Edward H. Thomas, who had been among the cadre who had scouted and planned the attack and then had been given field command after the taking of Difensa. The shallow cave that sheltered the wounded men had been labeled "Thomas Hotel."

Our Difensa reconnaissance continued as the guides let the tour group rest before heading down. Further circling the bowl, Susie, my sister Karen, and I ventured over the ridge that had first come into view above us as we summited. At the northeast edge, looking nearly into the Mignano Gap, a flat pad was cleared of rock, with a thigh-high wall of stones encircling the downhill side. We stepped into the German defense, and I felt even more like an interloper on this auspicious spot and also, surprisingly, like a conqueror. The rock wall had withstood the decades, a man-made testimony to the occupation of this aerie. From here, crouched against the wall, you could survey the slopes down the northwest side of Difensa and even west to the adjoining saddle to Remetenea. But if you wanted to see over the rim to the east edge of the bowl, you would have to turn around, and this is what the Germans did not do, until it was too late and many of their foes were atop the wall and marshaling at the edges of the bowl. Nature's sculpted ridge and human nature to orient toward a vista combined to leave the occupiers open to the rear attack.

Growing up, I had never heard the word *Difensa*, but I'd heard a secondhand story about a battle where two of Dad's closest friends had been killed in one mountaintop firefight. My images of that battle site had been formed through the pages of the family's copy of the Force history book of which we kids were allowed a rare look. A muddy aerial view showed the adjoining peaks, as did a hand-drawn map, elevation lines curling around the lettered location names. The most evocative image in the book still had not delivered anything near to this perspective. It was a painting created for *Life* magazine and reprinted with the permission of that premiere periodical of the day. Over a two-page spread, the rubbled ruins of Mignano village and one bare tree trunk were the foreground to a looming, fog-obscured hump that was Difensa. All three of those distant images would be replaced forever by the menacing ridge, the piled battlements, and the shallow cave that I had seen by putting my own boots atop the mountain.

I pictured my father's devastating moment, an explosion cratering the ground in front of him and fellow Forcemen crumpling over in the smoke. Now, as I stood on the soil where that had occurred, I began to understand why it was never described to me. Why would you tell someone, especially a child, how the worst day of your existence unfolded half a world and half a life away? We hide our horrors from our loved ones, to shield them from pain. If your restless, relentless memory brings it back, you instinctually tamp it down and lock it up.

Chapter 14

December 1943

Recuperating from Difensa and rebuilding the unit's strength took all the efforts of the Force after the mountaintop campaign. Erick and his fellow soldiers hunkered down at their Santa Maria Capua barracks, healing and training, but it was a brief respite. As 1943 was coming to a close, new orders arrived. The Force was to participate in another push into the mountains intended to destroy the last section of the Germans' heavily defended Gustav Line, about which they had been briefed for the Difensa attack. There it was also called the Winter Line, and it stretched from coast to coast, one hill to the next and across the strategic highway. The fight would prove to be a prelude to the largest campaign of their career. To crush that fortified Nazi defensive line was paramount, but to liberate Rome, which would be one of the largest and bloodiest campaigns of the entire war, was supreme.

They were to join a massive Allied effort to assault the German defenses that bristled alongside Highway 6 to Cassino, where the Rapido River cut north-south through the valley containing the highway and met the Liri. The rivers, the highway, and the hills—along with all the villages perched among the rocky slopes—composed that objective, and it was seen as the last major hurdle for an Allied army determined to push the Nazis out of southern Italy's mountainous terrain.

The Force was to take part in clearing the hill mass called Mount Sammucro. Sammucro was another treeless redoubt. It loomed over Highway 6 on its eastern edge, northeast of Mignano, and had been a key position along with Difensa for the Germans covering the highway. With the Difensa hill mass on one side and the Sammucro hills on the other, the highway had been unusable. But that was changing. Difensa was conquered, and Allied attacks had pushed the Germans off Sammucro's peak (also called Hill 1205), but the Nazis were dug into the adjoining hills—Hill 720 to the west and Hill 950 to the north—thwarting further Allied moves.

San Pietro Infine clung to the slopes of Sammucro, which was in the Allies' gunsights. The Germans covered the hilltop and filled the town's narrow streets and stone dwellings. San Pietro, dating to the twelfth century, had been built for defense, its stone towers overlooking the valley and steep streets rimmed with high walls. Nearby, the Germans had dug in on Mount Lungo, just south of Highway 6, and again held the high ground. After a week of battling in the hillsides below San Pietro, a surge of Allied troops knocked the enemy off Mount Lungo, which triggered the German retreat from San Pietro. But they still held Hill 720 and the surrounding peaks. For the Allies to push north along the foothills toward the next village of San Vittore, on the way to their ultimate goal of the town of Cassino, Hill 720 would have to be captured.

On December 20, the Force once again set out from their Santa Maria Capua base toward the hill towns. *Here we go again,* Erick perhaps thought as the weather beat on the men packed into their 6×6 trucks. Working their way north into the mountains, they found a nasty winter scene. Erick would see contours of the hills draped in a heavy, cold fog, and they jumped from the truck beds onto slopes covered in snow. The dim light wasted early into long nights that would drop to freezing temperatures. Erick wore the winter gear that became familiar during training in the Rocky Mountains the previous winter. His white parka sported a hood fringed in wolf fur, which layered over baggy wool pants. On top of his boots were rubber-soled, buckled overshoes. The traverse into the hills was rough, and the camping was even worse. Soldiers bivouacked among the rocks, stretching tents between boulders and lashing them down where the hillsides flattened. Each short day they moved ever closer to Hill 720, and for three nights they suffered on the icy slopes. The effort sapped every bit of energy from cold, hungry troops.

The hardship did not thwart their determination. Force leadership set up headquarters in the bombed ruins of nearby Ceppagna, and the diminished Force regiments were bolstered by additional artillery and infantry units. Battle plans were laid, and the FSSF's First Regiment was set to lead the charge up Hill 720 on an auspicious day, Christmas Eve. The battle flared into action in the early hours of Christmas morning and resulted in heavy casualties among the First Regiment before the combined forces took the hill later in the day. Erick's Second Regiment, its manpower decimated by nearly half after the bloody Difensa battle, served as supply packers and litter bearers during the attack. Gaining ground foot by foot, the Force cleared the surrounding hills of German resistance, then the hard-won land had to be freed also of the perils left behind by the enemy: antipersonnel mines and other "booby traps" that could blast through a soldier in an instant. It was tedious, nerve-racking work, and they would be at it for nearly a week, commanding those hills until tasked to move forward again in a blitzing wave that was intended to wash the enemy out of the area, finally destroying the Winter Line.

On the first day of 1944, orders came for the next move: up into the hills again, this time to secure the village of Radicosa and a series of peaks north of Sammucro, chief among them Mount Majo and Mount Vischiataro. From that high ground, the army would finally move westward and take the prize of the region that sat astride the Rapido River at Highway 6: Cassino.

While three of the Second Regiment's six companies engaged in supply services for the attacks, Erick's unit and two others were assigned to climb and capture Hill 724, which lorded over Radicosa. The village, which they were told contained only six stone huts, would serve as the Force's new advance command post. As night settled on January 3, Erick and his comrades stormed the village and quickly occupied it. Fighting raged through the next day, but as the next night fell among the forested hills, 724 and its nearby peaks were in Allied hands. Colonel Frederick and his officers took up residence in Radicosa.

While Erick's regiment was at work, their brother regiments crested Mount Majo, Hill 1270, and Hill 1109, each occupying the captured territory for a period of days until relieved by other units, which included a French cadre complementing the combined British and American forces. From Radicosa, the Force service battalion resupplied the advancing troops, aided by a growing number of pack mules. The soldiers would eventually be relieved of much heavy hauling duty by nearly seven hundred of the sturdy animals.

The fight for Mount Majo turned into an especially desperate and protracted struggle. Companies of the Third Regiment battled through the night on January 6 to take the hill, crawling up the slopes of the mountain under sometimes intense mortar shelling and fire from German machine-gun emplacements. And while the hill finally was gained before dawn, the respite from fighting did not last, as the Germans, realizing the strategic value of the lost position, plunged their reserves into the fray. The counterattack was effective in scattering the Forcemen and confusing their defensive response. Their struggle was further marred by a lack of ammunition, as many of the soldiers had used their supply on the initial attack. But their training was to be their savior. Forcemen seized upon the enemy weapons left on the battlefield from the first fight and turned those German guns back on the Nazi troops. Over the next two days, forty-two German counterattacks were mounted, and ground battle and mortar shelling left dead men mounded upon the hillsides. The grueling Force defense of the mountaintop was aided by reinforcements from the larger task force, and Force companies began deploying down the sides of the neighboring hills to push back enemy positions.

The protracted battle, along with fierce weather, was taking its toll. Nearly half the men returning from the front had frostbite and exposure injuries, related a Canadian Forceman's journal entries of early January in the 2000 book *The Supercommandos*, and almost as many were treated for battle wounds. "There won't be much left of the Force," said a January 9 entry, "if casualties keep at this rate."

Erick's constitution suffered under the bitter weather conditions. On a long trek through the mountains to Cassino, he contracted jaundice and was sent back for medical care. The official medical term was hepatitis B, which was widely spread to soldiers through a yellow fever vaccine. Reluctantly, he mounted one of the Force's mules to join those departing the front through the rugged country. *Most of these men are gone*, he would have realized, seeing the mules draped with dead soldiers. The few live soldiers were those leading the mule train.

Perhaps my father felt this trip away from the front as a retreat, a failure. The ignominious mode of transportation would not have helped. *All our preparations, the training, everything focused on getting fit for the coming battle,* he might have thought, *all being undone by some invisible virus,* an enemy not defeated by brute force or cunning maneuvers. In a unit as fiercely connected as his, he would know that every man was essential. *I'm not laid over this mule, so how can I justify turning back from the fight?* But the virus that spiked a fever in his head and an ache deep in his bones would not let him do battle, at least not on the field of war. Every inch of the plodding trip to base must have sent pain through both body and mind, but there was no choice. Atop the slow mule train, he followed orders.

As Erick recuperated in an army hospital, he faced a situation that he found difficult in a different way than battle. Many of his fellow patients were Arabs, and he was disconcerted by their unfamiliar religious practice as they prostrated themselves day and night to face Mecca and pray.

Back at it, and hungry again, he thought upon return from medical leave. His unit was still fighting over the road to Rome, pushing through every village in the foothills. At dinnertime, he lined up daily for the bowl of food ladled out by the company cook, who slapped a hunk of bread over the top. If the wind blew the bread off the bowl as they walked back to their tents, the ravenous soldiers would just pick it up, shake off the mud, and eat it anyway. But the muck was only a few inches deep; in the winter of their mountainous war, the ground beneath that layer of mud was still frozen. A cold wind traced every movement over the icy landscape, adding to a Forceman's misery.

The Second Regiment was tasked with one more maneuver to secure the Mount Majo area. Storm and capture Hill 302, Frederick ordered the Second, and it would drive the Germans from a crucial line near Highway 6. They moved out before first light on January 14, climbing the slopes into the fray. By 8 a.m. they had crested the hill and were raining fire down upon a surprised—and quickly retreating—enemy. Other elements of the Force, bolstered by additional American units and Colonel Bonjour's French groupment, widened the front toward Cassino, pushing the Germans off the last occupied hilltops along the range facing the town and the highway.

Inching forward, securing the front took three more days of fighting until the Force was released from the Majo campaign on January 17. It would be nearly midnight before the final Forcemen loaded onto the trucks to depart their temporary quarters at Ceppagna. But the convoy back to Santa Maria

Capua was sparse because casualties had been devastating. Of the Force's 1,800 combat soldiers, 1,400 were dead or hospitalized. The Canadian contingent was especially hard-hit, and one man in two of the service battalion went down. The entire outfit was bone-weary. They would need massive reinforcements and restorative rest before being sent back into the fray.

1. FSSF soldiers skirt a minefield along a barbed-wire fence in a raid of a German-occupied farmhouse in Anzio, April 14, 1944. National Archives.

2. A plaque honoring the FSSF is embedded in the plaza wall at Piazza della Vittoria in Artena, Italy. Author photo.

3. The author, hiking the countryside from Anzio to Cori. Courtesy Susie Thorness.

4. Virginia Agnoni assists in interviewing Eugenio di Giacomo, a survivor of World War II who resides in Cori. Author photo.

5. Susie Thorness (*left*) and Karen Leisy stand in a German gun emplacement atop Monte la Difensa. Author photo.

6. The Monte la Difensa cliffs that the FSSF soldiers scaled to mount the surprise attack on the Germans, December 3, 1943. Author photo.

7. The grounds of the Sicily-Rome American Cemetery and Memorial near Anzio. Author photo.

8. The ruins of the church at San Pietro Infine. Behind the stone tower are the bare cliffs of Monte la Difensa, which the FSSF scaled in its attack. Author photo.

9. Erick Thorness (*right*) and fellow soldiers suited up for parachute training at Fort Harrison, Montana. Thorness family archives.

10. After the liberation of Rome, the FSSF was tasked with protecting many of the Tiber River bridges, such as this one, Ponte Sisto in front of St. Peter's Basilica. Author photo.

11. Italian historian Gianni Blasi greets a man reenacting the FSSF's liberation of Rome at a commemorative parade down the Via dei Fori Imperiali. Author photo.

12. Erick Gabriel Thorness. Thorness family archives.

13. Ivano Bruno (*left*) assists the author in interviewing Euginio Loreti, a survivor of World War II, in Zagarolo, Italy. Courtesy Susie Thorness.

PART 3

Anzio

Chapter 15
May 2011

Clouds marshaled in the sky like an army on parade and the sun shone through to warm my shoulders as a military band erupted into a melody of horns paced for marching. It was the American Memorial Day, but the commemoration was being held a few miles from Rome. Although such a foreign celebration was new to me, I realized that the scene was being played out around the world, as it had for many years. With the United States acting as a military partner with (and often protector of) people in far-flung places for many decades, our armed forces were deployed to many countries. I balanced ambivalent views about that, as American political motivations and self-interest sometimes replaced allyship. But the United States had fought around the world, and following battles and wars had come memorials and cemeteries scattered over the globe. On our second trip to Anzio, once again I found myself walking the grounds of the Sicily-Rome American Cemetery and Memorial. The green acreage stitched with white crosses had been my first stop on that initial Italy trip, when I knew so little about my father's war. Returning this time to walk his battlefields, I was beginning the task by taking part in a ritual of group remembering.

    I recalled my first trip to the region, where a visit with the cemetery's director had inspired an idea to visit the fateful spot where my father fell in the campaign's final push to Rome. What's more, an audience with a member of the storied Borghese family had sparked my understanding of the area's lore. During that visit, incredibly, Signora Camilla Borghese had offered rooms in her family's seaside villa on the Anzio coast on my return. For the second visit, with Susie and a contingent of family by my side at the sober ceremony, I was ready for the *a piedi* exploration. As we prepared for our stay at the villa, I related our visit with Camilla to Karen and Steve and their spouses.

"At the time of the war, many residents of Anzio were recent transplants," Camilla had told Susie and me. We were seated in a modern office. Camilla, stylish in a tailored business suit and with wavy blond hair, had agreed to meet us in the corporate headquarters of the pharmaceutical firm she and her husband helmed in Aprilia, a small city between Rome and Anzio. She had succeeded her aunt as the managing director and chairperson of the firm some years earlier. Johannes Kevellenhueller, a tall, silver-haired Austrian who was the firm's chief executive, received us in his office, offered us coffee served on a silver tray, and sat back to listen as we talked with his wife.

Camilla related the theme of a recent book, *Canale Mussolini*, which unfortunately for me was published solely in Italian. It recounts, she said, the history of the public works project to reclaim the table-flat swampland for agricultural use by dredging a network of canals, a visionary project by the country's dictatorial leader, Benito Mussolini, head of the National Fascist Party in the 1930s.

"Many came from Veneto," she explained. "Every family was given property and cattle," and they pursued agriculture as they knew it. "They brought the idea of vineyards from their homeland, where wine grapes had been grown for centuries." Veneto, a northeastern Italy region—naturally with Venice as its capital—had grown to produce more wine than any other region in Italy. The region hugged the Adriatic Sea and bordered Austria and Slovenia. Picturing Italy's boot-like outline, Veneto would be on the upper back side of the wearer's calf.

With a smile, she inquired about her American relative who had put us in touch with her family when I mentioned my research trip and book project. Paola, that distant relation, had opened the door not only to Camilla but also to another branch of the family, headed by Andreas Borghese, who still occupied an ancient family castle in the village that we heard had been key to my father's final battle, the tiny hill town of Artena. When our walking tour took us to Artena, we would visit with them as well.

Camilla gestured out the window to the land stretching away from the second-floor office. It had been uninhabitable, she reminded us, impossible to farm and plagued by malarial mosquitoes. Before the canals, the land had minimal value. The canals that drained the land made it not only pliable for farming but also suitable for flatland towns like Aprilia that could host industry. As the farms flourished, they provided a new food source to the people of Rome, she said, and in that sense the canals were a success. The series of sloping ditches carved into the swamp drained many square miles of land, connecting to a main canal that led to the sea. It was Canale Mussolini, of course, that was to define the Force's battle on the Anzio plains.

There had been a society along the edge of the sea that eked out an existence. Though bolstered by the wealthy Romans who summered there, Anzio was a struggling village. A contingent of new residents sought to settle in Anzio from Ventotene, an island in the Pontine chain off the coast of the Lazio region. But they were reportedly a group that had just been released from the island's jail, Camilla related, and the people of Anzio did not want to have such low-class neighbors. So the Ventotenians moved a few miles down the beach and settled in the town of Nettuno, named after Neptune, the god of the sea. Today, she said, some bad blood still exists between the towns.

Also existing between the towns, physically, was an oasis that had been in the hands of Italy's ruling class for many centuries: a seaside castle currently owned by Camilla's family, known as Villa de Borghese Nettuno. With the roasted aroma of coffee still wafting in the office air, Camilla had delivered her generous offer: stay at the villa when returning for the battlefield trek.

My family and I turned our attention to the memorial ceremony, where soldiers of two countries in their sharp and shiny dress uniforms had gathered to pay their respects. Three of my father's descendants would represent him for the day. Steve, Karen, and I, along with our spouses, were to parade in with a stream of civilian guests, crunching down the wide gravel path that lined the reflecting pool in front of the cemetery's verdant grounds. We gathered before the marble memorial building, white-columned and solemn. During that holiday weekend, we had hiked up Monte la Difensa, we had dined with a group of Force veterans and descendants, and we had peeked into hillside towns on the fringes of Mussolini's grand experiment. Standing on the former marshland, memorial flags rippling in the spring breeze, the consequences of the war seemed momentous. The pool mirrored the sky, a blue portal connecting the earth with the heavens. Shoulder to shoulder with Italians and our extended Force family, we walked in step along the precision-cut edges of the path, manicured lawns fanning out with lines of crosses. I felt a kinship with those other descendants of immigrants. But were there locals among us who remembered the upheaval that battered its way to their doorstep? Were the elderly soldiers in our group reliving their moments of service? I gazed across the grounds, considering the place where our ancestors had marched to defend freedom from oppression and aggression and defy the visions that fevered into the heads of dictators.

Reverberations of the war had echoed back to North Dakota and through two generations of my family. My parents were both battle-scarred, and while my father's agony was apparent in his limping gait and disappearances through the dark portal of a smoky bar, my mother's struggle was on display at home, laboring to raise the family with scant resources and facing the late-night rage that would periodically take over her wounded soldier. And we, their children, grew up in the shadow of that hardship, the unspoken pain.

I recalled the night of his stroke, a bewildering moment. I was with my cousin, whose family also had retreated to a house in town to ease the difficulties of a long winter on an isolated farm. Her mother stepped through the door to the playroom, a storm clouding her face, and beckoned me to come and take my older sister Maggie's hand. Accepting my aunt's brief hug, Maggie hustled me down the block to our house, whispering that something had happened to Dad. Nervous activity filled the living room, and I sat on someone's lap as people crossed back and forth, in and out the doors, all wearing that same troubled visage. I looked over the comforting shoulder through the window into the dark November night, a pale streetlight barely able to cut through the murk.

The letters that had set me on this path swam back into my mind, with Dad's precise cursive and words of endearment to Mom. The love and hope in their union were evident, and I imagined that they'd tried to face their challenges with an optimistic outlook. That was my mother's matter-of-fact attitude retroactively, anyway. In her era, you just played the hand you were dealt, and it made no sense to complain. Being back in our hometown for her funeral and burial, which became a rare convergence of all my siblings and their families, I had seen her achievement. It was in the faces of my family, in the words of her friends and admirers. Shirley's legacy was to endure the loss of her spouse, forge a path through hardship, and find a meaningful way. It was to raise us children and stand by us into adulthood while standing in front of a grammar school class as a teacher of the community's next crop of youth.

Walking through the memorial grounds, my thoughts went back to the other cemetery, where we laid my mother's body down next to my father's grave, returning them to unity. The act hadn't erased all the pain and hardship, but it had put it in perspective, echoing the hope with which they began. I had not attended my father's funeral, as the youngest of us were deemed unable to handle the situation. My father was gone and would not return. I knew that, even if I didn't feel it. His last few days had been spent in a hospital bed, unaware of the family hovering nearby. I was not among them. When he died, our tiny living room was filled with bodies, our kitchen heavy with comfort food handmade and delivered by grieving friends. When everyone left, the silence was thick like the air before a summer storm. When my mother died, succumbing to cancer a lifetime beyond his passing, I was three states away, trying to envelop her through a telephone line. We cried for our loss, and when the grief overtook her, she gasped out one last line, "I can't... do this anymore." As we lowered her casket into the prairie, the painful side of love had never risen so high.

An Italian honor guard ushered us into an area set for the family of American servicemen, and walking past a line of locals, I felt myself to be a symbol, on display as an embodiment of the service that had been delivered by my father and his compadres. I sensed curious, considerate appraisal as we took our places, as though others were envisaging my connection, wondering whether their family members somehow had contact with my father. I looked at everyone that way as well. The citizens of Lazio, to me, symbolized an unconsidered aspect of war, where everyday people struggled to survive in the madness between dueling armies. In that respect we all shared one purpose: a personal connection to the blood and anguish that had taken place there seven decades previous. Their landscape was populated with the ghosts of those connections, the untold stories of survival and procreation. We stood as the hopes and destinies that were made possible by the triumph of the Allies on the future memorial, the former battlefield.

Chapter 16
December 1943

"I wonder if the Allied landing shocked the locals as much as it surprised the Germans," I said to Susie as we stood again on Anzio's modest waterfront, the waves a dull brown against an unseasonably gray sky. As 1943 waned, the sleepy seaside town was about to become a hot spot of the war and, almost overnight, a major port. Nero's fiddling while Rome burned was probably a metaphor, but wartime descendants of his hometown could have been as cavalier, not expecting their out-of-the-way village to become the nexus of anything.

"How could they not expect it?" she asked. "The war was all around them."

"From what I've learned," I said, "there was hardly anybody living around here, so few that the German occupation basically amounted to a squad of sentries."

Inland residents nearby would have been the first generation, still scrabbling to get established, and the rest of the country would likely know Anzio only from news reports about the canal project two decades earlier. As the war began, Anzio and its sister port Nettuno, along with a few other coastal towns, were the primary inhabited lowland locations on the landscape south of Rome. Mussolini's canal infrastructure had resulted in scattered villages inland as well, but mostly the region was just dotted with farmsteads.

We had been poring over maps to plan the battlefield walk, which I expected to take a week. Like my father had done after memorizing the terrain of Kiska Island, I sketched out the area for Susie on a notebook page. The largest canal, named after Il Duce himself, formed the southern border of the agricultural region. I drew a dot for Ninfa, a village famed as the source of mountain spring water that dated to the medieval era, and a curved line southwest for the Ninfa River, which flowed from the Lepini Hills onto the marshes, and continued the line to the sea, to show where the Mussolini Canal was cut. Onto the page went a series of carats to represent the hills south and east of the plain. Twenty miles north of Anzio, another set of hills, the Albans, formed the farming region's northern border. It was famous for hosting the pope's summer residence at Lake Albano, an oasis as round as a Roman coin and ringed by hills. A circle for the lake, a cross for His Holiness, and more carats for the Albans. Beyond that, fifteen miles of rolling hills led to the Tiber River, which flows through Rome. A squiggle for the river and a star for the Eternal City.

Two main roads from Rome accessed the new farmland. Highway 7, which my reading suggested was the route of the ancient Appian Way, cut through the Alban Hills in a trajectory toward the coast and crossed the Mussolini Canal near Foce Verde, a tiny seaside resort where the canal emptied into the ocean. Highway 6, the much-fought-over direct route from Naples to Rome that included the Mignano Gap, formed the region's eastern border. Between Highway 6 and the sea at Anzio stretched nearly thirty miles of farmland that was destined to become my father's last battlefield. I dotted my paper along the coastline to indicate the villages of Anzio, Nettuno, and Foce Verde.

But Anzio was not just a dot on a map to the architects of the Allied assault. It was calculated to be the location where an amphibious troop deployment could deliver a kidney punch that would leave the Axis powers gasping. At the time the plan was conceived, the "Axis" was a confederation between Nazi Germany and Fascist-controlled Italy. Planning that would lead to the Anzio operation had begun a year prior, in a January 1943 gathering of Allied leaders at Casablanca. The meeting came toward the end of a campaign that had been raging in North Africa since mid-1940. Late in 1942, the Allies had surged in Operation Torch, which signaled the beginning of the end of the Africa fight. As the leaders gathered in Morocco, the Allies—with colonial French corps (rebelling against the Vichy government that complied with Germany) and Greek, Polish, and North African troops at their side—were engaging the Germans in final battles in Tunisia, the African country closest to Sicily and Italy. The rest of the continent's northwestern border—the countries of Morocco and Algeria—were firmly in Allied hands, so the leaders could hash out plans for using North Africa as a base of operations from which to engage the Nazis in European theaters across the waters separating Africa and Europe.

At a summit in a Casablanca villa, Allied leaders and their top military advisors debated their next moves. Prime Minister Winston Churchill and his British strategists conceived of an Italian invasion as a diversion that would draw German forces away from fighting in northern Europe. Across the table, President Franklin D. Roosevelt and the American generals advocated for a campaign across the English Channel. But they settled on a plan to mount Allied attacks on Sicily and Italy in 1943, with the northern European invasion to follow.

The Allies pushed the Germans out of Tunisia in May 1943 and then in August took Sicily after a monthlong battle across the island's tumultuous terrain. The landing on Sicily had been a jab in the backside of leaders of Italy's Grand Council of Fascism, who voted Mussolini out on July 25 and returned power to King Vittorio Emmanuele, who then appointed a new prime minister. An armistice agreement with the Allied powers shortly followed, and before the Allies began swarming ashore, Italy became a country under Nazi occupation.

Landing on mainland Italy at the toe of the boot, the Allies progressed northward with victories to Naples. They battled against bands of defenses laid by the Nazis across the country as protection for an eventual withdrawal north if necessary. The German plan to slow the advancement of the Allies was most effective at their Winter (Gustav) Line, which separated the Lazio region along the Garigliano River (as it merged with the Liri just south of Cassino) from southern neighbor Campania, which had Naples as its regional capital. Those multisyllabic names had grown familiar to my father and his FSSF mates. The Force had advanced with Allied comrades in the rugged Campania terrain that lined Highway 6 all the way to Lazio. But in hill-to-hill battles at places such as Radicosa, San Pietro Infine, and Mount Sammucro, it became evident—in land studded with deep, wooded river valleys—that it was impossible to mount a sustained, progressive attack. Battle results were isolated, costly gains against well-defended high ground. The Allies, with the

Force contributing through their mountain warfare, pressured the Germans along the fortified Winter Line and inched closer to the Italian capital city. But if a knockout punch was to be delivered, another angle of attack would be crucial. When the commandos headed back to Naples, their next move was to join the beachfront landing as the roundabout blow.

Operation Shingle, as the coastal engagement was to be called, was the brainchild of Churchill and his advisors. Shingle called for the Allies to remain engaged on the inland front along Highway 6 while they launched a flotilla from Naples that would land on a beach near Rome, thus outflanking the Winter Line defenses. The landing would occur seventy-five miles north of the Garigliano. This one-two punch, they hoped, would weaken the German capability on both fronts, causing them to abandon the Winter Line and withdraw north. As the Allies increased pressure on the weakened or retreating German forces, Churchill hoped it would trigger an influx of reserve troops from northern Europe, thus also sapping the strength of the Nazi response to the coming Allied attack across the English Channel.

Although Operation Shingle was viewed skeptically by the American contingent, they agreed to the plan. As the Allies took firm control of southern Italy in the last half of 1943, preparations for the coastal invasion continued, and as the year ended, Churchill again journeyed to North Africa. At a Christmas Day meeting in 1943 in Tunis with American General Dwight D. Eisenhower and other military leaders, an invasion date of January 22, 1944, was set. After a review of possible landing spots along the coastline near Rome, Anzio was chosen. It sat close enough for a push into the city, and it was within reach of the Allied aircraft stationed near Naples to allow for air cover during the invasion. In the week preceding the landing, a renewed thrust toward the Garigliano River would again test the Winter Line, hopefully drawing German resources away from the coast. And that would be just what the Allies, and my father's unit, would need to land safely and begin the final push toward Rome.

Chapter 17
May 2011

To say that I was a bit intimidated by our upcoming stay at the Borghese villa in Nettuno would be an understatement. I'd never felt so much like an interloper and tried unsuccessfully not to project my nervousness to my family, as the six of us were imposing on Camilla's hospitality.

The House of Borghese, one of the noble families of Italy, traces its roots in Siena to the thirteenth century. The seat of the family's power moved to Rome in the mid-1500s, and in 1605 the son of Marcantonio Borghese, Camillo, was elected as Pope Paul V in the Roman Catholic Church. Of course, Camilla did not elucidate that history, but she did share the background of the villa, which was a summer home for her family. The mansion, which she called Villa di Bell'Aspetto, was built around 1650. Acres of forested land surrounded its "beautiful aspect" on the seashore between Anzio and Nettuno. It had been owned by her family since the early 1800s.

The villa had joined the ranks of many large properties operated in cooperative arrangements with the Italian government in order for the owners to afford upkeep and taxes. It was still a Borghese holiday home, but when they were absent, rooms were offered for rent to vacationers through the organization Dimone Storiche Italiane. Nearby but tucked away on the villa's grounds sat a stylized small castle with manicured landscaping and an event facility provided as a luxurious location for weddings and other celebrations. We were not asked to book rooms through the organization or to pay any fees, just to contact the villa housekeeper so staff could be on hand at our arrival time. Being invited into that seaside home was an honor and perhaps a testament to the place that my father's commando unit had held in the memories of the Lazio people, as well as to the graciousness toward Paola, their American cousin who made the connection to Camilla for us. Packed into our two tiny rental cars, we sped up the motorway from our previous night's lodging with the Force families at Cassino. On the phone, I haltingly informed the housekeeper, whose English was no better than my Italian, of our approximate arrival time. My stomach fluttering, I aimed the car down a side road to cross the former swampland toward Nettuno.

The villa appeared grand and slightly crumbling, a statement of the challenging, storied Italian life. Four floors of shuttered windows across a blocky front facade were topped by a series of small oval windows just below a flat roof with an open railing made of squat stone columns. Similarly stout and square wings pushed off into the trees to broaden the front of the manor.

We pulled out of coastal traffic and punched at the intercom next to a tall iron gate facing the road. As the gate opened we were directed up the curving drive. An allée of trees shaded a lane of hard-packed earth. The grounds in early summer were dense with shrubs and clipped hedges and highlighted by flowering plants. The housekeeper, with individual English words matching my lonely Italian nouns and greetings, clasped her hands and nodded a greeting. Above the door, three stone stars and a snarling bust of Neptune were set into carved flourishes. The exterior walls varied from tan to cement gray, with hints of previous gold paint still visible in protected areas. Occasional cracks and patches could be seen between the architectural features, lending the building an impression of an aging watercolor painting.

We were shown into the manor's elaborate foyer and offered a look at the adjacent sitting room and dining room. The dining room's chandelier sparkled above a modest round table with chairs for five, and two sofas flanked a fireplace in the sitting room that had voluptuous gold statues, male and female, arching into poses to hold up a marble mantelpiece. Our rooms on the next floor were more sedate, well-used but utilitarian furnishings topped by recently refreshed textiles. The marble-tiled bathroom gleamed through a gilt-framed mirror. Although this large home echoed with empty rooms and we saw only the few staff members, in the next two mornings we would be made to feel welcome with a breakfast of coffee and homemade cakes, served on a terrace bathed in soft morning light that put the home in shadow.

The villa's prominence in the beachfront battle campaign made its appearance even more wondrous; how did this manor avoid annihilation during the war? Its rural placement between the towns and surrounded by forest perhaps protected it, or maybe it was a recognition of the building's beauty and historic value. Its value to the Allies, we discovered the next day, was to be found literally beneath the surface. After much persuading, we were allowed a guided walk through the tunnels below the home. Carved out of the solid rock beneath the castle lay an extensive series of tunnels and rooms, which were used as the Allies' headquarters during the Anzio campaign. Tunneling had been undertaken in the prewar years to connect Anzio and Nettuno with a railway, a side spur of which served the castle from beneath. The staff said that train traffic could be felt regularly from the home and its grounds. During the war, the tunnels were expanded and extended to an exit on the seaside facade of the home, some distance from the front door.

The groundskeeper led us through the front gardens to what seemed to be an earthen mound. A dense layer of trees and bushes shielded an overgrown gravel path, at the end of which was a yawning archway beneath a knoll. The half-dome cave entrance was ringed with cement block. At its center was a red-trimmed door behind a rusted steel gate. The door creaked open with a hard tug. Out of the shadows came a gust of chilly air. With my first steps, I could not picture how these rough caves could become an army's nerve center. Tunnel walls had been formed by chipping away the solid rock to the height of a tall man and a two-person width. The gray stone was streaked with yellow, which I suspected leaned toward a common mineral (sulfur?) rather than a precious one. An exposed black cable fed naked bulbs at intervals to cast pools of light down the main shaft. Walking along the central tunnel, we shined flashlights into carved-out rooms and down narrower side shafts. Slowly the clues appeared. Bolts and spikes at intervals along the stone walls and ceiling held now-crumbling wood posts and beams, to which were attached fraying, brittle communication cables. There was evidence that more electrical cables had been strung to power and light the operation. One large cavern had held desks for radio equipment, the groundskeeper explained in pantomime and English nouns. Another larger room was the cinema. It would have sported rows of chairs and a projector to inform campaign strategists with daily films shot from cameras in reconnaissance planes. Scratched into the stone was evidence of life and work: one room was designated as headquarters for Company B, and another likely held a lonely sentry or soldiers' bunks, as the repeated name "Maria" in faded script was stacked high on a wall. Recessed further were bricked-off exits that led to the train tunnel. As we aimed dim lights at the mortared wall, a rumble came from beyond as a train was evidently moving beneath the Borghese property.

A chill raised gooseflesh on my arms. We were deep in rock below the afternoon heat, but before I had even set foot on the battlefields, I was a visitor in the war's former nerve center. The caverns were rarely contemplated now for their part in the war, as the family was concerned about liability and being overrun with tourists and military history buffs, so our look behind the scenes of the campaign existed somewhere between an after-hours museum visit and an archeological dig. I tried to picture Erick's high leather boots treading on the rough-carved floors. Perhaps he had been tasked with duties that caused him, too, to enter the unreality of coastal caverns beneath an Italian mansion.

Chapter 18

January 1944

The Allied flotilla steamed north from Naples on the long night of January 21, 1944, a nearly unbroken line of ships shadowy along the dark horizon. Coming to rest at midnight off the coast of Anzio, with British ships five miles north and another American contingent of the VI Corps a few miles south at Nettuno, scout boats turned to the shore. Firing bursts intended to roust Germans from their defenses and explode expected mines hiding in the sand, Allied destroyers began to pound the shoreline. Using the docks at Anzio and Nettuno, they began landing operations at 2 a.m. Long lines of soldiers streamed off the ships, crossed the beach on mine-cleared lanes, and swarmed into the town. Overwhelming the docks, the ships also disgorged their cargo of men and matériel from the shallow water as the LSTs (Landing Ship, Tanks) opened their bows like the maws of giant sharks into the surf. Soldiers stepped ashore nearly dry as tanks and trucks splashed and churned to the beaches. The sand was quickly compacted with tracks, but where it was too soft, men muscled their wheeled gear out of sinkholes.

The landing indeed caught the Germans by surprise, and American GIs bested the single company of German soldiers that had been left behind to guard the coast. The port villages were secured, and Allied forces made initial thrusts inland toward the larger towns in the center of the former marshland. By the afternoon of January 22, beachfront roads had been laid so that LSTs could speed the delivery of invasion forces and supplies. By nightfall, troops were three to four miles inland. By midnight, more than thirty-six thousand troops and 3,200 vehicles were ashore, representing 90 percent of the invasion force. The beachhead had been established with little resistance and few casualties.

In the days after the landing at Anzio, the Allies, by many accounts, dithered when they should have taken advantage of catching the Nazis flat-footed by pushing forward with the attack. The German troops were scattered thinly and had insufficient supplies. Plans called for the Allies to sweep inland toward Rome, but the advance faltered, as leadership worried that the forward forces would become trapped without adequate reinforcements and a resupply corridor, and planned advances toward inland German positions were halted. The operation's American commander, Major General John P. Lucas, sent out exploratory raids but ultimately decided to gather his forces just inland from the coast until supply ships could ensure the troops would be able to sustain a forward push.

Meanwhile, the German commander, Field Marshal Albert Kesselring, in a posh command post in the hills north of Rome, was awoken at dawn on January 22 with reports of the onslaught and immediately ordered thousands of troops into defensive lines all along the Mussolini Canal and in the towns along the hills bordering the flat Anzio plains. He supported the troop movement with an aerial bombardment that kept Allied forces ducking for cover. That decisive response from the Germans resulted in the Allies becoming pinned down at the coast. Reserve ground forces did indeed come up from the Winter Line and down from Rome, and Adolph Hitler sent reinforcements from Germany, Yugoslavia, and France. In that respect, the feint worked as Allied leadership had hoped.

Coastal towns were flattened as the artillery flew and both armies dug in. A buildup of troops and firepower increased on both sides. Lucas's meek approach after storming the beach meant that when the battle was finally enjoined—two days after the landing—each side faced an army of comparable strength, resulting in a stalemate and ongoing campaign that would stagger through the next four months.

The people of the Anzio area—who had streamed out into the streets to watch the occupation unfold from the sea—were rounded up for evacuation. Mostly women, children, and the elderly, they were marched to the shore, some balancing bundles of belongings on their heads, and loaded onto Allied ships to be ferried south to Naples. Children bawled as they were led through the decimated town, where the waterfront shops and holiday hotels had been so thoroughly destroyed that in one case a wooden window frame stood bare as the building around it lay in piles. Many buildings along the beach had been reduced to heaps of rubble, while those remaining sported gashes that exposed their interior rooms. A massive portrait of Mussolini that had been mounted on a building leaned against a ruined wall, stitched with bullet holes. Soldiers of the Allied armies guarded the port and the camps, British troops distinguished by their "turtle shell" helmet ringed with a wide flared brim, Americans sporting the M1 helmet with its high bowl and short front brim.

As the invasion continued, the Anzio port became, by tonnage of cargo unloaded, the sixth-largest port in the world. The Allies found ways to cope with the artillery and air barrages. "On the third day VI Corps burrowed itself into the wine cellars of Nettuno," reported Robert Burhans, the Force historian. Army leaders also commandeered spots like the caves under the Borghese villa between the towns because "German long-range 170mm artillery and railroad guns were concentrating their power on the port."

The Allied landing had not immediately crushed the Winter Line or pushed back the occupying Germans, but it did have the effect of getting Berlin's attention. Hitler called the incursion "the abscess below Rome." According to Burhans, "[The Anzio beachhead] was an area which, by Hitler's personal order, twice publicly repeated, was to be completely wiped out."

Chapter 19

May 2011

My feet were on Italian soil, specifically a jasmine-lined walkway along the beach at Anzio. But my thoughts on the first day of the walk through my father's battlefields were about navigating a road across the North Dakota prairie. Just two tracks in the dust, weeds sprouting from a center ridge. Dad walked down one, while I skipped along in the other. Ahead, across the asphalt of the state road, our old wooden grain bin leaned downwind, its siding silvered and gouged after years of being scoured by blowing dirt. Beyond, a wheat field dipped and stretched away to a stand of trees that contained the shell of a farm truck perfect for a kid's imagination. But for once, I was alone with my father, a rare event with none of my eight siblings around.

"Stand up straight," he told me, and I looked over at him, striding along in his farmer's uniform of striped gray bib overalls, two shiny silver buttons and U-shaped clasps on his chest connecting the shoulder straps to the pants over the stomach. As usual, you could barely see his eyes under the long bill of his railroad cap, made of the same striped gray cloth. That cap came down so far over his forehead and was worn so incessantly that when he removed it, he had a stark line above his eyebrows where the tanned, dirt-caked skin ended and a pasty white forehead began. His neck was red under short-cropped hair. His arms swung slowly as he walked. His calloused hands were at rest. I did not recall a limp on the lanky frame of this stoic farmer who was my father. His exact words beyond that moment were gone, but I recalled how he proceeded to show and tell his seven-year-old son how to walk with good posture, shoulders back, looking forward, not at the ground.

"Stand up straight" would be the army way, no other possibilities. Keep your eyes ahead, know what's coming at you. Advice as good for a man in middle age as it was for the little boy who could barely tie his shoes. And a rare memory of instruction from a father who was more ghost than man in my life.

As I set off from Anzio, I tried to square my shoulders against the straps of my pack, as he would want me to do, as he must have done, marching in a long line of helmeted soldiers, under a much weightier pack that contained all the necessities of life except for his weapon, which would be in his hands and ready for duty.

I walked alone on the first day of my trek. Susie and I had decided that she would travel by bus to the village near our agriturismo, and I would tackle the first—and longest—leg solo. My siblings and their spouses had departed for the Rome airport, comically cramming their luggage into the tiny rental car. After the group events of the weekend, I just wanted to be alone for a bit with this project and see what transpired. We hoped she'd be okay figuring out her travel, because she didn't speak Italian any better than I did. But we were comfortable phrase-book tourists, and we thought she'd have a better start with the bus and an easy short walk to the farm B and B than a very long walk burdened by the backpack on our first day out.

I walked next to an oceanfront road, opposite a cement breakwater separating me from the sea. The pack straps pulled my shoulders back like invisible hands. Thinking of the eighteen kilometers on plan for the day, my pace was quick as I moved into Nettuno, which seemed a larger and more successful vacation destination than Anzio. On the waterfront shopping street, I navigated through pedestrians, then stepped into a small store selling basic groceries and general supplies, with a front window sporting a very American icon: Mickey Mouse, for sale as a plush toy. On such an eventful trip, my travel notebook was filling quickly with impressions, so I purchased another. I didn't buy the Disney mascot. As the morning's trek was to be mostly in the country, I provisioned myself with some backup lunch items. Wanting to cut my fruit and cheese as if on a picnic, I also bought a small folding knife. Palming the items, I thought of Dad's few soldier's relics that had fallen into my hands: a thin, leather-bound notebook; a crumbling shaving kit embossed with his name; and a telescoping tin cup with a lid. No knives or other weapons remained in his belongings.

I imagined that the proof of his service lay heavily enough in his head and his gimpy leg.

Wood smoke wafted in the air of the late-May morning, which had started chilly along the water. The twin briny smells of fish and seaweed hung just above the smoke, thicker and more prominent. If the brimstone of battle could have been avoided, Dad would have very likely encountered those smells as well, as foreign to a prairie man as the lilting syllables of the Italian language I heard from shoppers crowding Nettuno's sidewalks. All was obliterated as I walked through a cloud of perfume swirling around local ladies showing off their finds and gossiping at a shop door.

The many small businesses of Nettuno, situated in two- and three-story buildings, offered the glassy visage of recent construction interspersed with the facades of the previous generation, cracking plaster and paint-peeled window sashes, waiting for the store to change hands or for another round of urban renewal. The scene betrayed scant history beyond my own generation. Just beyond the town center, however, a bit of old Nettuno appeared. A circular stone tower, its top ringed with notches above arches, rose behind a stone gate. The entrance revealed a thick stone wall, and the way it sloped outward at the base seemed to indicate a very old construction style, before techniques to stiffen a vertical wall were discovered. A historical marker identified it as the Palazzo Pamphilj, said to date to 1600 and once owned by another family whose ranks included a pope and whose name blazes over one of Rome's premier art museums, the Doria Pamphilj Gallery. The palace changed hands to the Borgheses and later was operated by a religious sect as a school. It was an emblem of history, somehow surviving the destruction of the war. It stood as a gateway to a Renaissance village, and a brief walk down its main street removed all the sights of modern Nettuno. I imagined this enclave of stone and pale-orange plaster buildings lining the cobbled street as the city of centuries ago, perched on the edge of the sea and looked after by its palace patron. The facade and dome of a church faced a small square, and views between the buildings revealed a bristle of sailboat masts in the marina. A block farther, the lane wound its way back out to the modern shopping district. I felt I had tripped over an unexpected threshold and landed in another time.

Opposite the castle entrance sat the seat of city government, which struck me as an updated addition to the castle. Its square clock tower sported a notched flat roof and half-moon arches, and the plaster and stone colors ran from tan to orange, seemingly the signature of the local stone. People in suits bustled by me to dash under the flags adorning the entrance.

A turn in the road away from the ocean was marked by an imposing church, and I searched for the entrance beyond a broad, sloping courtyard. Granite cobbles set in fan shapes led to an arched covered walkway. I walked through the copper-clad doors, adorned with significant scenes in the church's history, into the hushed chapel, muted lighting setting a gilded altar to glow.

I had stepped into Santurio St. Maria Goretti, the sanctuary of a local girl elevated to sainthood. I surveyed the modest design of the church, built in the decades following the war, and the brief but proud history of the local saint from an earlier century. I could not help but filter my impressions through the lens of my father's war. He would not have seen this church; it had been built in the years of reconstruction, and Maria Goretti had not been canonized until 1950. Because her remains were in this grand new edifice, had her previous resting place been bombed into rubble? Had my father heard the story of this peasant girl, whose heart was so pure that she came back to comfort the townspeople after she had tragically died? Was his response like mine, trying to picture the village in her era and how the townspeople processed the circumstances of her death and subsequent happenings in the context of their beliefs? I could imagine that their grief over losing a revered community member would have them seeing her in the faces and deeds of their friends, for surely her spirit lived in their hearts, as do all lost loved ones. That she died at age eleven no doubt heightened their grief. The merging of Maria Goretti's historic tale with the precise brick and concrete church construction spoke also of the resilience of the local people. The war that destroyed their town did not erase the village's history; it was their task to build it back and give it context.

I turned inland from the town's rebuilt cathedral and navigated through a multiroad intersection, soon seeing Nettuno's traffic and homes thinning to a rural scene. Once in the country, my senses became attuned to the rigors of the highway, as the only way to trek through the countryside was on the edge of the road. Rural communities there, just like at home, often were linked by just one paved thoroughfare. Warily, I walked facing oncoming traffic and stepped onto the grassy edge whenever trucks approached. But it was mostly small cars, whining along. I passed acres of field crops, green rows waving in the breeze. A wide tractor lumbered into view, its knobby rear tires spilling off the asphalt. I stepped farther off the side, which gained me a respectful nod from the old farmer atop the bouncing seat.

I tried to imagine what this land looked like seven decades earlier, when it was contested by warring armies who staked their claim with sudden air strikes and artillery shells that would carve holes into the earth and send men tumbling for cover. Rough gravel would have been under Erick's feet, and the ditch would be littered with mangled metal and even twisted bodies, face down and awkward in the mud until the corpses could be retrieved for a more respectful last chapter. In the distance, smoke would rise from some skirmish. Off across the field, unplanted that year by the fleeing farmers, mounded soil would signify bomb craters, mud holes where soldiers could dive for a bit of cover if their position was discovered and targeted. They would curse as they landed in the ditch, just as they did when trying to dig a foxhole in the swampy terrain; chop just eighteen inches below the surface and your hole would start filling up with groundwater.

I scanned up the road and then looked down at my map in futility. I should have reached a turn, and I sensed a mistake. I crumpled the map and then released it, smoothing the creases and squinting into its lines. Seeing structures along the road ahead, I pushed on, vowing to resolve my concerns at the next corner. At the crossroads of tiny Tre Cancelli I tried to correct course, veering off the road at the combined deli / gas station that seemed to be most of the town. I reconnoitered a bit before sitting down at a plastic table next to the gas pumps and pulling out maps, and luckily found my location. And where I'd gone wrong. I needed to hike the highway to the next intersection and then head south. I squared my shoulders, which tightened as I had shrugged free of the heavy pack, and eyed the trek ahead.

After the way forward had been plotted, I suddenly felt hungry. I picked up a wrapped sandwich, stammered out thanks to the clerk, and took it to a small table next to the espresso machine. The sandwich did a stellar imitation of processed factory food, meager and bland, its plastic wrapper slick with corporate logos. Nobody but me was eating the stuff, and this was clearly a place for grab-and-go, not sit-and-snack.

The shop buzzed with travelers and laborers, though, and all were more interesting than the food. Everybody but me was drinking coffee. Espresso, to be precise, while standing, leaning against the coffee bar. They ordered it so fast the syllables flew, and it arrived almost as quickly in tiny ceramic cups, the saucer blooming with a miniature spoon, a slender wrapped chocolate, and a slim paper sleeve containing sugar. The sugar packet was quickly dispensed into the steaming cup, the espresso agitated with a tink-tink of the spoon and then just as quickly lifted to the lips and tossed back. Many left the chocolate behind as they strode out the door, hopped into their vehicles, and sped away.

Finishing my lunch, I crumpled the plastic into a garbage can, then stepped up to the bar and ordered an espresso. Into it went the sugar, tink-tink-tink. I downed it with my best imitation of casual Italian flair, regarded the empty cup with appreciation, then palmed the chocolate, hoisted my pack, and headed for the door. The sweet shot was indeed an enticement to get moving.

As I was the shop's only customer for the moment, the matronly clerk gestured to the empty road and said sympathetically, "No rides to city." She pronounced it "chitta," but I got it. She smiled with her eyes, searching to see if I understood.

"No," I said, pointing the other way. "I, ah . . ." I tried to recall my speech. "Io a piedi, in memoria di mio padre, who was a soldato in la guerre due."

I was ashamed that my memorization was so atrocious. Nicoletta's hard work was nearly forgotten in the moment, at that crucial point where I could have described my project. "I am walking," I wanted to say, "in memory of my father, who had been a soldier here in World War II."

But when I stammered it out to Italians, it would inevitably come out garbled and incomplete. They would respond incredulously with "Piedi?!" which I knew meant "Walking?!" So that, along with the basic word for "I"—*Io*—replaced the grammatically appropriate *Sto*, or "I am," and *camminando*, which is the verb for "walking" instead of *a piedi*, the adverb meaning "on foot." You'd think a writer and editor could grasp the distinction. It was truly "non parlo l'Italiano" for me. Yes, even after the class series and Pimsleur's rhythmic repeated audio prompts, my efforts prior to the trip proved not to settle the Italian language into my brain or onto my tongue. Beyond the basics that did tumble out of my mouth, conjuring up further details, such as my destination being Rome or that my father was injured before the city's liberation, well, those got a little lost before they could even be blurted out for consideration. I had once pulled out the written statement and read it, which certainly worked. But even if I stammered it out, however little squeaked through, the message always provoked a response.

The clerk's eyebrows rose to the hairline of her auburn bouffant, and she leaned back to regard me. Clearly, she understood. She bolstered me with "Molto bene!" and a couple of other encouragements delivered with a shake of the head. She handed me a banana and asked "Aqua?"

I shook my head, holding up my full water bottle, and with "Grazie mille!" and a slight bow, accepted the banana. I called up my other killer Italian: "Ciao!"

It was so encouraging to make a connection, even if it consisted of fumbling through a prepared script and being unable to actually have a conversation or know for sure I'd been understood. The encounter echoed in my thoughts as I strode along the edge of the road, facing the oncoming traffic, trying to return to the route the Force had taken to its first encampment after disembarking on the Anzio beachhead.

Back on the highway, I stepped onto an approach to pull out my music player and plug the headphones into my ears. The beats of the British trip-hop band Massive Attack pulsed. With an extra four clicks due to my detour, it was going to be a long afternoon, and I needed percussion to quicken my pace. Double time, wasn't that what the army called it? I smiled inwardly and considered that my fastest walk was probably time and a half.

If I thought I was going to see evidence of battles that had taken place seventy years previous, my first hiking day was clearing up that idea. The vista across the road to my right was all agriculture, plowed fields or undulating wheat, broken occasionally by a cluster of buildings around a farmhouse. There were no repaired old churches, cratered fields, or industrial ruins. To my left, a ditch with long grass fronted a high chain-link fence that seemed to stretch for miles. Only more grassland was visible beyond, but its galvanized steel gleamed in stark contrast to the low, rusty farm fencing opposite. Finally, I spotted a sign mounted high, "Zona Militaria," with a warning to keep out. There was no further explanation, but at least, I mused to myself, it was a bit of a connection to my purpose.

Paralleling the fence, I reached my first canal bridge, low and concrete. The military fence angled down to the water, warnings posted everywhere. On the far side sat an old shed, probably a pump house, twenty yards off the bank. Judging by its decrepitude, I saw it as one of the few landmarks likely in place during the war. I stopped for a picture but also to conjure images. The soldiers used landmarks like this for cover or reconnaissance. It had survived the continual warfare, but through my camera lens I imagined that I could make out a series of bullet holes piercing its crumbling walls.

As I stood on the bridge looking across the canal, a delivery truck lumbered by with one significant word writ large on its side in red and blue: "Norge." Startled by coincidence, I thought that maybe I was not alone on this trek after all; my Norwegian ancestors were with me. "Tuk" I said in thanks to the receding truck, raising my water bottle in a mock toast to the Scandinavian-branded company. Strangely, this reminder of another land caused me to feel more at home.

Swallowing a drink of water and considering the fields, I saw another link to my dad: the land did look like the prairies of home. The horizon's unbroken line, above a table of soil and below a dome of sky, was as familiar as the effect of espresso on the brain. My farmer father had traveled farther than he'd ever imagined and set his feet on Anzio mud that was obviously familiar with the plow.

To that smooth plane of bottomland, Erick and his fellow Forcemen had come to face their most challenging battles, but their previous fights in the cold, rainy winter of 1943 had been in the forested slopes and flinty heights of the mountains massed around Monte la Difensa, many miles south. On my horizon I could see the Lepini Hills, where the enemy had again lorded over the Allies, until the battle sent them running. I would try to keep the Lepinis on my left as I headed south to skirt the edge of the farmland bordering the sea.

Sticking to my directions, I turned off to a narrower paved side road. A stand of trees signaled a driveway, no doubt leading to a farm. This road carried few vehicles, but now one sped by, and I jumped, having not heard it due to the music in my ears. I blinked back to the scene and was startled to see a woman standing by a copse of trees, a bit back from the road. I was on the other side and still many yards distant. She looked at me, then looked away, and I wondered if she might be waiting for a ride. Coming closer, I saw a metal folding chair set in the shadow of the trees, and I realized there was no driveway, just a gravel approach that dead-ended in the small grove. Was this a rural bus stop?

I strode farther, and once more we regarded each other. I got close enough to realize, again with some alarm, that she looked starkly out of place. Bright colors glowed on her lips and eyelids, and her hooded eyes fixed a challenging stare at me. Her arms were bare, as were her legs, olive skin dark in the summer sun. I was trying not to stare back but realized that she was barely—and provocatively—dressed. A battered leather handbag leaned against the metal chair, its top gaping open.

Then I was across the road from her. She raised one hand to plump, pursed lips, two fingers extended and slightly parted. Her eyebrows went up. No, I shook my head. I didn't have a cigarette. I smiled a little, politely I hoped, but I did not break stride.

As I walked on, I could feel her eyes still on me, no doubt wondering what I was doing walking out there, where I was going. Possibly wondering what anyone would be doing there, if not seeking the services of a prostitute along a remote stretch of road that almost certainly carried a reputation. Surely all her customers arrived in cars.

I've noticed that when blood rushes to my head, sounds become echoey, distant. My beat-heavy music played on unheard. The disconnection was akin to grasping at a memory but fanning the air, imagination reduced to a hazy closed window. A truck caught me in its slipstream, and its rumble was gone as fast as the hot air that washed the grasses into a frenzy. I pulled the headphones from my ears, self-conscious that I should look so strange, an American with a backpack blithely walking along this clandestine road, naively unaware of reality.

Scanning the way ahead, wondering if there were more women stationed on chairs along the rural lanes of the Anzio plains, I realized with a start that I could envision another connection to the war. Hundreds of thousands of men were sent into combat far from home, possessions on their backs, loneliness weighty on their shoulders. They might seek any rare comfort available in the upheaval and offered by desperate or opportunistic people. Prostitution was so widespread, the men were counseled on it and treated for its accompanying diseases. Although not a relic of the war, the sight on that forlorn road reminded me that some struggles were as eternal as the cobbled streets of Rome. Perhaps I was not as far from the battlefield as seven decades led me to believe.

Chapter 20

May 2011

I confirmed that local drivers were not used to seeing pedestrians on the Anzio roads. A semitruck driver warned me with his horn, while one member of a carload of youth yelped out the window. I crossed paths with a few bicyclists who, as a touring cyclist myself, I expected to be more friendly. A few waved, and meeting one at a stop sign, I chatted with him. He mirrored some of my Seattle cycling friends, a lean man clad in a bright jersey, taking quick breaths through a trim gray beard. A local on his daily training ride, he assured me that I was now on the right path to the coast.

Another interaction was less satisfying. A car slowed next to me, and the passenger leaned out to ask for directions. From me! I so wished I could converse with him, and even more—confidently route them on. "Dove di mare?" he asked.

"Si, di mare," I could at least say, pointing in the general direction of the sea. No doubt, across the fields and beneath the sun that had started to make its descent, the ocean could not be more than a few miles away. Asking a further question—perhaps if I wanted a ride—he exchanged looks with the driver when realizing by my stammered response that I didn't speak Italian, but they pulled out and headed off in the right direction, toward the beach, and toward my goal of Foce Verde. Finding "di mare" might be their quest for the day, and it was comforting to think that even Italian visitors would get turned around in a landscape as featureless as a blank stare. But sighting the Tyrrhenian Sea would be only my first triumph, and even then a poor substitute for my true goal. I plodded on, blinking away the salt dripping off my brow. Could an outsider ever dig any deeper than bringing mapped coordinates into three dimensions? Under the punishing sun it seemed doubtful, even without considering the fourth dimension, time, that erases so quickly the evidence of our history.

By midafternoon the horizon shimmered with waves of rising heat. Late May, in this Mediterranean climate, felt like midsummer. I hadn't passed another town since lunchtime, and my water bottle was getting light. I regretted not taking the backup bottle offered by the deli clerk but immediately discounted the idea. It would have added a couple more pounds to the pack now chafing my shoulder blades. I'd been training for the walk, carrying around my pack with a load of rocks, but it hadn't been a true test. I should have used boulders.

I knew I could hike for hours without water, really. At the end of the walk, well before dark, would be a local dinner at the farm B and B with Susie, where we'd share our day's adventures. If I had brought my backpacking water filter, I could have dropped it into one of these canals I was crossing and pumped out a refreshing bottleful. The canals were another feature of this place that no doubt had been in my dad's memories. Tree lines could be seen hugging the canal banks and lining the neighboring roads. Just like at home, a plume of dust rose and fell when a car cut across the plains on an unpaved lane.

In the war, the big Mussolini Canal became the center of no-man's-land after my dad's unit beat back the defending Germans. Cutting through the countryside from northeast hills to southwest shores, the canal served as a natural barrier for each side to use to defend their territory. The Allies had landed at Anzio north and west of the canal, while the Germans were still ensconced south and east of the waterway that angled to the sea from the hillside town of Ninfa. The Germans also held the high ground beyond the plain, where Allied troops were still putting on pressure from the other front.

I squinted into the fields, trying to envision how this meek, flat land I was walking had become the drawn-out trial and source of battle-weariness for my father's unit. Would he, also looking over the land, have experienced a jolt of recognition? Landing somewhere new, especially in an extreme discovery mode on your first trip abroad, would trigger comparisons with lived experience while bringing anything foreign into sharp focus. Erick could have felt at home on these flat plains, their countenance so similar to where he'd grown up. When able to tear his thoughts away from the concern for his own safety and that of his Force brethren, surely his mind placed him back on his own familiar land, striding amid the wheat or eyeing the weather on the horizon. With many fewer distractions and no danger, even I had trouble staying in the present, my mind doing mental calisthenics so I could perhaps see this place through his eyes. Mussolini's public works project had created this land, fertile and largely uninhabited. Erick had seen his own corner of the Dakota plains similarly occupied by the settler and the plow, still a sparse smattering of humanity clinging to it, trying to make a new life. I was again the interloper among these visions, able to see the movie but as a spectator, not a character.

But when Erick would look across the flatland to the north or east, he would see in the distance the steep hills and jumbled rooflines of the ancient villages that clung to those rocky hillsides. That's where the comparison to his homeland ended and the terrain veered sharply into the now-familiar territory that he and his Force compatriots had been slogging through since landing at Naples three months earlier.

When Erick encountered boot-shaped Italy, he also discovered a climate quite different from the hot-and-cold dry prairie of North Dakota and certainly unlike the chilly Norway of his parents. Influenced by latitude and the warm waters of seas on both sides of the peninsula-shaped land, the south of Italy, especially the low-elevation coastal areas, held a climate generally more moderate and forgiving in winter and more oppressive with heat and humidity in summer. But the boot, in the winter of the war, was reared back for a kick, to be inflicted on many thousands of fighting men and women deposited on its land. The winter of 1943–44, when Allied soldiers debarked at Naples and pushed north, contained plenty of misery for fighters and their medical and support personnel bivouacked near the ever-changing front lines—cold days, some barely above freezing, and rain-soaked, mucky soils. Fighting in the higher elevations, the Force had already suffered through the spitting cold rain that turned to sleet and snow and the cold fog that enveloped the craggy battlefields.

As I sweated my way toward the coast, aiming to find the mouth of the big canal, I imagined being in the war, walking the edge of our defensive line and surveying the actions of the enemy beyond the watery border. A staggered line of soldiers in olive green spread through the field off the road, arms bent to hold their rifles gut-high and ready. Another line formed behind me, their boots crunching gravel and the low thrum of a jeep engine slowly gaining on our position. *Let's do it,* I imagined my soldier-self saying, hair rising on the back of my neck. *We will show them the true meaning of determination and what Americans think of an invading dictator.* Hand gestures prompted men to step out of line and drop to the ground by the canal, eyes narrow as they crawled rifle-first into position. Shadows moved behind the thin tree cover far beyond this water ditch. *We know they're watching us, and they surely know we see them. It's just a matter of time . . .*

The canal along my road, however, did not match my imagination or the news reports of the dictator's big channel. In fact, it paled in comparison. Perhaps Mussolini's canal, abandoned and dried up, was no longer a prominent feature on the map. I could have been looking at subsidiary waterways, maintained out of necessity to feed thirsty crops. The modest streams that I'd seen on the first day of walking the battlefields were not grand enough to hold back armies. I kept watch ahead as I mirrored my father's imagined step.

The heat of the summer day seemed most intense in the late afternoon, perhaps because the sun had just been burning through the sky for so long. A haze had turned the blue of the noontime sky into a pale glaze above my head. The azure color only returned as my eyes panned the horizon. I was down to the last precious swallows of warm water in my modern-day canteen, the reusable plastic bottle, when I finally sniffed a whiff of the sea. The smell, so familiar from my home at the edge of Washington's Puget Sound, spread from my lungs through my torso and down into my tired leg muscles, seeming to stretch and loosen them. I scanned the sky for seagulls but instead saw the spire of a church in the distance, then a grove of trees announcing, finally, the next town. This must be Foce Verde, I thought, the first Italian land defended by Dad and his comrades on their path to help liberate this occupied country.

The narrow road widened, and I began to cross side streets that led off into shallow groups of homes set in modest grids among trees. The developments were all recent, no styles older than perhaps twenty years, wear and tear just starting to show on sooty chimneys and dented road signs. Soon I set my feet on a sidewalk, and the traffic slowed and increased as the town loomed. At a large intersection I spotted a sign for the beach and turned right again—and back into the countryside. Instead of an ocean beach, squat industrial buildings and clusters of homes edged on the field ahead. Looming over it all was a square white building surrounded by a complex of smaller structures, all encased in another tall chain-link fence. As I passed, I guessed that it might be a nuclear power plant, its massive vents visible along the tower's open side, with the other side devoid of windows. With no activity or sounds coming from the plant, it looked out of use, but giant power lines set on orange and white steel scaffolds hummed overhead.

Expecting to arrive at a village with shops and activity, I walked instead nearly to the sea itself, coming first upon parking lots for the nearby beaches. They were fronted by clusters of condominiums, and one of those, thankfully, contained a small shop flying colorful flags from its awning. Gelato! Praise the pope and pass the ammunition! This was an Italian treat that would be delightful on any day but absolutely exceptional for a hiker advancing slowly toward the end of a long day on the road. I luxuriated in the air-conditioned shop, taking my time to review the many ice cream flavors on display while begging the idling clerk for a water-bottle refill. Finally deciding on a large scoop of "limone," I stepped again into the sunny day to slurp down the creamy lemon ice, which began to melt at an alarming rate. I crossed the parking lot and sloughed off my pack so I could sit on a bench by the sea, facing the crashing waves and stretching my legs in front of me. Yellow drips went off my wrist to my shorts, but I couldn't be bothered as I reveled in the delectable respite. The gelato was too soon gone, the water bottle again empty, so I returned to the store for an encore as I determined my next move toward Susie and my home for the night. The second round held crunchy pistachios.

It had taken me all day and one mistaken detour to reach my first goal. I had indeed found Foce Verde, an unassuming collection of a half dozen buildings and a one-sided lane of homes huddled around the intersection of two roads, next to a small park. Beyond the condos, a row of holiday villas and low-slung motels stretched south along the beach. But as I sat on a cement wall at the edge of the park, I realized what made this destination significant. In Italian, *foce* means "mouth" or "outfall" (thank you, Berlitz pocket dictionary), and *verde*, of course, means "green." This was the mouth of a waterway. Could it be the end point of Mussolini's big canal, emptying into the sea?

The little spot of land, edged to its west by the ocean and to its south by the green-fringed waterway feeding into it, was surely near the first campsite of my father's last battleground. This was where the Force encamped as they took up their duty to guard this liquid border and not let Hitler's army pass. From the beach inland two kilometers was the front line of Dad's war for nearly four months in 1944, raw winter into muddy spring. His determined unit held the Germans from advancing toward the Allied command base. Not only that, but from this spot, Force raiding teams—my father among them—would slip across the canal under the cover of darkness, gather information about the enemy, take prisoners, and build a reputation as ruthless fighters so stealthy that they came to be known as the Black Devils of Anzio. *They never heard us coming.*

I set out along the beach road, passing a campground and a couple of restaurants, their parking lots empty on this late afternoon. Two modest breakwaters formed a pincer into the surf and protected a small boat launch. Reaching the next intersection, which included helpful street signs, I turned away from the rhythmic thrum of the surf and scuffed along sandy sidewalks, my back to the sun. I had come to the center of the small resort town. There were absolutely no indications a war had ever been fought over this burg, which seemed as sleepy as the waning day. No need to pull out the maps; I could picture it in my mind. It would be just two more kilometers inland along the road toward Latina before reaching the next village, beyond which, in another quick kilometer, lay my agriturismo—a working farm that rented rooms. I double-timed.

I exited the next village, walking by the only shop that looked slightly like a grocery, which was closed, and venturing back again onto the edge of the road as the sidewalks disappeared. It would be farmland until the outskirts of Latina, ten kilometers ahead. I began to scan for signs of a farm B and B but instead spotted a person walking toward me, swinging two hiking poles and taking the decisive strides of a Nordic skier. It was Susie, of course, coming out to meet me. My ski-instructor wife had no pack, so she must have found and checked into our night's accommodations. Indeed she had, after a long day on slow buses. A few minutes earlier she had dropped her pack but decided to shake off her travel tedium and see if she could find me on the road. We embraced gratefully, smiling proudly at our abilities to navigate two different paths through this foreign land and end up together at our destination.

We hiked the last stretch together, Susie leading me in and telling me how she was barely able to communicate with the young farm woman who was alone at the agriturismo. "In fact," Susie said, "we might be the only guests. The parking area was bare, and the rooms adjoining ours seemed empty." We stepped off the road into the wide gravel driveway fronting the low building that housed our accommodations. Across the road, plants pushed at white fabric that was stretched over lengthy rows to protect whatever crops lay beneath. This was a technique I used on a small scale at home in my garden to shield our wintering vegetables. Surprised to see it here, I looked forward to exploring the farm but breathed deeply at being in sight of the day's destination.

Susie pointed to the office in the small house situated in front of a long, brick-red building with a motel-like layout. The rooms faced away from the car park, looking instead to the fields and a series of horse pastures. A half dozen horses grazing in a far paddock were the only signs of life. I recalled from the online brochure that the guest rooms were actually converted horse stables, so the horses were no surprise, although I hoped they were stabled elsewhere. Staying on farms in the Anzio countryside not only met my desire as a former farm boy to experience rural life there but also resonated with my quest to see the land as my father would have done. He very well might have rested on haystacks in an actual stable; ours would likely be a stable in name only, without a pile of straw ticking in sight.

My shoulders willingly gave up the pack, which skidded to a halt as it hit the gravel entranceway. We stepped into the office, and I rang the bell to summon the young woman, who mocked a relieved "whew" that Susie had found me and smiled a welcome. Susie had not yet done the paperwork or paid for the room, so I handled the business, and we both produced our passports for photocopying.

"Could we have dinner here?" I asked, pointing at the restaurant door across the empty parking area.

"Unfortunately... no," the young woman said. "It does not open on weeknights until the summer season, and that is in two more weeks."

"Is there dinner in the village?" I asked, looking up the road. But again it was no; there were no services yet open in that small town. The closest would be Foce Verde. Hearing that, my tired back muscles spasmed slightly, and I looked at Susie, shaking my head and telling her that was too far to walk after my long hike.

The desk clerk thought for a second. "Alore" (Well then), she said, holding out her hands. "Do not be concerned. I will bring you dinner." It would be added to the bill.

I could have hugged her, a sentiment that must have come through as she shooed us out of the office and said simply, "Go. Relax." Clearly she knew enough English to satisfy guests.

An hour later I was sitting on the tiled patio attached to our room, reviewing the jottings in my new notebook and looking at the row of young trees that paralleled the rooms and cast long shadows our way from the setting sun, when a rhythmic clack-clacking got my attention. It came from around the end of the building, and I looked down the row of empty patios for each room, which were bordered on each side by a three-foot stucco wall. The tiled surfaces of our decks ended in a third wall with a gate, nicely enclosing each patio space without sacrificing the view. It felt private but not unfriendly.

The clatter got louder, and into view along the tiled walkway came the young woman pushing a cart with large wheels, on which was transported our dinner. The cart was rattling noisily every time the wheels went over a grout seam in the tiles. She rolled the cart through the gate onto our deck, lifted white cloth napkins off a series of plates, set out china and cutlery for each of us on our small table, then wished us a good dinner and a good evening before departing. A scruffy farm dog stayed behind, peering across the deck from beyond the wrought iron gate, clearly hoping we were the type to toss a guy a bone.

I didn't blame him; the spread represented a minor feast. Quarters of thin-crust pizza adorned with various toppings were stacked upon one platter: tomato sauce and cheese, chopped vegetables and sausage. Another plate held thin slices of prosciutto, the ham reddish and translucent and veined with white fat. Next to it were piled thick slices of rustic bread. A third platter cradled wedges of ripe melon, rounds of kiwifruit, and a pyramid of fat cherries. A fourth revealed a deconstructed caprese salad: generous slices of red tomato and an arrow of spiky wild arugula surrounded two mounds of glistening mozzarella cheese. The stunning display centered this bounty of local goodness, and I blinked to realize the salad's color scheme perfectly mirrored something I had seen regularly flying in the breeze roadside: the red, white, and green Italian flag. The trays were edged with bottled water, Peroni beer, and a bottle of local red wine. On the shelf below were desserts. My long hike had left me powerfully hungry, and I had expected to receive takeout containers of unremarkable dishes, scooped up at the last minute from the dregs of a deli case. Instead, I was surveying five-star room service. I cued up the DJ musician Danger Mouse on my iPad, whose new recording "Rome" cast a modern electronic soundtrack over the cooling breeze that wafted across our laden table.

As the horses munched grass quietly and the trees' long shadows softened the setting sun, we enjoyed a meal that soothed the aches of the long walk. The travels of my soldier father were absent from my mind for the first time all day, but any comparison to Erick's plight would have been laughable. I decided to live in the moment. There would be plenty of opportunities to reach back in time in the days ahead.

Chapter 21
February 1944

Spending my first night on the Anzio plains, perhaps as close as I would get to my father's encampment, I thought about the strategic plan that married the Anzio beachhead campaign with pressure on the Germans' inland defenses and considered how Erick and the Force could have been deployed quite easily to the other end of that pincer attack.

Two weeks of rest and relaxation after their mountainous campaigns had rejuvenated the soldiers of the Force, and incorporating 250 replacements had put a dent in their diminished numbers. While recuperating at Santa Maria Capua, word had spread that they would be sent north again to become part of the II Corps assault on the Winter Line across the Rapido River. They prepared for another trip up Highway 6 to continue the fight, wrote Burhans, and had "fairly completed plans for the operation against Mt. Cairo," another high redoubt in the Cassino hill mass. But new orders arrived; they were to trade their mountain fighting for a sand assault. On January 29, they prepared to debark for the beachhead at Anzio, and by 3 p.m. the next day, they were packed into their trucks and convoying to Concentration Area 3, west of Naples at Pozzuoli. The Force contingent, after two months of hard charging, numbered sixty-eight officers and 1,165 soldiers of other ranks, including Staff Sergeant Erick Thorness.

At dusk on January 31, the Forcemen boarded LSTs and LCIs (Landing Craft Infantry vessels) at the port of Pozzuoli and cast off north, hugging the coast. Enemy aircraft did not bother the long convoy moving in bright moonlight. Sailing through the night within a massive contingent of Allied ships, they reached Anzio on the morning of February 1, 1944. The ships were anchored off Anzio by dawn, and at 10 a.m., they set foot on the main pier.

The Anzio port, even a week after the initial assault, was filled with ships unloading on the piers and from hastily built beach landing sites. Out in the bay, anchored freighters offloaded DUKWs, the amphibious troop carriers. Force fighters could spot a freighter and lesser ships south of Nettuno looming as sunken hulks, beached and burning. The three Force combat regiments, service battalion, and headquarters staff disembarked from the ships and set about to quickly disperse. Their 6×6 trucks loaded with gear lumbered out of the gaping steel cargo doors of the LSTs and rolled down the army-engineered corduroy roads. Troops unloaded and scattered quickly because "there was, in fact, no safe area on the beachhead, since every foot of the ground held by Allied troops could be observed by the enemy and reached by his guns," recalled military historian Charles M. Wiltse. By noon the Force had unloaded and double-timed inland into an open field two miles west of Anzio.

As they were receiving their orders, a dogfight took place overhead, and a German bomber and Allied fighter both crashed into the sea. "We are to defend the front line of the Mussolini Canal," Frederick told his troops, "eight miles of it, from the crossing designated Bridge 5 just west of Sessuno to where the canal empties into the Tyrrhenian Sea on the south side of the town of Foce Verde."

For a unit the size of the Force, the assignment meant their personnel would be thinly stretched. Combat strength—just half of its original 2,400—included many replacements new to the unit. Both the First and Second Regiments were cut to one battalion each. New reinforcements had been attached to the Third Regiment, so it was fully staffed. Two of the three combat regiments were assigned canal guard duty, spreading themselves in a thin line along the waterway. Erick's Second Regiment was to be held in reserve and used for intelligence-gathering raids, patrols, and responses to any German attacks. They were to find an encampment spot well behind the front line. The service battalion decamped to a rearguard position northeast of Nettuno near the village of La Ferriere, which held a central location on the beachhead. Its position on a treeless plateau offered a sloping view to the Third Regiment, close enough for quick resupply of frontline needs.

The canal was a formidable obstacle, so it provided an effective defensive barrier. At spots it was up to sixty feet wide. It was eight to ten feet deep. A flat flood zone spread out on each side, edged with a slight rise. Sparse copses of trees and the occasional pump house stood lonely on the expanse. A branch of the canal split west at Bridge 5, one of a series of bridges that had crossed it, including five within the Force's defensive area, but most of those had been destroyed by the Germans. Any further crossings would have to be improvised with temporary bridges or boats.

With such flat terrain and sparse cover, any offensive actions were in clear view of the other side, so they expected skirmishes and raids to take place under the cover of darkness. As the Force settled into place on the first night, in fact, small-arms fire and grenades began to rain down on the First Regiment. The Germans had evidently observed the installation and decided to test their new foes. The move spurred the aggressive unit to action, and the Force responded with concerted fire, driving the Nazi patrol back from the water's edge. On the next night, using a hastily built bridge, Force patrols dashed across to, as recounted in the book *The Supercommandos*, "probe the German outpost positions and generally raise hell." That began a pattern that would be perfected by the night raiders of the Force to chilling and deadly effect in the months to come. The Black Devils of Anzio were about to be born.

Chapter 22

May 2011

Hiking Anzio's shoulderless roads presented me with a conundrum. I found it necessary to study the high grass lining the road, being careful not to step wrong onto hazards or off the edge of a concealed embankment. A twisted ankle or a rusty nail through the shoe could easily put a bad end to the day, or the trek. As usual, Susie accepted my risk-averse admonishments with patient good humor. But we both kept watch on the road ahead too, scanning for signs and turns and eyeing the oncoming traffic for its own very real hazards. It was a tricky combination, I thought, as we set off northeast at the crossroads nearest to the agriturismo's horse pasture to begin the second day of the hike. I imagined a soldier's lot to be similar, trudging along in a long line of dogfaces. The idea triggered my memory of a playful letter Erick wrote to his sweetheart Shirley during their early courtship while he was still recuperating from repeated surgeries in the army hospitals. I think she'd told him that she wanted to get a dog.

Dogs! That's kind of a touchy subject for soldiers. There was the Blaze incident you know and besides a soldier is a dogface, his shelter is a pup tent, he wears dog tags, his feet are dogs, he gets dog tired of the army and he has a doggone good reason as he is treated like a dog. But as pets, I like them ...

I smiled, as I know my mother surely did when she read that punny diatribe. I discovered that "the Blaze incident" was an embarrassing travel situation involving the dog owned by Colonel Elliott Roosevelt, President Franklin D. Roosevelt's son. Elliott had brought Blaze, a 130-pound bullmastiff, back to the United States after acquiring him while deployed in England. He left instructions for the pet to be sent by cargo plane to California when the military had space. A clerk gave Blaze "A" priority, which put his transport above that of soldiers. Naturally, that didn't go down well with the press or the public.

The "incident" triggered thoughts of the family dogs on the farm—most notably a scrawny mutt named Fritz, a dog that figured in my own incident, whose name must have sprung from another nickname for German troops. When I was perhaps five, I surprised the dog as he snoozed on the barn floor, and he snapped reflexively and bit me on the cheek. The bloody wound triggered a trip to the hospital and a woozy night ride home in the car, watching the yard lights dimly pierce the blackness on neighborhood farms. Soon after, Fritz disappeared, with a family line that perhaps he'd run away.

I considered my own feet, not yet dog-tired but certainly destined to be, given the pack on my back and the miles on the day's schedule. We'd not gotten an early start from the agriturismo, having had a nice conversation over coffee with the young clerk, Bernadetta, while she showed us the family's operation. They had run the agriturismo for eleven years but had been farming on that land since about 1978, the year I ended my farmwork and went off to college.

"We have been farming," said Bernadetta, choosing and pronouncing her English carefully, "since my grandmother's grandmother." Their farm, she said, was run by her parents, herself, and her three sisters. That reminded me of Italy's matriarchal society, curious but familiar from my own upbringing, as I was principally raised by my mother and my older sisters after Dad passed away when I was just nine.

As we walked to the field behind the agriturismo, our hostess, who looked to be in her midtwenties, described how her family came to be on this land.

"Like many people of Anzio," she said, "we are from Veneto." The northeastern region, as Camilla had told us, was recruited heavily by Mussolini's managers who were trying to populate the newly arable land. Many more homesteaders came from Emilia-Romagna, the region adjacent to Veneto. "They came here in the 1940s," she said, "after the war." Although they were not among the first wave of settlers, it must have been a momentous occasion to strike out into this cratered, battled-over land. I thought of my own grandparents, leaving a land where subsistence was the way of life and opportunities were few to start anew in a place where the land, the farming, and the people were the definition of foreign. Even within Italy, this would have been the case after the war. And just as my Norwegian ancestors, Bernadetta's grandparents would essentially be traveling to an unknown land, also foreign in many ways. It was only in the mid-nineteenth century that Italy became a unified country in the Risorgimento, or "resurgence," when regions combined into a kingdom and chose Rome as its capital. As the European settlers spread out over America, opening frontiers to homesteading, people of Italy's diverse regions came together. The move from north to south would trigger another challenge, as those regions were still in many ways separate entities populated by fiercely independent people, and there was a well-known prejudice by the industrious northerners toward their perceived indolent southern cousins. Even today, my Italian friends tell me, people of the north are very different from those of the south, and there exists amazement and even disdain for each other's way of life. How would a family make such a move, involving not only body but also soul?

"It must have been a big change for your family, moving here," I said.

"Yes," she said. "People in Italy stay in one place for many generations."

We stood on the edge of a field sporting a variety of crops. The floppy lambs-ear leaves of eggplant, a crop just beginning to sprout cheery purple-and-yellow flowers, alternated with rows bursting with salad greens and orderly with tomatoes, their main stems tied to a slender stake in the production method.

"The farmers leave the wine grapes for other regions," she said, clearly relieved at my interest also in the fields, "because the soil here is too sandy." She told of the family tending "twenty-five hectares," and I quickly tried conversion in my head, picturing a significant operation that stretched far beyond the fields we saw.

"Across the road," I said, pointing at the white mesh we saw covering the row crops. "This is a technique we also use at home." The mesh was stretched tightly over low hoops and anchored in place every few feet. With my background growing food year-round in our mild maritime Northwest climate, I recognized this hoop-and-fabric technique. We called it "floating row cover" and used it to keep our crops warmer, but here it was no doubt used to keep destructive insects off the plants, or possibly shade them.

"That is not our land," she said, her eyes narrowing. "It is not... pleasant to look at."

We said a cordial goodbye and stepped onto the busy Strada Sabotino, the road to Borgo Piave. In our wanderings through this countryside, I had learned that it was difficult to tell when you had crossed from one "borgo" to another. The term equates to the English word "borough," which in the United States is used to denote the administrative boundaries of some big cities. For instance, New York is made up of five boroughs, the most famous being Manhattan. In Italy, the *borgo* denoted the area of a town outside the ancient town's borders—essentially the newer part of town. But I found the designation was mostly used for the area around small villages, which were sometimes so tiny as to be only at a crossroads. Perhaps annexing the adjoining countryside allowed town leaders to collect taxes and control growth. I have always been in favor of keeping farmland in production and limiting the human tendency to sprawl.

So Borgo Piave could have begun well before we ever reached the town itself. We passed a series of small shops where the area's principal roads met at a roundabout. On offer was bread, then fruit, and finally meat. We stopped to consider the fare, wondering whether this was where Bernadetta had provisioned our previous night's feast. With such specialized shops, it would take a lot of effort to assemble a varied dinner.

The flat country road was not without traffic, dodged as we proceeded along the "verge," the British word for the road's edge. I mused on it as an evocative term, connoting an image of balancing on a tipping point, which would be an apt description for our walk. The pavement ended abruptly at the edge of the driving lane, leaving no room for comfortable walking, so we were literally in the weeds, which were sometimes knee-high, and on the slope of the ditch, sometimes precarious. Daydreaming or sightseeing was a sketchy option.

At every stop, I took off my pack with relief. The full load, probably just thirty pounds, was still quite taxing. I was hoisting a combination pack and rolling bag, and the suspension and straps were not up to the standards of a quality backpack. I should have committed to one type or the other, but the trip also included a lot of time in cities and on public transportation, making useful a wheeled bag with a telescoping handle. Now I was paying the price, as the straps cut into my shoulders, and the thin pad shielding me from the bars of the handle rubbed my shoulder blades. Guilt accompanied every tired curse, though. My father and his fellow soldiers endured so much more weight on much more primitive gear, so who was I to complain?

The Forcemen hoisted a framed rucksack that was an olive-drab canvas bag consisting of one large compartment and three outside pockets. A tubular metal frame spanned horizontally across the hips and curved up to form an inverted U between the shoulders. Flat, three-inch web straps held it to the shoulders and around the waist. A rifle and entrenching tool were strapped to either side. But here's the kicker: the Force soldiers stuffed their packs with gear weighing seventy-five pounds or more, including their wool clothes, leather boots, food rations, bedroll, and extra ammunition. They would routinely hike dozens of miles in training, making my one dozen look just like a warm-up. And their marches in war were often up steep inclines or through icy, sucking muck. I had enough knowledge of their struggles to offset the aches and pains caused by my aging body, soft physique, and inadequate training. Although I saw myself as an active, capable guy, the effort got to me. I suffered mostly in shameful silence.

Stops became more frequent, and at each one I found it a bit more challenging to ignore the sharp pain between my shoulder blades or the dull ache in my neck. Behind my knee grew a gnawing throb, as though a muscle was being stretched too far. I swore to do more conditioning before another trip and kept reminding myself of the maxim that I'd heard about repetitive physical activity: the first few days there would be pain as your body adjusted; with time your strength and endurance grew. Your body gave up eventually and said, "Okay, we're doing that again? So let's go." That thought got the pack back on my shoulders.

We strode along into the heat of the day. Ahead, the asphalt appeared to flow like ripples on a calm sea. By early afternoon we reached a crossroads outside of Borgo Pogdora, a hamlet that looked mostly like it had lost the battle against suburbia. Probably, I thought, it had succumbed to the needs of workers from nearby industrial Cisterna. We lunched on very white sandwiches from another roadside convenience store, tuna salad and tomatoes on one, ham and cheese on the other. No crusts on the bread. Considering the care and uniqueness of Italian cuisine available in cities and restaurants, these ubiquitous sandwiches were an affront. How could self-respecting lovers of great food allow them to even exist in the country? Sitting at yet another plastic table festooned with an ice-cream company's umbrella, I suddenly saw the reason. Once again, we were the only ones buying and eating these sandwiches, the modern equivalent of a soldier's MRE. This was not the way Italians had lunch; civilized people would enjoy their midday repast at home, sitting next to their burgeoning garden or leaning over a white-clothed café table, leisurely attending to a carefully composed plate.

Washing down the meager bites with my second sweet tea of the day, I leaned back to at least enjoy the shady tree spreading over our picnic table. Susie reached into her pack for goodies left over from Bernadetta's gourmet cart, and the bland bread was quickly forgotten.

Packing our things for the last leg of our hike, I realized we would be breaking with Italian tradition in a second significant way. The way of the locals would be to let the lunch settle and the heat of the day pass over you with a rest before tackling the remains of the day. But we would brand ourselves the clueless Americans by rising up, hoisting our load, and sweating out into the afternoon sun. I pulled a hat from its clip on my pack strap and settled it onto my already sweaty forehead. Silence pervaded the steamy countryside, as though the world had curled up for a nap. Very few cars swept by us to wash a breeze over our clammy T-shirts. We walked a side lane that unfortunately had no trees to shade the baking asphalt. The fields were full of baled hay, dried a crispy tan. The farms, the few buildings, the scant infrastructure—none gave a hint of the war in the region's history. Homes dotted the route, as though many more people lived in this country than farmed the land, a trend we could use more in U.S. farming regions.

Chapter 23

May 2011

By midafternoon, Susie and I had skirted the larger town of Borgo Flora, and I knew that the night's destination was close. I also realized that we would be crossing one of the most famous ancient military installations: the Appian Way.

As we waited for a break in steady traffic to cross Strada Statale 7 (SS7), I looked up and down the two-lane highway. Cars streamed along under a canopy of trees, limbed up to allow distant views across the farming fields. Waves of orange poppies topped undulating grass. I scanned the scene for evidence of ancient influence. History describes the area's first road as an arrow-straight path heading south from Rome to the Alban Hills, where it then shot across the marshes, which, of course, at the time were hated malarial swamps that leaders had again and again tried to tame. So the Roman builders erected the road over the marsh, building up the roadbed to rise above the water level. They aimed for the coast at a point southeast of Anzio called Terracina. Reading current maps, I deduced that SS7 would be the obvious Appian route, and I thought it safe to assume that such a valuable asset would not have been abandoned by a country that revered history. So, I thought, we were about to cross the ancient road.

The Appian Way had been key to the Roman Republic's expansion and successful battles against the other powers of the day, including the Greeks. Begun in 312 BC by a leader named Appius, that first Roman road was undertaken at the same time as a massive aqueduct was erected to give Rome a fresh water supply. I had seen remnants of the aqueducts, just as I had viewed the roads trodden by the people of ancient times. But usually, such artifacts betray their history. SS7 did not appear historic. If you ventured onto the Appian Way at Rome, you would find a rough road consisting of layers of gravel and rock topped by large, flat stones set closely together. SS7 was smooth, paved asphalt. We found our break and crossed, looking south down its arrow-straight path as we reached the middle. On the far side, our night's goal nearby, we slowed our pace to relax.

The flat open road sent my thoughts back across the Atlantic to the middle of America and a recent trip to dig up family lore. That visit to North Dakota confirmed a sense of loss: in my home area, as in much of America, most people had rejected rural life. A few extended family and friends still enjoying rural or small-town living would be dismayed at my observation. As I had driven through the empty landscape where our farm buildings once stood, I considered the massive national infrastructure projects that happened when my father was coming of age that leveled out life for rural people to put it on par with the advantages of urban living. An updated grand plan to refresh the infrastructure for contemporary rural communities, I thought, could again balance the benefits.

And I wondered, as we crossed the historic road that bisected flat farmland with no homes in sight, if the Italian people grappled with the emptying of their landscape. Evidently, one way was to lay in a fast modern road to replace the history, the better to whisk people from one metropolis to another. Who, in the fast-paced modern world, would desire a slow, historic journey? Who would need to even pull off that road and stop?

Today, with industry being more decentralized and remote work more possible, rural people could have more choices than just driving through the landscape on their way to city life. The reclamation of the Pontine Marshes that turned it into agricultural land was a massive public works project for its time, and in the United States, rural electrification was happening at roughly the same time. As my father was seeking work as a young man during the Great Depression, the federal government, under President Franklin D. Roosevelt's New Deal, brought electric power to rural America, which turned on the lights at millions of farms and enabled modernity to take hold. In fact, my sleuthing through his letters had uncovered one from his sister Ruth in 1937 where she reported, "The radio and lights are working fine. It doesn't seem to be that it is the same house as it used to be, with the lights and all."

Similarly, paved roads and sturdy bridges connected communities and allowed the interstate transportation of goods, opening markets for farm commodities as well as bringing urban-made goods to rural people, not to mention the widespread purchase of automobiles that fueled a world-changing American industry.

Walking down the side road with the SS7 traffic noise receding, I thought that the equivalent today would be a reclamation of rural infrastructure, renovations like a modern communications grid and deep mass transit. It had been a common thought as I bumped along the American side roads that took me through towns that had become merely a wide spot in the road with a rusting sign. Improvements to the physical and virtual grid would allow not only rural people the choice of staying in their community but also urban people the option of moving to a rural area without experiencing a slippage from their accustomed lifestyle. With a more distributed workforce, rural communities could again be formed, the populations rising to support schools, community centers, churches, banks, newspapers, and grocery stores.

Such a refocus on the American heartland would reduce our modern experience with silos. It used to be, the only definition of a silo was a tall vertical structure that held grain or another farm commodity. Today, the term refers to people sequestering themselves (or being pigeonholed) into an insulated community with no view or connection to fellow Americans who are living a different experience. The only similarity between the old definition and the new is that neither structure has windows. Would bringing more people back to the rural and small-town communities trigger the building of more of the former type of silo and the destruction of the latter?

Those thoughts, rather than the war, occupied my mind on the second day of my trek across the Anzio plains. To my father, such ideas would not have been utopian, would they? *These fellows need a decent road to get their wheat to town too*, he would have thought, *just as those Romans need their bread*. He could easily relate it to his own family's farm, his parents sitting down after supper to read the Epping paper by electric light. *Maybe if they'd had electricity brought out to these old stone houses, they could have learned of the danger to the world and wouldn't have been so quick to throw in with the Fascists*. My visions, colored by city life, came more into view on a personal level: a pair of brothers gulping the fresh country air as they smacked a baseball or bicycled a dirt road. Yeah. I shook my head. The heat must surely be getting to me.

I had booked another agriturismo, Ali e Radici (Wings and Roots), a modest farm that offered a couple of rooms. A mile beyond the SS7 crossing, a sign poking through the ditch grass announced the farm, and we turned down the long driveway. I waved to a worker piloting a small tractor heading away from us around the stucco farm buildings with their red-tiled roofs. We dropped our packs and stood to catch our breath and wipe our brows. A young woman appeared from around the barn, long curly hair pulled back to reveal a large smile, and at the end of a slim tanned arm was a strong grip to shake my hand.

"Ciao, I'm Francesca!" she said and gestured to stairs that led to a side entrance above the kitchen. We entered a spartan, modern apartment and gratefully shed our belongings. "Walk. Look," she said simply. "Come for dinner later after you rest."

We took her advice, strolling the perimeter of the farm after the heat in the sky and on our bodies had dissipated. Crops radiated smartly from the farmstead, and a small herd of cows stood expectantly near a pasture gate. The odor from the cattle was strong but not offensive, which was fortunate because we'd need to leave our windows open overnight for relief, expecting a hot night with very little breeze.

Chapter 24
February 1944

Came all this way to camp in a field! Erick might have thought, as the flat Anzio plains stretched away into the darkness beyond the camp. After two months of fighting in the mountains, he could have felt useless on that treeless farmland. *Makes about as much sense as using a thoroughbred to pull a farm cart.* After all, the Force's deadly leadership in the mountainous campaigns was becoming a legend. *Reminds me of that phrase from the marines, which just about says it all: a typical SNAFU, situation normal, all fouled up.*

Normal or fouled, his platoon and all the rest of the Second had started on their foxholes. One guy got ahead on the project and found when he came back from chow that the darn thing had filled up with water. *Dig too deep and you hit another SNAFU,* Erick may have thought, considering the high groundwater table. The Second wasn't asked to guard a section of the canal; that was tasked to the First and the Third, and they would be stretched thin. His unit was in reserve initially but then expected to see the most action. The job of the Second Regiment, they were told, was for raids and other advanced maneuvers.

It was February 2 when Force regiments stepped into place to relieve the Thirty-Ninth Combat Engineers Regiment along the west bank of the Mussolini Canal, defending the right flank of the beachhead. The Force operated independently, under orders directly from VI Corps headquarters. As they fanned out and dug in, night fell, and Erick could see the tactical problems they would face. No cover and no light, and stretched thin along that murky waterway. *No wonder they call it "the billiard table,"* he thought, *but who's the cue ball?* When muzzle flashes from the long barrels of the German 88 mm antitank guns lit up the First's new defensive line and grenades—too easily lobbed over the waterway—began exploding around them, the commandos scattered like pool balls after a break. They quickly learned how battle would be out there. They would need to get themselves some breathing space.

"Orders went out the first night to start kicking Germans out of the front yard," wrote Force historian Burhans. It was clear that the enemy held positions too close to the canal. The first raid was ordered, under Third Regiment command. Soldiers skittered across the canal on improvised footbridges. They probed along the line as the enemy responded with flares to expose their positions. The Germans launched all manner of firepower, from machine guns to tank fire, to push back the interlopers. The horizon was lit by muzzle flashes periodically throughout the night. By daybreak, the Force raiders had returned, with casualties but also carrying intel on enemy positions that was quickly put to use by the artillery batteries. The next night it was the First Regiment's turn. They pushed even farther into German-held territory, gaining significant advantage when First Lieutenant Gus Heilman took thirty-two men of the First into the area near the mouth of the canal, below a village called Borgo Sabotino. They flushed the Nazis out of the canal lockhouse, then combed through the town for German night outposts and continued past it, pushing the enemy back into the countryside. The patrol "took a shine to Sabotino and duly declared it the new home of 2 Company," Burhans reported. Further, they renamed the town Gusville in honor of their leader and voted Heilman the mayor. They held the town as an Allied prize, and it even would become a place for soldiers to take some R&R at the newly minted Gusville bar. Army photographers would come in and snap an image of Gus and two comrades smiling broadly, drinks in hand, leaning on an improvised bar decorated with pub signage. It could have been a night out in downtown Helena, Montana.

Repeated raids all along the Force's frontage paid dividends, and by the end of the first week the Germans had pulled their line back 1,500 to 2,000 yards from the canal. The effort effectively created a "no-man's-land" where future Force raiding parties could operate and push farther into German territory. It was an eventful first seven days of the ninety-nine that the Force would see in their positions along the canal. The action begun, Erick's Second Regiment picked it up. The commandos trained by day, raided by night, dodged air and artillery attacks, and planned future campaigns that would further hinder the German army's ability to control the area.

We've got three flavors of raids, like Neapolitan ice cream, Erick may have thought, rehashing the information from the daily briefings. It would fall to him, in his role as staff sergeant, to make sure his squad understood the training. He might go over things as they pulled up a piece of cold ground at chow time. *We'll be heading across that canal for combat, reconnaissance, or demolition.*

Combat patrols would engage the enemy in close-range fights. *We'll push them back from forward positions where they're going every night to guard their own front lines. That will prevent them from launching their own patrols into our territory. When we catch them by surprise, we'll take prisoners and hold the ground.* The captured Germans would be sent back for interrogation. *Meanwhile, other teams will set traps, and we'll ambush them before they can say "Nein!"*

Reconnaissance patrols would target a position where they could observe enemy activities. *We'll take a spot, such as a farmhouse, in no-man's-land or beyond and set up a forward listening post, sending a guy to string a telephone wire back so we can call in reports.* While they were at it, they would map the enemy outposts and equipment movement in the area.

Demolition teams would strike at strategic locations. *Targets will be roads and buildings we expect will be valuable to the enemy,* he might have thought in planning his training speech.

The raids would begin just after dark, which at that point in February fell at about 8 p.m. Sometimes they would strike quickly and be back in their camp by midnight; other times they would be roaming the dark battlefield until dawn. Close attention would be paid to the cloud cover and phases of the moon. *We'll be moving on earth when the heavens allow,* Erick perhaps noted. As a farmer, he was always reading the sky to plan or worry about what was to come. Weather evident in cloud cover and moon cycles would determine planting and harvesting duties. "Red sky at night, sailor's delight," they'd tell one another back on the farm. "Red sky at morning, sailors take warning." Perhaps the landlocked family was echoing their Norwegian ancestors in using a nautical metaphor for homegrown forecasting. Spitting distance from the seashore at Anzio, the rhyme might echo for a former farmer looking skyward to see what to expect. *Dark sky at night, Germans take fright*, he might have thought.

But even the dark was not enough. The Force raiders would blacken their faces with shoe polish, feeling more like warriors with such masks. A Force soldier cut an unusual figure, garbed in baggy mountain trousers that were tucked into high combat boots and a multipocketed field jacket with its distinctive red-and-white spearhead logo on the shoulder. In extreme cold, they pulled out their fur-trimmed parkas. On their backs and in close-fitting packs were wire cutters for the German barbed wire, entrenching shovels, and clearing tools like a pick-mattock or an axe. Strapped to the leg was the specially designed double-bladed V-42 stiletto knife in its horsehide sheath. They wore steel pot helmets, some covered in mesh or camouflage. The soldiers carried the Johnson light machine gun or the Thompson M-1 submachine gun and strapped extra ammunition and hand grenades onto a broad belt lashed to their suspenders. Some would hoist a handheld flamethrower with its backpack fuel; one of Erick's sergeant duties was to direct flamethrower assaults. *They may have us outnumbered,* Erick perhaps thought as his heavily armed squad struck out across the dark terrain, *but they might not.*

Chapter 25

May 2011

From our tiny second-floor apartment, the orange sun slipping past the horizon cast a harvest glow onto the rows of crops fanning out from the farmhouse. Sitting for Francesca's simple farm dinner had settled an ache into my joints, and the satisfying meat and potatoes further tamped down the energy left from the day's *piedi* explorations. I leaned with both arms against the window frame to appreciate the setting sun, then pushed back and made for the door. Pulled by the glow to have one last view of the slumbering farm, I slipped on my shoes and stepped carefully down the stairs.

As I walked out of the yard to the edge of the field, I pictured my father having a similar nighttime stroll on one of his early days at Anzio. Picking his way through the foxholes, Erick could venture to the edge of the camp enclosure and look toward the front. Scanning the pockmarked landscape, he could see a portion of the canal that his comrades were guarding. The frontage totaled fifty-two kilometers, just over thirty-two miles. The Force guarded one-fourth of it, about eight miles, that stretched from what they called Bridge 5 to the sea. The full-strength Third Regiment lorded over the first five miles of it inland from the sea, while the half-strength First Regiment, just three companies, stretched out over the remaining three miles to the shards of Bridge 5.

Erick likely reconnoitered the canal frontage in preparation for the raiding campaigns. Traversing the front, he would see meager defensive coverage: one man stationed about every twelve yards. A dangerously thin line. "An accurate estimate of this opposing strength, on intelligence gained from prisoner interrogation, placed 1,250 enemy fronting the FSSF," Burhans wrote. "Further, a minimum of two regiments were held in Cori and Ninfa, reserve pockets in the mountains within easy striking distance of the Force sector." My father's unit at that time held just over 1,100 combat troops, including his Second Regiment in reserve, so a rough tally with reserves could mean the Force was outmanned at least two-to-one.

It wasn't just a problem on the canal. Overall, the Allies were vastly outnumbered, but most of the troop concentration was along the area's two main roads, the Anzio-Albano road, which was defended by British troops, and the Nettuno-Cisterna road, defended by the masses of the Third Division. Fortunately, the German sector facing the Force was "removed from the main enemy axis of movement and communication," wrote Burhans.

Erick and his mates had not fought this kind of battle before. "Anzio meant a complete reversal of the former Italian situation," Burhans explained. "The Force went on the defensive, and was down to sea level on the Pontine Marshes, the flattest piece of ground in Italy." The dredged waterway provided defensive benefits and offensive challenges. It was "a prime tank trap," Burhans recalled. Flat bottomland rose from each side of the canal into earthen berms that provided the only high ground to hide behind. At its widest points, the canal ditch was sixty yards wide. Numerous small canals, drainage ditches, and irrigation channels connected to the main line. Since most of the bridges had been mined or destroyed, attacks or raids were done via improvised transportation. Soldiers built temporary bridges or ferried across in small boats tethered by a cable. Once you forded the swampy waterway and clambered up the muddy bank, you would have to attack across the open farmland that stretched away from the canal.

In the last of the day's light, I scanned the undulating outline of the Lepini Hills beyond the fields. Clusters of lights revealed the villages. Erick, too, could have looked into the distance and understood that the Germans once again held the high ground for observation. Perched in the hills that paralleled the canal and the church towers and taller buildings in larger towns behind their front, the Germans could observe all activity along the canal. The front-line Forcemen dug foxholes and set up machine-gun emplacements into the leeward side of the canal berms, slightly less observable than the horizontal land behind them. But there was scant cover to prevent them from being sitting ducks along that made-up river. Chafing at this exposed situation, they itched to take over the high ground, and Force leadership pursued ways to go on the offensive. Right away, General Frederick sought permission for the Force to take Mount Arrestino, a pivotal high spot in the Lepini Hills above Highway 7. The campaign's cautious leader, Major General John P. Lucas, nixed the idea.

So it would be another fight where the numbers were not in the Force's favor, and again they'd be battling unfriendly terrain. Comparing the frontline need to his unit's depleted numbers, Erick would see a chilling shortage. But a steely defense from Frederick's fighters was to be paired with deadly offensive maneuvers. Coiled behind those lines, biding their time day after day until the sun went down, waited the battlefront's leveling factor. The Force's extensive night training was to be put to use in near-constant raiding into the canal's no-man's-land under the cover of darkness. The Second was to be the sharpened tip on the spearhead's relentless offensive.

I walked farther down the narrow gravel lane toward those distant shadowy mounds, which were to be the next day's adventure. Aiming for a full-dark experience, I kept my back to the farm buildings and unfocused my eyes into the gloom. What if the canal was right there in front of me, water churning and gurgling down from those hills and headed for the sea? What if just beyond a shallow rise, the inky river, and the far shore's twin-mounded bank, gun barrels were aimed squarely at me, their operators scanning the dark horizon for any signs of movement? I froze on the road. I wanted to drop to the ground and skitter over to the shallow ditch. To conjure up the scene one night in peacetime, surrounded by calm, triggered a chilling, frightful image. To live with that feeling nightly, and then to strike forth into that darkness and walk headlong toward those aimed weapons . . . I could not conceive of it. Dad pulled from a reserve of bravery and determination that, if he passed it down to me, I could not detect in myself. Perhaps he didn't realize that he carried it, and maybe it only surfaced in the presence of such unavoidable obstacles. Perhaps the same would be true for me, in the unlikely instance that such a situation would arise. I could no more know that than know the heart and mind of my long-dead father. All the roads toward him, the source of his courage, his experiences, were shadowed, gravelly lanes leading to blackness. The sole light was my hope that, standing on the land where he stood, contemplating his path, I could catch a glimmer of his spirit, moving purposefully behind the enemy lines of my desolate thoughts, my barricaded memory.

The stars came out over the Italian farm and took me there. A North Dakota evening as warm as my mother's embrace, the air finally still and fireflies winking beyond the window, drew us onto the farmyard's lawn. I could hear the ringing clink of dishes as my sisters washed and stacked the dinner plates, and the open window sent their chatter into the quiet darkness. Dad stood by us, the youngest of his brood, his weight on his left hip, casting an angular shadow onto the lawn. We walked farther from the house, the girls' voices receded with the light, and then we sank down onto the lawn to end the day in my favorite summer way, gazing up at the stars. On a clear and moonless night like that, your thoughts navigated star to star, marveling at the brightness of a scattered few amid the vast quilt of dimmer pinpricks, uncountable, unfathomable. Lying back, completely at rest except for our searching eyes, we inched ever closer to sleep, which was very likely the goal of this quiet excursion. But it was also a time for the feeling of being together, not needing language, sharing the twinkling image above, the warmth of the ground below, the itchy grass on our bare legs, the heaviness of our bodies at rest. "There is the North Star," Dad would say. "Follow it up to the Big Dipper. See how it is pointed upright? The cup won't spill out. No rain coming."

Chapter 26

February 1944

On the night of February 10, the Second Regiment began to earn its stripes. Orders were to cross at Bridge 5 and close in on Sessuno, the village at the edge of Nazi territory. A company of Second raiders swept across the canal, and two dozen men advanced undiscovered, their movements preceded by strategic artillery strikes. Nearing the town without having flushed any German troops, they called for additional shelling to cover their entry, then platoons flanked the town's perimeter and moved in. Their movement along the town's main road triggered return fire, staccato flashes bursting from each ditch. As the Force soldiers advanced from each side upon the machine-gun nests, with covering fire from a Force platoon situated off the road to the rear, the German machine gunners accurately targeted the rear platoon, and three Forcemen went down. Swiftly responding, the combat patrols silenced the German guns and began to sweep through town, scattering the resistance. By midnight, Sessuno was clear. The commandos took seven prisoners and counted forty to fifty German dead. They continued to skirmish with Nazi reinforcements and dodge a heavy artillery barrage, but finally, seeing tanks and other vehicles descending from two directions, they withdrew back to the canal, taking more casualties but again inflicting greater pain into the enemy ranks than what they suffered.

Some of the German guns were too powerful and too distant to attack. The Nazis operated two "railway guns" secreted in the hills and caves around Velletri, to the north, and Cori, the closest hill town to the Force canal front. Those 280-millimeter guns, nicknamed Anzio Annie and the Anzio Express, would periodically appear from their lairs to sling massive, 562-pound shells onto Allied positions.

Nearly a week after the Sessuno raid, a patrol of four German raiders had infiltrated Force forward defenses when they were detected by a Force machine-gun sentry and dispatched. A search of their uniforms revealed a diary kept in the pocket of one soldier, a lieutenant. A February 11 entry noted, "Reports from Sessuno of Black Devil raid last night." An entry from two days later noted, "We never heard these devils when they come." News of their nickname among the German troops spread, and the legend of the Black Devils of Anzio began.

The raiders were quick to capitalize on their mystique. Red spearhead stickers were printed to leave behind after the raids on dead Germans or their property as a Force calling card. Some contained the phrase "Das Dicke Ende Kommt Noch!," often translated as "The worst is yet to come!" Two weeks into their tour of duty, the commando raids not only had instilled fear into their foes but also had yielded maps of many of the enemy's field positions, which made it easier to slip through the German defenses. Reconnaissance reports also revealed enemy buildup or activity, which spurred the raiders to investigate. On the night of February 17, Erick's Second Regiment company, under the command of Captain Frederick T. Hubbard, set off across the canal to explore a rock quarry south of Sessuno where significant activity had been detected. Perhaps an attack would be marshaled from the quarry, or maybe it was an ammunition storage location.

As the Sixth Company raiders approached the quarry, a large, tracked vehicle lumbered into view. A shot from a Force bazooka—a shouldered tubular rocket launcher that the Force pioneered as an antitank weapon—hit the cab of the vehicle and caused an explosion that lit up the entire quarry site. That opening salvo set the blazing half-track and the surrounding land afire "brighter than Broadway on a Saturday night," said service battalion member Lester Merha, on the raid as a litter bearer. Erick's company exchanged fire with the Germans in the quarry site for a half hour before pulling back along an adjoining road. Three Forcemen had been killed, as had fourteen enemy soldiers.

Such raids were duly reported in the secret "s-2" reports typed up daily by the Force intelligence officer in strings of military shorthand. But Erick's recall of one raid strayed far from battle jargon; it was triggered by the popular song

"Lili Marlene," which was on the radio much at home as well as, evidently, in the minds of soldiers on the Mussolini Canal. Sung by the sultry German actress Marlene Dietrich, it was a soldier's love letter to his girlfriend while slogging through a cold, wet night march:

> My love for you renews my might
> I'm warm again, my pack is light
> It's you, Lili Marlene.

The song "brings to mind a night patrol . . . on the Anzio beachhead," Erick explained in a letter much later to Shirley while he was convalescing in an army hospital:

> We were given the mission of going out and getting prisoners. We had penetrated the German main line of defense when we came upon a farmhouse which was occupied by the enemy. It was very evident that they had no thought or fear of Yanks nearby as they were having a party, or spree, I should say. While we were lying near the house studying the best method of raiding the joint they were singing this song, in German of course. It was the first time I had heard it and I liked the melody. Oh yes, we got our prisoners too—three of them—without much difficulty.

That unnamed raid likely happened on February 25, against a house in Borgo Piave, noted dryly in that day's S-2 report.

Erick would shy away from recounting most of those night battles. Nothing romantic about sloshing across the plains through deep mud and standing water in the icy night air. Many a night, the task was to pick through the rubble of a former farmhouse shelled by their own artillery to flush an enemy outpost. Stepping among the rough stone piles, my father's eyes and the bayoneted muzzle of his gun would swing from one darkened crevasse to another partially standing wall of the newly useless buildings. He might order explosives to be set, as they finished the job of demolishing the buildings as they went. He would give wide berth to the crew setting antipersonnel and antitank mines, and in their wake, road culverts or improvised bridges would explode, thwarting the enemy's road access. Or they could deploy a fragmentation grenade, the soldier's throwable explosive, which sent searing steel shards thirty yards in all directions five seconds after the pin was pulled.

He would be alert to grenades thrown by the enemy, as both sides tossed the explosive calling cards. "I was hit in the knee by a piece of hand grenade tossed by a Jerry that I had mistaken for my friend California, who soon dispatched that chap," recalled Jack Martin, one of Erick's 6-2 platoon mates. Martin was evacuated to the field hospital, and the injury put an end to his combat duty. Meanwhile, as the Second was practicing nightly raids and returning with enemy position information and prisoners to be interrogated, the front-line troops from the First and Third Regiments were facing repeated assaults. Four times in February the Forcemen repulsed German attacks across the front line.

Which way are we headed today? Erick perhaps thought as he emerged from his foxhole into early spring sunshine. *Too bright to sleep anyway.* After the early raids had mapped Nazi camps and troop movements, the brass had given the Second some nighttime shut-eye and shifted to daytime raids. The Germans were responding in kind. As he looked down the line, he would see new foxholes and gun emplacements forming like gopher holes along the canal berm as the frontline troops worked around a new set of craters just laid down by Nazi mortars. Machine-gun chatter echoed a new skirmish just beyond view. And it was just turning to March, their second month on the line. That last day of February saw action all across the plains. The Germans had launched an attack against the army's Third Division in the Cisterna area while also driving against the 504th Parachute Infantry and rupturing their line. But on the Force front, tactics shifted successfully. To push into Nazi territory in daylight, clearing houses and dispatching enemy machine-gun nests, Force strategists would call for artillery to lay down a smoke screen beyond the action, eliminating the chance for German long-range spotters to zero in on their position.

The front line would remain unchanged along that water barrier that sliced through the billiard-table terrain. But the battles, though becoming less frequent after the intensity of the first month, would continue through the spring.

In early April, a dozen Second Regiment men occupied a building they called House 13, on the beach at Fogliano and just one hundred yards short of two houses held by the Germans. They settled into House 13 under the cover of darkness and intended to stay throughout the following day and observe enemy activity. But by midday the Germans had spotted the occupation and began to fire upon the house, a close-quarters fight that left several Germans dead as the Force team repulsed the attack. They remained in the house as night fell, and darkness brought a lull, but the next morning the Nazis renewed their attack. Again, they were repelled. However, artillery from far beyond the Pontine flats sent a barrage raining down on House 13, flushing out the Force patrol, who finally withdrew with casualties. *We were sitting too close to the pocket on that one*, Erick perhaps thought. *Best to get out before getting knocked into the hole.*

Returning from a winter raiding campaign, Erick's rubber overshoes would have been caked in mud, with even the thick wool socks unable to stave off the ice-cold water that oozed into the boots around the tall tops where the pants were tucked inside. Wool trousers hung heavily with accumulated moisture and muck, and the stiff canvas of the winter parka—when he was able to wear it—shielded the rain for only so long before it too became slick and heavy. Erick's knit hat and balaclava wrapping his neck would serve extreme duty, becoming stinky with sweat. He would have returned to his camp from an effort such as the House 13 siege and have sunk wet and cold into a clammy sleeping bag, surrounded by his dripping gear. Storming Nazi positions was a deadly challenge, but frequent rains and temperatures near freezing sent the soldiers burrowing into the landscape to fight another foe. Bitter winter weather—the flatland version of the ice and snow that caused such suffering in their mountain campaigns—continued through February. "It apparently is difficult for anyone not here to understand the full effect of the combination of terrain and rainfall on the battle," said General Ira C. Eaker in a letter to General Harold "Hap" Arnold. "The land is a complete quagmire.... We shall go forward and capture Rome when the weather permits ... and not before."

So the dogfaces fought winter in their beachhead shelters, shallow trenches ringed by a hill of mud, some with salvaged wood as a leaky cover over part of the foxhole. In land as flat and exposed as Anzio, they also were careful about occupying their canal-edge foxholes and gun emplacements. To avoid becoming targets by staying in fixed positions, they dug trenches along the lines, allowing them to move back and forth within their defensive fortifications.

But water pooled in those trenches where the men were posted for ten to twelve hours a day, and there often wasn't a stretch of decent weather long enough to dry things out. That triggered prime conditions for a malady called trench foot. A feared ailment during World War I, where protracted infantry battles were called "trench warfare," trench foot would start with numbness from being constantly cold and wet. Sharp pain could be experienced, similar to a frostbite injury, when recovering from a trench foot episode. Fungus could develop, as well as sores and blisters, and the foot would turn red or blue from the lack of blood supply. Prolonged exposure could cause necrosis, or tissue decay. It could lead to gangrene, which often required amputation. So it was essential for medical staff to see trench foot and treat it early, causing many soldiers to rotate out of active duty to recover.

Day after winter day, the Force soldiered through routine: set defensive barriers, guard the perimeter, repel incursions, strike out on raids, and keep one eye and ear cocked for the air being cleaved by an artillery strike. New recruits to the Force were quickly, if not comprehensively, trained at the Force's rear quarters at Santa Maria Capua, then shipped up to Anzio. After a devastating battle at Cisterna where another elite unit was cut off from reinforcements and decimated by superior enemy force, that special forces battalion known as Darby's Rangers was disbanded, and its few remaining ranks were transferred to the Force. By midspring those replacements bulked up the regiments close to full strength.

After weeks of intense clashes, the facing armies each settled into a defensive crouch. Daily life took on a routine for the many thousands of Allied soldiers encamped on the open land. When not on the line, Forcemen participated in physical conditioning and weapons training, and tank-infantry exercises aimed to incorporate all the new recruits and bolster unit teamwork. Into the long standoff, days would include opportunities to take comfort in meals, relaxation, and rest. The soldiers even participated in sporting activities. Letters and packages from home began to arrive regularly.

The rains finally began to abate in March, and by then Erick had spent significant time exploring the small patch of land where his company was bivouacked. Beyond the camp and rearguard positions, his roaming duties meant that his gaze also surveyed the area and its people, and he looked through a farmer's eyes. He commented on the plight of the agrarian Anzio people in a letter to his eighteen-year-old sister Helen, to whom he wrote most frequently:

March 30, 1944

From: Sgt. Erick G. Thorness, 6 Co., 2nd Rgmt., 1st Sp. Sv. Force
To: Miss Helen Thorness, Epping, N. Dak.

Dear Helen,

I have received two letters from you now since I last wrote, one written March 3rd and one the 8th. I was glad to hear that everything was O.K. at home. I am getting along fine also and we have it pretty easy at times. For our recreation we have softball and volleyball games with the other companies and skirmishes with the Jerries for a little excitement.

You were asking about the Italian people. Well the ones I have seen around in these rural communities are poorly dressed and hard working people, very far behind us in so far as modern conveniences and machinery goes. The farmers use oxen for farm work and hauling and most of their implements are hand made. Most buildings are made of stones.

I hope this finds you all well. Greetings to all.

Love,

Erick G. Thorness

Although it was difficult to tell a resistor from a Nazi sympathizer, the Allies sought to safeguard the civilians caught in the middle. By mid-March, eleven thousand people had been evacuated by sea to Naples from the Anzio and Nettuno areas, leaving about eight thousand locals scattered across the beachhead, huddled in the stone farmhouses that were regularly contested by the warring parties seeking an observation post or dry bivouac on the flat, rainy land. By the end of April, those last residents had been removed too.

The farmers and ranchers among the Force soldiers found familiar comforts to add to their lives on the line. Departing local residents left behind their farming implements and livestock, so chickens, pigs, horses, cattle, and even Brahma steers (to hitch to the plows) were tended behind the front lines. Sometimes the departing Italian farmers got some money for it, but every usable thing was commandeered, from bicycles to farm carts and tools. Like their families at home, soldiers planted "victory gardens" of vegetables as the weather warmed to add fresh food to their prepackaged rations, in one instance growing entire fields of cabbages and potatoes. A debate broke out among front-line platoons over whether, when relieving a departing company, they would also gain the rights to eggs from the henhouses in that company's sector. Soldiers also looked out for herd animals who had met an unfortunate end by walking over a land mine and recovered their carcasses to send to the cook tent.

The Second Regiment had a particular specialty: fresh milk. Bivouacked well away from the front, they tended a herd of cows and even experienced cattle rustling—until they posted night sentries. Commandeered bicycles allowed unit chaplains to roam the lines and hold Sunday services, which also were held for a time in a chapel in Borgo Sabotino, until it was discovered and shelled, at which time the effort was relocated far behind the front lines. A barber from the service battalion, Technician Fifth Grade Manuel Garcia, also plied his trade by bicycle, cutting hair up and down the front.

Erick and his fellow commandos must have felt their energies bolstered by activities that varied the drudgery marking a soldier's day. The Force also had its own newspaper, published each afternoon. Known as the *Braves Bulletin* after their early nickname, it included news of the world and of the war. Local color was added as humorous tidbits gathered from the soldiers. "Sergeant Nick George," went one report, "fugitive from malaria, jaundice, Neapolitan nights and oversea-ism, returned to the fold yesterday." Another item poked at twin brothers Claude and Paul Christian, maintenance workers from Sharpsville, Indiana: "Since the Christian twins bought that cow they are having trouble finding room for her in their foxhole."

By April, life began to heat up. As the Mediterranean spring warmed, both armies bulked up to combat strength. The Allies fielded approximately 90,000 men on the Anzio plains, and their leaders prepared to go on the offensive. The Germans opposed them with an estimated 70,400. The winter cross-canal stalemate was nearing a violent end. After more than three months of holding their beachhead line and in preparation for the planned assault, the Forcemen handed off their canal guard duties to another unit and relocated to a rear headquarters on May 9, 1944. In their ninety-nine days at Anzio, they had provided a morale-boosting offensive thrust in what was otherwise a defensive parry against formidable, well-supplied enemy forces.

The lore of a deadly, professional commando force left the Anzio beachhead with them and would lead them into the battle for Rome. "The Force worked hard and bloodily to maintain the legend, pasted their divisional stickers on the bodies of Germans they knifed and on enemy equipment they disabled," said "The Black Devils" article in *Time* magazine's September 4, 1944, edition. "When Allied forces broke out from the beachhead, the Force spearheaded the attack, led by Robert Frederick wearing a bandage around a neck wound."

Leaving the front lines to rest and reequip, the Force would have two weeks before leading the breakout to Rome. For Erick, it was to be the last field of battle.

Chapter 27

May 2011

As I rose and looked out over Ali e Radici, squinting into the sunrise, I tracked dryland agriculture in all directions, grains and vegetables and lines of fruit trees. We had traveled from the coast into the heart of the former marshland. Beyond the fields to the southeast hunched the shadowed bulk of undulating hills, our destination for the day. We planned to climb from the plains and continue through a series of hill towns from which the Force had been tasked with sweeping the Germans as they helped secure the road to Rome.

It was to be a shorter hike, so I was persuaded to allow a little tourism along the way. Francesca had furrowed her brow when I told her of our route. "Cori is a wonderful city," she said about our next destination, "but you must see Sermoneta." She gestured to her car and up to the hills. "I will take you there."

The village walls seemed carved from a rocky promontory, windows hatcheted high into the black stone cliffs. In the crisp morning light, my eyes could trace even the iron hinges grasping weathered shutters. The cluster of buildings, their facades smoothed together by eons of weather, looked more like an outcropping of rock than a town with modern plumbing and paved streets. During the war, Sermoneta had been an overlook for the Italians who were with the Nazis, and they peered down from its fortress onto the exposed Allied regiments fighting to gain ground or raid villages like Sessuno. The thought of their radios blurting troop movement details to Anzio Annie sickened me.

We departed right after a typical breakfast. I sipped a silky cappuccino and, through its steam, eyed the generous bowl of yogurt appreciatively. A hint of beige and almost-liquid consistency led me to think it was made just a few feet from our table, confirmed when I discovered a taste that was grassy and nearly effervescent with tanginess. Strawberry jam showed chunky outlines of its fruit, the perfect accompaniment. A long baguette was centered on our table, next to a jar of butter so yellow it too must have come right from the field. The food made me think of farm breakfasts growing up, when a thick slice of warm bread with butter had fueled me on summer mornings before I kicked back from the table and headed out to play. Soon we were zooming off in Francesca's tiny car along the winding farm roads. Peering through the dusty windshield, I considered how crazy it was for us to walk along the road, with so many sharp curves and narrow spots. The young farmer drove fast—and hit the brakes only when necessary. Meeting another vehicle meant slipping to the verge and balancing one set of tires upon the grassy embankment. If she had come upon us ambling along the edge of the shoulderless road, she would really have to stand on the brakes, especially in the face of oncoming traffic, which would be invisible until just seconds before it appeared. And if she was like the other local drivers—which seemed likely judging by a number of startling traffic encounters—there would be little time to react to a blind-corner interaction. Her style of driving seemed insane: zero to fast in no time, and then back to zero almost as quickly. She consistently hit 110 km in a 70 km zone. As I distracted myself by silently converting the numbers, I considered reprising a word that budget travel guru Rick Steves taught us to use to get the attention of an Italian taxi driver: "Vomito." As in, "If you don't slow down, I will throw up." Reconsidering my breakfast, I glanced back at my companion, wedged a bit sideways with our packs in the back seat, holding on to the armrest and looking steadily out the front window. Susie seemed to be trying to find a fixed point on the horizon to steady her stomach.

We attacked the twists and turns up to Sermoneta, and I was amazed that the layers of dust covering the car didn't just fly off into a cloud behind us. The little car strained on a couple of extreme hill climbs, and I blamed my big Americanness. At a gated arch, towering stone walls disappeared above our poster-size windshield, and a tour bus filled the sky in front of us. Francesca clutched noisily around it, continuing up into the town's narrow streets. They would be impassible to the behemoth bus and formidable to most American cars. Our driver hopped from one wide spot to another, coasting around small groups of pedestrians, her eyes scanning the openings to consider how far into the village she could get without having to call it a day. She finally rocked the car to a stop with the yank of the emergency brake, and we tumbled out underneath a large street sign with no words but a red circle with a red X through it on a background of blue. The car engine clicked as I noted the countrywide symbol for "No Stopping."

She pointed up the street, and we followed her quick steps through a small square and up to the castle, which was closed. Gesturing at the iron gates, she grabbed the camera from my hand to take a couple of pictures of us. We stood dwarfed by the stone walls, which surprised me with their tan color, as they had seemed chocolate brown from the valley. The wall was broken up by occasional white rock inserts, with dark wood doors and window shutters also stark against the light stone. Shadowed by the castle walls and ensconced along this narrow street, we could see nothing of the valley below. Haltingly, we discussed the history visible in the ancient, pitted stone and the beauty of the fortress rising behind the gate.

We turned to walk back toward the car, once again crossing the square. Francesca stopped and begged us to wait a moment, saying she must do a bit of shopping. We drifted to the fringe of the cobbled plaza. It was bisected by sunlight, the morning chill quickly disappearing as you stepped from the shadows. Shopkeepers were sweeping entryways and rolling out racks of postcards. Locals sat on the edge of molded plastic chairs at an outdoor café, cappuccino cups in hand. Francesca returned with small paper bags. She'd gotten pastries, her husband's favorite, she said. It was charming to see her fulfilling his special request. I considered that most farmers don't often get away from the land during the growing season, so it pleased me that our insistent outing would also result in a treat for them. On the way to the car she handed me one of the bags. "For the road," she said, swirling her hand clockwise. "It is typical of this area." I peeked into the bag, which held two palm-sized pies, crisscrossed with golden crust and filled with glistening ruby-colored jam.

This temporary tour guide and crazy driver had won my heart. I reluctantly asked Francesca to drop us at the crossroad roundabout that linked her farm with the local village of Doganella and the hill town of Cori, which was to be our destination. Shortly our feet were back on the road, and we waved goodbye to her cloud of dust. I hoisted the pack. It did not seem as heavy or challenging as the previous day. Maybe the training mantra was true, and my muscles would stop complaining as my body adjusted. The thought would carry me down the road a ways.

But the morning's diversion had a drawback. Before we had put any miles under our feet, the day was growing hot. Commerce buzzed around us. We walked facing the traffic. We soon were on the edge of the valley, farm fields to the left and the Lepini Hills with more rock cities to our right. Sermoneta quickly faded out of sight behind us, but other hamlets appeared clinging to the distant hills, and I wondered which one was Cori. Traffic moved fast, but the road had fewer twists and turns, so we could see what was coming, and fortunately, drivers could see us. As the main thoroughfare, the lanes were more generous, giving drivers a chance to hug the center line and afford us a couple of feet of airspace. Still, we stepped off the edge to let trucks pass. One driver waved at us in thanks. Small farm tractors passed going in each direction, slowing the flow as they lumbered along. I appreciated them for that, and for another sign that farming life was alive in this valley. Once, a small car passed a tractor coming up on us from behind, and the tractor's rattling engine was so loud that I hadn't heard the car. As it passed, I could only feel the windy rush of it. Had I stepped another foot out into the road at that moment, I would have been catapulted into the ditch. Protectively, I had been keeping Susie near so I could "run interference," and I was glad the startled driver had inched away as he passed.

We walked by a modest farm compound—house and barn; a crumbling, roofless outbuilding; a rusting mound of vehicles in the weeds; a copse of trees shielding the scene from the traffic—and it triggered memories of the farm where I spent my youth. We rested on the rock wall defining the property's driveway and pulled out refreshments. Francesca's "typical" pastries had soaked a sheen onto the folded paper bag, but we found them dry and flaky, the jam holding the crust together until it crumbled in our mouths. The fruit and the wheat could have come from the very farm over my shoulder. Gazing down the two dirt tracks to the house, I realized that our North Dakota homestead had basically the same layout, off a similar two-lane road ... but on the other side of the world. We kids had played in a ramshackle former chicken coop, just as the Italian children here probably explored the tumble-down stone cottage that was likely the farm's first barn, or maybe even the original house. We had danced through the shade of our few trees, which here were lined up as ours had been, sentries along the edge of the field that protected the buildings. I pictured the Allied invasion pulsing into the gravel farmyard, soldiers behind each tree, all eyes intent on the rough-wood window frame that could reveal a gun muzzle. I imagined today's farm kids here, running along the allée of poplars, aiming their slingshots at the birds in the branches.

Most of the farm buildings looked recent, but the old shed sat as a witness, mute with memory. Had its roof been shattered by Allied artillery? Had it shielded my father as he tromped by or wove through the trees?

We continued down the road and into the heat, where you could nearly hear the waving wheat ripening. I stopped to mop my brow and look back across the field behind the farmyard, imagining the soldiers who made their way along this obvious route. The tree cover here was sparse and scrubby, because most land was given over to production. Would it have been cleared by the time of the war, taking agriculture to the edge of the valley? Or perhaps the old stone cottages had sat in the midst of a tangle of scrub vegetation and trees rising out of the drained wetlands, yet still fed by water sources streaming out of the adjoining hills. This far from the coast, this close to the mountains, I could imagine the area as a swamp. We had not seen a canal since we crossed the Appian Way, which, as I recalled from the maps, was where Mussolini's canal split. I had learned also that the ancient Romans had built a canal too, just along the other side of the Appian Way, which served for some centuries to keep the road open, although eventually the main route south became the Via Latina, a road along these foothills, which literally paved the way for the hillside settlements visible to us. The area we crossed was a checkerboard of cropland, clearly fertile and very likely in production for some time. An overexposed photo from a Force history book came to mind. In it, the soldiers were fanned out across a field of grain, which came up nearly to their waists. That single crop provided no cover for their advance.

The Allies' infantry was exposed to long-range artillery spotters hiding in the hills, like those collaborator Italians in Sermoneta, and the Germans rained down fire on the flatland, gouging out the landscape, setting the buildings, roads, and trees into smoking piles of rubble. And through this landscape Erick and his comrades needed to move, keeping an eagle eye out for hazards from the hills—sighted first as puffs of smoke before the bang reached their ears—or from any farm structures in their path. My father surely found no comfort walking through a wheat field, however familiar. He would just soldier on, shouldering a massive pack, aiming a rifle, trying to stay alive.

The road began to rise, and not in the way of the Irish proverb. It was rising not to meet us but to challenge. My feet felt more vulnerable in the heat. Encased in thick socks and leather hiking shoes, padding along on the hot pavement, carrying the weight of me and my shouldered pack, my dogs barked under the pressure. The wind also was at our back, again not with a lilting Irish whisper. The breeze that washed over was tainted with diesel. We began to rest more often at road approaches and gulp water at each stop.

"It is so green here, so full of color," I said to Susie at one of our stops. She gave me a patented quizzical look, and I quickly was embarrassed at the statement. Why was I surprised at a colorful landscape? I realized that it was because I pictured this area at the time of war. "In my mind, it's all black and white!" I told her with a laugh. "All I'm thinking of are the news photos." Even the color ones were so effused with smoke and grime that the scenes were gray or sepia toned. The verdant land and blue skies around me were out of sync with those memories. I was trying so hard to see through my father's eyes that his era, represented in grainy history book pictures, struck me as more real than my own.

So once again I sipped from my modern canteen and considered what Erick would have experienced out there and what his reactions might have been. He'd be mopping his brow too—their breakout campaign clicked at the same time of year as our walk, my deliberate choice. I was sure we were both relieved to be moving. I had chafed through a long winter of studying maps and practicing Italian, and surely he tired of the many weeks tethered to a static battle line along the canal. Just to be doing something was gratifying.

Of course, they would also encounter the green landscape, I thought as I looked across yet another swath of roadside grass and vining weeds choking the highway edge but delighting birds flitting in and out. Perhaps he'd even have been able to hear the birdsong at moments when war's cacophony subsided. Wildflowers and sparrows would be resilient even in the face of battle.

If they had stormed Sermoneta, the soldiers would have stared at the same old castle walls that we'd seen that morning, delivering feelings of insignificance. Looking into the hills, Erick would have seen the tiny farms that were still cut into the hillsides there, clusters of stone huts and low walls. The cascading flowering vines smothering the old gate to a once-fine homestead could have been around and blooming then too, emitting their sweet scent.

Their feet would have scuffed the brown dirt roads cutting along the hillsides. The shapes of the hills or the contours of the land were not much changed by bombs. Erick would view, as I was seeing right then, the low spots in the terrain where water would settle. Would his eyes narrow as he suspected a Nazi hiding place? A fast little lizard like the one that scurried through a crack in the old stone wall in front of me might have skittered in front of Erick too, diving for cover like an infantryman.

But I was viewing paved roads cutting up the valley, surely not there in the war era, and a dry landscape, where likely it had been marshy after the war's wet winter. Telephone and electric poles lined the roads, along with blue road signs and welcoming town signs. During the war, many of the old directional signs had been taken down by the Germans to keep the Allies confused.

Three hours into our walk, we took a break for refreshments and rest at another roadside gas station and grocery. Between the gas pumps and the door huddled the typical scrum of plastic tables and chairs with the bright awnings and double red heart logos of Aglida, a popular ice cream brand. This indicated the presence of coffee and snacks, so we dropped our packs on two chairs at an open table, murmured "Buon giorno" to the men crowding another table, and walked into the store. Behind the counter, a woman with dark heaviness around her eyes greeted us, and we responded in kind; we were tourists, yes, but trying to follow the customs. The simple greeting often opened the doors to conversation, or at least relaxed suspicions about our appearance. We purchased espresso and sandwiches.

"What are you doing, out on the road?" asked the clerk.

"Walking to Cori," I said, "part of a long walk in honor of my father." I tried a bit of my speech.

She regarded us, nodding her head and considering the idea, a familiar response. We seemed to encounter thoughtful people. Some, like she did, expressed their admiration for the task or a war connection; even though I was not seeking it, the recognition always made me feel good. Or perhaps that was what I sought, to represent my father there and give people another view of the modern American, the next generation beyond the one who helped save their country. Maybe they think we had forgotten or didn't care about our shared history. More and more, I was feeling the need to show the opposite. Or maybe their acknowledgment just fed my ego.

"Would you like a ride to Cori?" she asked. "My boyfriend comes soon in his truck, and he will make deliveries there."

"No, grazie," I said. "We prefer to walk." I meant I must walk, although I didn't say it so starkly. We enjoyed our snacks under the shade of the ice cream awning as the traffic sped by.

Chapter 28

May 2011

Rounding a curve in the road after another hot hour on the verge, I spotted clusters of buildings that seemed to sprout from a line of stone cliffs. This was surely Cori, looming on an outcropping above the valley. The road got steeper, with more homes and buildings alongside it. We contemplated a small side road as we passed, wondering if it would be a back way into the city that would take us off the commercial route and allow a gentle entry into the town. Though the road looked promising, we sailed forward at my urging. It was the source of a somewhat heated disagreement, made hotter by the radiating pavement. As the conservative one, I wanted to stick to the most likely route, following the road signs. Stubborn and cautious, I frustrated my walking partner. Susie was willing to take the road less traveled, with the risk of a longer route or having to retrace our steps worth the benefits of a quiet road and the spike of adventure. Too hot and edgy to concede, I trudged forward, and she followed, silent and frustrated. The atmosphere approached the boiling point. Surely I would have been too predictable to have survived a wartime assault on the clearly fortified city.

At long last, we entered the town at a roundabout built for heavy traffic. Another road converged halfway around the circle, signed as the same lane that I insisted we pass by. Clearly, we could have taken that way, and I was mortified, but my apologies were quickly outdone by the anticipation pulling us into the narrow canyon from which the city climbed, rows upon rows of stone buildings stacked one upon the next, stepping back one lane width at a time up the cliffs. Curtains fluttered in open windows, and vehicles moved across the gaps between the buildings. I pulled out my paperwork and my phrase book and entered a roadside coffee shop to attempt to get directions.

Our goal was a small B and B operated by an artist and a teacher. He was a painter, and she taught English in the schools. We had the B and B's name and what I thought was an address, but as the clerk puzzled over the scant details of my website printout, I realized that I should have asked the lodging for directions instead of just planning to walk up and find it. In the warren of streets that surely made up this ancient town, which was much larger than I expected, we had little chance of just happening upon our destination. Another error in judgment, I thought as I returned to Susie, who had sunk into a shaded chair outside the café. "No luck," I said, my tone trying for another apology. We rejuvenated with cold drinks, then continued up the road, which rose along the sheer stone wall defining the edge of the city. Cars swerved around us. There were no other pedestrians. Every time a truck went by, its engine straining from the climb, we were left in a cloud of acrid exhaust. A man leaned out his driver's side window and indicated the passenger seats.

"Go up?" I think I heard over the roar, as he pointed up the road.

"It's okay," I said, waving and smiling. "We will go there." I pointed at a side road a few yards on, taking care not to glance toward my long-suffering wife. The side lane angled up more sharply than the main road, but it looked promising. There the traffic was less, but the exposed stone walls lining the street also radiated waves of heat. We stopped at the intersection, and I pulled out a skimpy map of the town. A small car coasted down to the corner, and the two women in it regarded us from open windows.

"Scuzi," I said, swallowing hard and pointing at my map. My attempt at Italian was inversely proportionate to the heat and unpleasant surroundings. "Directions?"

"Yes," said the woman in the passenger seat, reaching for my map. I pointed to the B and B's name on my paperwork, apologizing for the inadequacy of my map. They conversed in quick Italian, which I watched like it was a Ping-Pong game.

"Just wait," she said and stepped out of the car. I thought she would point at the map and tell me where to turn, but instead she walked around the car, where the other woman had also jumped out. She got behind the wheel as her friend came around to us.

"I think I know this place," she said. "Come, I will walk with you there." The two women tossed a quick "Ciao" to each other, and the car folded into the traffic going down the hill.

I could feel my shoulders relax and Susie's relief as well as we fell in behind our new guide, grateful for the generosity of a person who would reverse course and interrupt her day to help us. As we walked, she pointed out the hospital and the elementary school. We stepped onto a quieter side street and continued to climb, now in the shade of looming buildings. Up and down the maze, then along a tiny side lane we walked, finally reaching a building with fresh white paint and a handcrafted wooden sign hanging above the entry. On the sign was the name and logo of our B and B: Casa Pinturicchio.

Signs of relief are universal, and our guide smiled at our overflow of gratitude. She graciously accepted our handshakes and my halting "Lei e gentile" (You are kind). She walked off up the street as we slipped our packs down from our shoulders to the narrow sidewalk. But no one answered the door at the B and B, again pointing out my tactical mistake on a level that would surely have turned us into prisoners of war. Looking up and down the street, I wrote a note saying that we had arrived and that we would explore the town and return shortly. As we walked in the most enticing direction, I nearly lay breadcrumbs like Little Red Riding Hood so I could find my way back. My version was to write every street name into my notebook alongside a crude map with arrows for each turn and take pictures of the street signs. The prospect of creating another humbling mess seemed as threatening as would Nazi rifle shots ringing out beyond the next corner. Our instinct was to find cold drinks and shady seating. I hoped for the town square, an old church, or some ruins that would distinguish the city from others we had visited. Somehow tying the sights to our exploration of the war's path through these narrow stone lanes would make our effort worthwhile. We agreed to aim for a place where we could overlook the city and perhaps even our day's trek.

Finally, we rested our feet at the very top of Cori, beneath a square church bell tower dating from the first century BCE. It was built, like many ancient churches, on the ruins of an older temple. Around its perimeter were glimpses of the ruins, dedicated to the ancient Roman god and hero Hercules. A plaza with thin grass and light shade from a line of limbed-up trees offered a place to sit and contemplate the scene. Sipping bottled iced tea atop a rough wood bench, the hills behind us, we looked down upon the valley to the west, the commercial road and roundabout clearly visible. Far vistas to the north and west were in view. The distance faded to haze, but on a clear day, I expected you could see the coast all the way to Anzio. The sidehills stepped down to the valley and the roads that linked Cori to another large town in the flatland, which I surmised was Cisterna. It dominated the middle distance beyond hamlets scattered across the fields. A mass of Cisterna's buildings, one especially tall, rose incongruously against the flat agricultural grid. We finally could relax. We broke bread and settled our travel argument with relief.

After several minutes, I removed my shoes and socks and regarded my tender feet. They were red from the day's exertions, which I assumed would go away with rest and elevation. But a bluish tint spread from the base of the nail on my left foot's big toe; perhaps I'd lose that nail. I'd rubbed some skin raw below that toe, and hot red spots appeared around the edges of my feet. Below my sock line, the ankle skin was very white, a hiker's tan that reminded me of Dad's farmer's tan and his pasty forehead.

Clearly my feet were pampered; I always had been a tenderfoot. But I also sported high-tech shoes and socks that should have protected them. The issue was exertion: where and when and how much, and my feet hadn't been toughened up. The soldiers had no special treatment except daily training, but even those commandos suffered. Perhaps our tired dogs have always been a weak point in our anatomy, a limitation on toughness.

Causing the slotted wooden bench to groan, I stretched my legs in front of me, splaying my toes into the breeze. In the distance, the haze blended the hills with the trees, the land with the sea. It was a restful and pleasing sight, a calming view that allowed the mind to wander. I imagined my father, so many days at the front during that long, winter stalemate. As always in war, there would have been much more slack time and boredom than actual fighting. "War is thrilling; war is drudgery," said the writer Tim O'Brien in the Vietnam War classic *The Things They Carried*, and I pictured Erick, contemplating the horizon as I was, thinking about where they had made camp in a wadi, the dry river washouts where the Force bivouacked behind the lines. His was a long, slow-motion battle, and there must have been much time to think. I imagined him reminiscing about home, daydreaming of the time when he would go back to his family's farming valley. What would the postwar hold? Marriage? A family? Was he actually contemplating the future presence of me, his son, who would someday sit on a high promontory of the land upon which he fought and wonder about him? Since I had no evidence to the contrary, I decided that he was indeed thinking of me, somewhere in his future, a child with whom he could share his experiences, talk about Italy and the amazing things he saw as they toughed out the long wartime hikes through the Lepini Hills. Or perhaps create bedtime stories, fantastic tales of adventures in stony mountain villages to divert my attention from the questions he would not want to answer, about the rage of battle and the spilling of blood.

Chapter 29

May 1944

The Allies' preparations to break out of the Anzio beachhead officially began on May 5, 1944. It was to be part of a three-pronged attack to repel the Germans from southern Italy. Tens of thousands of soldiers on the beachhead would sweep north and east toward Highway 6. A second front would work along the Winter Line, which had been pushed back but still stretched from the Cassino area across Highway 7. A third assault would be mounted along the coast by Terracina, seeking to break the German hold on the coastal end of the Mussolini Canal. The Force would join that first front line, charging across the Anzio plains. The three assaults were to meet and form a unified Allied line coursing north. On a map of the battle plan, broad arrows would arc from all directions, pointing directly at the Eternal City. For the Allies, an old Italian axiom would be true: all roads would indeed lead to Rome.

Allied operations engaged in the stalemate on the Anzio plains prepared for the breakout, code-named Operation Buffalo, by ramping up their training. I expect that Erick, hearing the plan's name, would have pictured a thundering herd of looming, shaggy bison that used to roam en masse over the northern plains, ruling the area of his birth long before it was a state named Dakota. Their movements shook the ground and raised a brown cloud of disturbed earth, surely as terribly impressive as an army on the march.

In the case of the Force, preparations meant handing over the duty to guard their third of the Mussolini Canal to another unit, the Thirty-Sixth Engineer Combat Regiment, so they could train for the assault. But so storied were the Force's reputation and their fierce night raids that Force raiders were tasked with continuing the nightly sweeps through enemy territory to bolster the illusion that the Allies were maintaining the status quo. By day, they drilled on tank-infantry collaborations, training that proved to be so effective that it was taken up by other units. While preparing for the operation, the Forcemen also had opportunities to relax and appreciate their days away from the action.

Erick would have woken on one of those sunny spring days safely removed from the need to duck and cover. The staccato announcements of gunfire skirmish would be muffled in the distance. And in front of him would be a stable of horses and a hastily built fence. Ringing the fence would be soldiers with smiles on their faces and money in their hands, leaning and pointing and wagering which horse and which cowboy was the best. The Force was holding a rodeo. Among their ranks were many who hailed from America's Wild West, and they would be able to put on a show that smacked of home. For the day, carnival would replace carnage, fun instead of gun, and the resultant spike in morale would be mercurial. It would be an opportunity for the cut-ups in the Force crowd to let loose their inner clowns as they worked the rodeo ring between events. *The softball games sure were fun,* Erick might have thought, *but nothing beats some calf roping and barrel jumping.*

As D-Day for the breakout came near, the Force raiders were charged with bringing back prisoners to determine whether the Germans had caught wind of the plan. On the night of May 21, two patrols slipped across no-man's-land and toward enemy concentrations at Borgo Piave and the abandoned quarry that had been the site of the bloody earlier skirmish. They met stiff resistance, and again Force blood was spilled, but they marched back to camp with seventeen prisoners. "G-2" divisional intelligence reports on the raid were silent on the results of their interrogations.

Finally, on May 23, the order came down the line. Force soldiers boarded trucks and moved into position for the breakout attack. They were tasked with protecting the right flank of the operation, holding the Germans back as the Allies passed the northern section of the canal, which began northeast of Cisterna at the ancient hill town of Ninfa. They deployed along a drainage ditch southeast of Cisterna called the Fosso di Cisterna, which emptied into the main canal. Beyond the ditch ran Highway 7, the ancient road that had seen the boots of Roman soldiers centuries before. Parallel to the Appian

Way ran the tracks of a railroad that bisected the town and headed through the valley, another key piece of infrastructure to capture.

Beyond Cisterna lay the Velletri Gap, a narrow bottomland where the Allies might again be at the mercy of the Germans high above in the Lepini Hills on its south or Monte Artemesio and the Alban Hills on its north. The gap was key to Operation Buffalo, as it was to funnel the Allied troops between the danger in the hills and to the strategic town of Valmontone on Highway 6. The Force was tasked with keeping the German troops across the canal from attacking the Allies as they took Cisterna and moved into the Velletri Gap. As the armies pushed northward, the Force would advance along the foothills, continuing to shield the troops below.

Toward the end of that breakout day, the Force moved into position along the Cisterna canal. The sun set on a summery atmosphere. Red poppies glowed in the field, and the air was sweet, a scene so notable that the Force historian put pen to paper. Even sweeter was the light resistance met by the advancing Force troops, so they settled down for the evening to await orders to proceed. Erick may have compared that night to the end of a long planting day at the farm, which was the definition of anticipation for a farmer. He might even have looked for fireflies glowing in the air, the surest sign of relaxation on a Dakota spring night.

At first light on May 24, artillery began its hammering blows, followed by mortars whistling toward the German lines, and the Force began their advance. Enemy mortar responded, and the Forcemen continued into the barrage. By midmorning, they had taken Highway 7 and shortly also seized the road's bridge over the canal. The next objective was the railroad. But forward progress was halted by a fierce and diverse German defense. Beyond the railroad, a minefield devastated many of the tanks that were accompanying the Forcemen. From a stand of woods beyond erupted a cacophony of machine-gun fire, bracketed by mortar explosions that shook the ground. The Force dug into positions along the railroad and around the bridges where the highway and the rail line spanned the canal. But they had outpaced their armored support and discovered they were running low on ammunition. Worse, a company of nimble German Mark VI Tiger tanks advanced to command the assault. Hastily recruited American artillery support, along with additional tanks and tank destroyers, put a dent in the formidable German armor, but the effort was not enough, and the first day's advance ended with regrouping back at the morning's jumping-off spot. For the first time in battle, the Force had been rebuffed from its objectives, and its units took heavy losses.

Throughout the next day, as Allied artillery pounded the German defenses, the Force reorganized and reequipped. But before they could again surge into the fray, the Germans began pulling back, as the continuous Allied assaults caused them to abandon the area. By the time the Force moved forward on May 25, the enemy had retreated to Highway 6 and to another line in the hills above the plain. They would continue to defend their positions in the high towns. So into those hills went the Force, heading first for Mount Arrestino, about two miles south of Cori, the first target that their commander, Frederick, had eyed months before. It was time to put an end to that threat. The Third Regiment took the lead, with the Second covering a line along the canal that led south toward Ninfa. The First covered the hill's other flank to the north. With resistance as light as the breeze, the Force topped Mount Arrestino by midday. From the overlook, Allied tanks were visible advancing on the valley road leading to Cori. The Forcemen held their position overnight, at home in the mountainous terrain. At daybreak on May 26, they moved quickly toward Cori, marching in uncontested. However, disabled Tigers and other German armament had been destroyed and littered the route with roadblocks in and out of the town. Cori had been so extensively shelled that it sat smoking, in shambles. Its ancient cobbled streets were nearly impassable with rubble. In the square at the village apex, the distinctive round tower that commanded the high corner sat pockmarked but still erect. Relieved villagers greeted the advancing Force troops with wine.

By early afternoon, the commandos were moving again, having reorganized and resupplied. Their next objective was Rocca Massima, another village, much smaller than Cori, perched at a rocky apex of the Lepini Hill mass. They departed in two sections, one group down the valley's main road and the other via the ancient mountain trail, accompanied by local men who volunteered as guides through the wooded hillsides. A mule train packed their ammunition and armaments. They trampled the footpath past Cori's cemetery and climbed into the woods.

Rocca Massima sat five miles farther by trail to its peak. The Force moved in as trained, swift, and stealthy. Among the town's narrow streets and high stone walls there was destructive evidence of German occupation, but again, no enemy to fight. As before, pockets of enemy soldiers could be seen through field glasses retreating toward Highway 7, just beyond the next town. The Force once again moved into the mountains, settling for the night just east of Rocca Massima under the cover of trees on a nearby hill called Mount Illirio. With the Germans in retreat, the battle had gone quiet, so the Forcemen spent a calm night in their mountainous camp. In the morning, they would proceed on the forested path to the final high objective between them and Highway 6: the town of Artena.

Chapter 30

May 2011

The historic plaque appeared to be wrong. Tracing the cobbled lanes of Cori, we stopped at a memorial panel bolted onto a wall facing the town museum in the Piazza Papa Leone XIII, a small square defined by a hulking church. High on a plaza retaining wall I spotted the red arrowhead of the Force, pointed toward the heavens. The raised lettering around it was edged in soot, and the FSSF logo was dulled with dirt. Still, here was a flag-sized permanent plaque commemorating the "Raggrupamento Operazioni Speziali Statunitense-Canadese," which roughly translated as the "U.S.-Canadian Special Operations Group." The wording unfortunately stated "22 May 1944" as the date the Force stormed through Cori; battle records set the date as May 26. I stood gaping at the scene, as I had done in the Anzio museum. The scope of the war—its battles, sacrifices, and heroics—deserved mountains covered in plaques, and yet the weathered stone held only one, memorializing a sliver of it all. From the iron and stone, the words and the insignia, came a humbling power.

"I have seen many old people come through to look at the places where the men had fought," said our local host, Virginia Agnoni, "but this is the first time I have seen a son come looking." We had returned to her B and B, where she'd read my note and had been waiting. Her dark eyes searched mine. "Such journeys are important," she said, "because we must remember, and we must pass on the knowledge."

I was taken by her sincerity and quick understanding of my purpose. Virginia had a matter-of-fact teacher's demeanor behind stylish glasses perched on a friendly face. She pulled back her long, dark hair when she welcomed us into her flat. Although she had just returned from Siena, where her daughter was in college, and she had a head cold, for which she had been aspirating sulfur steam, she set about to get me connected to locals who might know more about the war and its effect on the town. As we breathed the sulfurous air in her living room, she picked up the phone and rang the town mayor—even though it was 7 p.m. on a Saturday night—and he suggested that she call an older gentleman who had grown up in Cori during that period. The man was not home, as it turned out, but his family said he could be found at the bar. So we squeezed into her Chevy Aveo, another tiny European ride, and motored up to a high square to check the bar. He wasn't there either—had just headed back home. So our determined host got the approximate location of his home, and we started walking, up and up through the dark streets into a newer part of town, where wider streets were lined with apartment blocks and homes built more recently, from the 1960s to the '80s. Not as attractive as the historic homes on cobbled streets, but no doubt with the comforts of modern construction that could outweigh the charm of narrow stairs and rusty plumbing.

We walked back and forth on the street looking for his home and caught the attention of an old woman watching from her balcony. She pointed a crooked finger down the street, and finally we located the man, just by pressing each of the buzzers in front of the two homes where he might be. On that street, every home was behind a gate with an intercom. I mused on the sense of Italian privacy on display: people lived on top of one another in cities, and even in smaller towns like Cori so many were found living on closely packed streets. Although people seemed outgoing and interested in one another's business, walled gardens and locked gates separated them. A man walked out to open the gate and greet us, and we stood in his driveway to talk. His white hair spoke to his age, but it was a full head of hair, and his sturdy stature, toothy smile, and strong grip showed much vigor.

Eugenio di Giacomo could remember when the Allies finally arrived because, he said through Virginia's translation, of the "terrible silence."

"The town had been bombed seven times," he said, "and then the bombing ceased."

Now eighty-four and a retired local traffic warden, Eugenio had been sixteen, and he fled from the Nazis to the hills above the town with his family and the rest of the townspeople. "We were there for four months," he recalled, "living in huts we built from straws and sticks. It was the way our ancestors had done." The people had been thrust not quite back to the Stone Age, but nearly, I thought. From the mountains, they periodically would go to town, sneaking in to avoid encountering the Germans. "We had left everything in our homes," he said. "We were always very hungry, and we would try to retrieve our goods and look for food." Eugenio made this trip multiple times with his father. On one such forage, a German soldier called to him and his father while they were walking on the road. "He made my father take buckets and go and get water for them. They were staying in a home," he explained. "They held me as a hostage." When his father came back with the water, he asked them for food for his son, who was hungry. "He knew he was endangering himself by doing that," said Eugenio. "The Germans pushed him hard to the ground." No food was given to the hungry boy.

The townspeople suffered that winter, which was "cold but not snowy," he said. "At least the ground never freezes in Cori." Their living conditions caused a painful, itching skin condition. "To treat it they rubbed on olive oil, which was made from their own trees and was one of the few things they had brought from the town," Virginia explained as Eugenio looked off into the gloom of the dark street and commented, "It was a very sad four months of life."

On January 30, all the churches of Cori were hit. I imagined the townspeople watching the bombardment from their concealed location, despair piling on top of their dejection. "The Americans had been told by an informer that the Germans were hiding in a Cori church," Eugenio recalled, "but they misunderstood. It wasn't a church but the ruins of an old convent outside of town named for a saint." Of course, in that Catholic country, many of the churches were named for saints. So American bombs rained "continuously" on all the churches, he said, "destroying even the oldest ones," pulverizing Cori's ancient religious history. He frowned as he called it "a sad, sad loss." I thought of my trek to the top of the town, to the ruins of the churches built upon churches revealing the layers of civilization, and how the lessons of centuries of life had to be pushed aside in the rage of war.

Before the bombing had begun, though, the Americans sent warning shots. "These exploded like grenades," he said, "to let the townspeople know that the battle was coming to Cori. But the people didn't understand the warnings." There was an American spy in town, though, known by everyone. "People would say, 'There's the American spy,'" Eugenio said, gesturing with his hands. "He told us the bombing was coming, so we left and went back to the hills." By that time, the Germans also had left the towns and were hiding in the hills as well. They forced many locals into service. Eugenio's brother was eighteen, and they tried to conscript him. "The German people were not nice," he said. "But not all were bad. One German, after the bombing had destroyed the leg of an eight-year-old Cori girl, put her in a car and drove her to get medical care in Rome." The family's father had died, but the mother was still alive, and she went to Rome to look for her daughter, Eugenio recalled. "She walked the halls of every hospital but could not find the girl. Finally, as she was walking through a children's ward, the daughter called out to her, and they were reunited," he said. "Hospital workers had shaved off all the girl's hair" to fight the endemic pestilence, "so her mother hadn't recognized her." The girl grew up in Cori, surviving with only one leg. "She might still live here," said Signore Giacomo. "She wrote a book about her experiences." I felt a surge of hope that I might be able to share the tortuous journey of such resilient people with more readers by also telling the story.

When the bombing stopped, after months of enduring the explosions echoing up the valley to their hidden huts, young Eugenio realized what the silence meant: "The Americans were coming" to free the town. And it was true. "American troops came through and pushed the Germans back, and the townspeople returned to Cori." They discovered chocolates and biscuits. The American troops had left boxes of sweets and tins of omelets, which Cori people had never seen before. "For fifteen days we ate when the Americans came," he said.

But Eugenio also remembered that the first troops to come into town were the Moroccans. "Their leader was riding on a horse," he said. "He kept yelling at the townspeople to hide their women." Many women were raped by the Moroccan soldiers, who he recalled as "huge, scary black men with nose rings and no hair and strange costumes." Virginia added that she remembered hearing about babies who were born after the rapes, and the children growing up as the offspring of a Moroccan father and an Italian mother, "with darker skin that you could tell was not from the Italian heritage," she said. Perhaps, as Eugenio observed, not all the Germans were bad people, I thought, but not all Allies walked with honor.

"These are sad stories," Signore Giacomo said to me, "but good to tell."

Chapter 31

May 2011

I said a grateful "buona sera" to the Cori elder, and we made our way back to Virginia's B and B. The night turned quiet, echoes of children's laughter the only sound wafting on the breeze through the high window in our loft bedroom. The next morning we would hike again to the top of Cori to continue our journey.

As the sun exposed the stone plaza to the morning's warmth, we happened to see Eugenio di Giacomo once again, taking coffee in the sun with his grizzled friends. We stopped to shake his hand and again offer words of thanks. We spoke of the beauty of Cori and the pleasant walking weather. I tightened my pack straps as I waved goodbye to him and to Virginia, who pointed up the lane and said to "go on to the stations of the cross." Instead of turning right at the blue road sign labeled "Rocca Massima," we forged ahead straight, to a steeper but shorter and more beautiful route. She had steered us well. The homes and paved street gave way to a set of broad stairs, each perhaps fifteen feet wide by six feet deep, with granite steps and infilled with cobblestones. It seemed the builders had patterned the path after the tiny town streets, but the open countryside gave the design a generous expansion. The dark cobbles surrounded an eight-pointed star in white square stones on each stair. At the path's edges appeared stone alcoves housing the stations of the cross. This was a religious path, created by the faithful to commemorate events in the Passion of Christ and Jesus's death on the cross. Beyond the alcoves, the hills fell away, and the country opened up to olive groves, trees set in grid patterns, and then dense woods filling the ravines. Cori receded as we climbed, and with every turn the view changed. A jumble of rooftops, most of them clad in terra-cotta half-moon tiles, clustered around the church towers and the ancient castle. Below the towns, homes dotted the countryside, punctuated occasionally by another crenellated compound, signifying a castle or a monastery. The sun was warm by midmorning, but trees canopied the stair climb on both sides so pilgrims could walk in shade.

Coming upon the fourteenth and final station, a zigzagging wall of brick and stone appeared through thin underbrush. We were arriving at Santuario Madonna del Soccorso. An amplified voice echoed on the stone, the sonorous phrases clearly noting a Catholic Mass in progress. On the final paved walkway leading to a central plaza, the sanctuary came into view. Imposing white stucco walls framed four sturdy corners, and the front facade was faced in red brick with white stone archways over the doors and windows and topped by a peaked roof holding a red cross. Mosaics underfoot identified the church and its creation date, and broad planter bowls of red flowers lined the plaza to the church doors. On the expansive brick cobbles in white stone were the words "Ave Maria." The hilltop breeze cast a floral scent from the blooming borders. Along one edge, a pole held a boxy speaker through which the priest could send blessings out into the peaceful atmosphere.

As we were not there to worship, we rested briefly in the shade before stepping onto the edge of the exposed road to Rocca Massima. We immediately encountered a flurry of leisure-day activity: cyclists pumping by, a jogger going up, and a man leading a fine riding horse coming down. As we hiked the road, we saw a car every few minutes, bikes almost that often, and a few other hikers. At the top of the climb, with the entire valley below the Lepinis open before us, we stopped for an early lunch. The road then flattened and hugged the edge of the wooded hillside as it snaked around a series of hills toward Rocca Massima, whose granite ramparts were becoming visible in the distance. Our new friends in Cori who had just hosted us had explained that local people used this quiet road for exercise, walking between the towns, and I could see why. A pleasant hike, possible for people of many abilities.

The streets of Rocca Massima were quiet and dusty when we stepped into town in early afternoon. We sought our locanda, a simple hotel common in such hamlets. I was certain that this one would be easy to find, because Virginia assured me that Rocca Massima was much smaller than Cori. Also, the lodging was in the shadow of the town's main church. Locanda dell'Archangelo was around the corner from a plaza facing the ancient church, San Michele Archangelo. The hotel operated a few rooms opening onto the lane behind the church, but its front faced the town's wider ring road. Entering our room, I looked through a weathered wooden window frame to the view across that road. A path of stone stairs led into the valley. The sky darkened, and it began to rain. Between rainstorms, we ventured out to explore the few streets, quiet and shuttered on a Sunday. The flat-fronted church—with heavy dark beams and a dim, rounded chapel—did not brighten the gloomy scene.

A series of terraces led to our locanda's front door, and upon those terraces were tables for its fine restaurant. Our hosts from Cori drove up to meet us for dinner, and we ate indoors in a spacious dining room, with soft pools of light that invited intimacy. Recounting our day's hike, we dug into platters of pasta and tried to deconstruct their sauces by flavor: one with cocoa and nuts, another with cherry tomatoes and light oil, yet somehow thick and hearty. All enhanced by a bright and fruity *vino rosso* and relaxed smiles with our new Italian friends.

Winds had washed the rain clouds from the sky, and after dinner we stepped onto a dark terrace to survey the valley. Yellow beads of light showed homes dotting the roads through the farmland. Towns glowed, and bright streams of light belted the distant shoreline. Beyond, bobbing lanterns indicated ships moored off the beach. As always in that landscape, my mind went back to the war. From our perch, in clear weather, especially with binoculars, you easily could have seen anything and everything happening below.

I leaned back into a down pillow on the creaky four-poster bed and considered our travel. The day's trek spanned an old religious path and a modern road. The Force came through much faster than we did, storming Cori in the morning and Rocca Massima by lunchtime, "liberating" the towns with no resistance. Then they bivouacked in the hills below Rocca Massima. Clearly there was scant room for even a few visitors like us in this carved-out aerie, so bedding down hundreds of troops in town would have been impossible. But as they slept among the trees, surely they thought of the fight ahead. They would eventually catch the fleeing German army, which would be expected to turn and fight. After months of back-and-forth brutality, nobody believed it would be a simple task of chasing them away. So as they rested for the coming effort, I did as well, looking over the crude map that was given to me by the locanda's proprietress. It showed a series of pilgrim trails through the hills, including one that went from Rocca Massima to Artena. That town, Artena, was finally in my sights as our next destination. We would venture down another religious path, it seemed, which would be a more direct route between the towns than dropping to the valley and walking along the road. The path stayed in the hills, bypassing the valley town of Giulianello. Surely this would be the way of the mountain-trained Force, I thought. We resolved to follow the pilgrim trail in the morning.

Only one corner of the locanda's dining room was lit when we walked in for morning coffee, and a few fractured sunbeams creased the floor in front of a heavily laden breakfast table. Platters offered cut fruit, rows of sliced meat and cheeses, and burnished baked goods. The array stretched twice the distance of the only table set for breakfast—ours—shining with china and glass. We could not do justice to such excess, but I was touched by the hospitable effort. With the pasta dinner still a fresh sense memory, we settled on cappuccino, pastries, and the juicy fruit. Our hostess insisted on wrapping thick sandwiches in stiff white paper for us, stacked for our departure with more fruit and packaged sweets. We walked the cobbled street buoyed by the gifts and goodwill wishes.

Perhaps the hearty breakfast distracted me from my duty, as the serpentine road out of Rocca Massima did not reveal the pilgrim's route to us. After just a few minutes of walking downhill, I stopped to peruse the map and decided that we must have missed the trail to Artena. Perhaps the route was accessed before reaching the village, I thought, and we should have backtracked in the direction of Cori to meet it. As Rocca was perched on a hilltop and surrounded by dense forest, once you headed off the winding downhill road it was easy to lose the sense of direction available from the high overlook. And then, of course, was the matter of my internal sense of direction, which too often failed me. Looking down the open road, which held few vehicles on that country morning, I saw a police car approaching. It turned out to be officers from the *carabinieri*, Italy's national law enforcement, which seemed to me to be a pseudomilitary agency that bristled with weapons and evidently carried on some of the policing in the countryside. The driver slowed to a stop, and we pleasantly greeted each other. I pointed to my map and haltingly told the two officers of our hike to Artena and our search for the *strada di pellegrino*, my attempt to convey the "pilgrim's path." They directed us to continue down the road, and in a few kilometers we would come to a right turn to Artena.

That was not a great revelation. They were sending us on the main road. We waved them on their way and considered the effort needed to retrace our steps—it would involve a significant elevation gain—and whether that work would result in finding the elusive route. In the end, we decided to just soldier on down into the valley. We would approach Artena the way most people—and most of the Allied army—did: via the highway. The sun arced higher as we descended along the treeless lane, the agricultural land spread out before us.

The burg of Giulianello appeared before the road to Artena, and we ambled along its sidewalks through residential streets. At the juncture to Artena, we shed our packs, sank onto the grass under a spreading tree, and cracked open the stiff paper to eat our sandwiches.

The town had quickly dissipated, but the valley road was busy with traffic. It intensified the closer we got to Artena, so we crossed the highway and walked facing traffic, one foot in the grassy slope of the ditch. I hoped for espresso at a roadside café, but their power was out, so we could only buy lukewarm bottled tea and sit on their covered porch for a bit before moving on.

Like other villages in the hills along the edge of this valley, Artena's rocky incline appeared first. Layer after layer of boxy stone buildings crowded the skyline above a forbidding density of dark green trees. Near the apex, a squat structure of great size loomed over the rock, two square towers rising from a sheer stone cliff and topped with shallow domes. The cathedral, holding the high ground.

Sidewalks appeared, and we gratefully stepped to safety as the cars sped by. Heat shimmered off the asphalt in the late afternoon glare. The town entry was familiar from our previous driving visit, where we had motored to it following the cemetery director's suggestion. We continued on the newer streets of the lower town, through its commercial center. Passing a heavily wooded park, I looked up at a soaring wall of stone above the trees and realized we were below the Borghese castle. The park held the ruins of the famous family's local granary, the grain elevator of an earlier era, where the area farmers would bring their harvest to be stored, ground into flour, and sold. On a rise toward the castle, we passed the local wine cooperative, a modern version of the ancient practice of farm folks banding together to sell their wares.

Although the modern commerce of the town bustled all around us, the old city above beckoned, and I had planned to stay at the only lodging I found in the crooked old streets of upper Artena. The B and B dell'Artista was run by Maurizio, "the Doctor Clown." Along with that vocation—actually a noble and serious job working in costume with children in the hospitals of Rome—the lanky physician operated the B and B with his wife, Giovanna. It consisted of a half dozen rooms in their stone-carved home and another building nearby. Our room featured a giant boulder jutting into the living space, with the bedroom crafted around it. To a foreigner, the B and B was well hidden. We called our host to come down to the municipal parking area so we could get him to show us the way. The cobbled street to their flower-filled entrance was cleverly disguised among an array of similar paths, and all too narrow for any transportation but your feet . . . or a mule. As Maurizio met us, three mules stood tethered at the end of the street, waiting to be loaded with goods to transport up the village's steep stone stairways.

The serpentine route to our lodging took us right past a bar—also the only one tucked away so high in the old town—that had a reputation due to its most famous visitor: Jerry Garcia. The barman was a drummer who was simpatico with the long-haired Grateful Dead leader. When Jerry found his way up to Artena during a free day on tour, he bonded with his fellow musician. Worn wooden counters, a smattering of tables and chairs, and a couple of jangly pinball machines composed the bar's small space. A ridiculously high ceiling opened above the chrome espresso machine and soda coolers. Mounted appropriately high on the wall was a signed portrait of the late, great hippie, clad in black leather, eyes hidden behind smoky sunglasses, hair frizzed to the edge of the photograph. By the time we discovered the place, the drummer had also unfortunately passed away, but his brother was tending the bar and telling the story.

After exploring our new neighborhood, I learned to take a left at the bar, continue on until the church was in sight, then, as the lane widened, make another left down a steep section of tall rock stairs to reach our lodging. On the way, I passed a greengrocer who opened her doors a few hours a day.

Further exploration of Artena would have to wait, because I had become determined to find the route that we'd missed. If it went between the two towns, I hoped we could access it from the Artena end and do a round-trip exploration to Rocca Massima and back. The route would not be long and could be done easily in a day. I pictured sitting down to lunch up there before turning around. I laid this plan out to Maurizio and Giovanna.

"That is the 'Il Muli,'" Maurizio informed us, "the old mule path between the towns."

"Can it still be hiked?" I asked.

"Yes, it is possible," said Giovanna. "But it is unimproved. People do not walk there too often anymore."

The curving hillside road that led to Il Muli went from pavement to gravel to dirt, and the view was a satisfying mix of hills, farmhouses, and pastures. Bugs floated lazily on a morning breeze. Trees layered over the hills above, while well-manicured fields were carved out of the forest that stretched out below and up an opposing hillside. We had stopped at the greengrocer's for fruit, and my small pack also held water and energy bars. Told it would take three hours to Rocca Massima, we had set off after breakfast. We walked lightly without the burden of our full packs, simply T-shirts and shorts. Susie wore a wide-brimmed hat.

On this return, I craved the elusive path, wondering if my father was among the contingent of the Force fighters that had traversed the Il Muli on that day in late May when the Allies were finally pushing the Germans north. Artena would prove to be a fierce, crucial battle that would change my father's future, and I felt the need to see it as he might have, through the wooded hillsides, not from the valley road.

We sought an open field below an agriturismo where our hosts had said we would find the trail's entrance. An hour into our walk, the lodging rose up on our right, and then the trail appeared as described. It began as a wide, grassy road but quickly devolved into a footpath that wound into the hills. The forest was mostly deciduous trees, rising dozens of feet above our heads. Under that canopy tangled thick flowering bushes, one with particularly prominent white blooms: blackberry. The vines climbed through the underbrush and reached out across the paths, their flowers and thorns in equal numbers.

The trail occasionally broke into pasture, and waist-high grass obscured our way forward. We would skirt the pasture's edge until finding where the trail exited, or at least a likely break appeared. In that manner, we followed a number of animal paths to dead ends, retracing our steps to the last known trail spot to find the correct way forward. The process took time and reduced my confidence in whether we were remaining on Il Muli. Repeatedly, we would traverse a rough section or bushwhack a shallow ravine and find ourselves again on a wide path that was clearly a trail, if not the trail, and so on we went. Late in the morning, the trail began to rise, and I eyed the treetops, looking for the peak of the ridge. But we would climb and then drop slightly, then climb again, always thwarted from a view by a dense canopy and another hillside before us.

Surrounded by forest and unbroken underbrush, I admitted that we were no longer on the Il Muli. Trails would only appear in short segments before we would once again have to traverse a ravine or break through a dense copse of woods. I had begun to worry that we'd gotten turned around when our trail intersected with a rusty barbed-wire fence. It seemed we were reaching some rangeland that, I reasoned, usually has road access. At that point I expected we would soon have a vista as well and be able to reconnoiter. We walked the fence line and just fifty yards farther came to a gate, its silvered tree-trunk posts wrapped in wire that looped over a shorter fence post. Lift the wire and free the lower wires from the ground tangle of brambles, and the gate would swing free. We stepped through the gate and onto a dirt road that paralleled the fence. I replaced the gate wire, and we quickened our pace in anticipation of our destination. I realized that our brief hours moving through only woods had made me hungry for the simplest signs of civilization.

The road soon led to the open edge of a boulder-strewn hillside, with only scattered trees impeding our view of the landscape beyond. Past another gate, a connecting road hugged the hills, and across a valley sat the familiar tower blocks of Rocca Massima, dominating the top of its scabrous terrain as though it had been carved as one piece off the top of the mountain. It was still distant, perhaps another half-hour walk, but the way was clear.

The rough dirt led onto a gravel road, which flattened and connected to a paved road, clearly the one we had taken on our previous hike. We turned left and began walking uphill, eyes swiveling. Facing a series of blind curves, we'd need to listen and watch for traffic. But more importantly, I needed to memorize landmarks to our route to the high pasture so we could return. At the intersection of the roads sat a tall sign, black lettering on a long white panel with the symbol of a sanctuary and the words "Via Francigena." This was the connection to Il Muli. It was also the path of the pilgrims and priests who traversed the land between missions and abbeys in medieval days. Although we had strayed through the overgrown woods, at least we had exited at the trail's juncture. I looked back to the level path that we'd take on our return instead of ascending through the pastureland. We quickened our pace into town.

It was nearly 1 p.m. by the time our feet paced the quiet streets. A dog barked from a backyard. In early afternoon, we were entering the traditional Italian time for rest, and I wondered whether we would find an open lunch spot. The few businesses around the plaza—really only a wide intersection where the road from Cori met the road to Artena—were shuttered. Down from a closed pizzeria, however, sat a coffee shop and bar, Cucina la Baita. A few people sat inside its screened porch, and music played over a tinny speaker. Here would be lunch. We ordered thin sandwiches and iced tea from the elderly proprietors: a woman who could offer individual words in English and her husband, who eyed us suspiciously and tended to his espresso machine and one other bar customer. We pointed to the glass case and waited for the paninis to be warmed, then took them outside to relax under a table-sized umbrella. A postal delivery van pulled up to park. Construction workers, their clothes white with rock dust, ambled slowly toward their truck.

Following that relaxing interlude, we hiked back through town, past the locanda and the church. This time we were chased not by rain clouds but rather by felines. Cats scrambled along the edges of the narrow lanes as we paced. The quiet was so complete that it silenced our desire to explore further, and we turned to face the hillside toward Artena. After refilling our water bottles and reapplying sunscreen, we were ready for the hike that would have been undertaken by the Force nearly seven decades earlier. I squinted to try to picture the scene through my father's eyes. Surely Erick and his compatriots observed the same church, the narrow lanes, and the same road toward the valley—probably gravel back then. And also the same trail, certainly much more heavily used in those days. I hoped that our return trip would yield a more obvious, correct route.

Descending through town, the first segment was on easy pavement, but my enthusiasm was dampened by the day's intensifying heat and by my concern over the disappearing trail. Given the dizzying result of the morning's confusion that was only solved by running up against the fence, I was resigned to very likely again enter the unmaintained portion of the trail and angle off to a mess of dead ends and forest bushwhacking.

We returned to the sign for the Via Francigena and aimed ourselves in its indicated direction, past a small utility building instead of uphill along the rancher's fence line. Beyond a clearing appeared a grass-covered road, trees leaning over it from both sides, no cars or other people evident. As I stepped onto the road, I felt it was right, and my idea was confirmed when, just a quarter mile or so in, my boot uncovered the remains of a hoof.

"Look at this!" I called to Susie as I kicked it free of the matted grass. There was no mistaking the shape of the sole and the formerly solid material, much like our own toenails enlarged a thousand times. "Most likely this came from a pack animal, right?" It was like unwrapping a gift. "A mule on Il Muli!" Susie smiled at me, and we both looked up the trail.

"We could use one now," she said, bending branches out of the path.

"Naw, this is my job!" I said, quickly stepping in front of her and pulling the underbrush out of the way. The overhead canopy was welcome, but not the young whips of trees and bushes encroaching across the path, which increasingly narrowed it. But the trail continued along a hillside, and I could see the wooded valley below, the forest broken only by a cleared field on a distant opposing slope. It was already golden with bales of hay arrayed across the stubble.

As had happened in the morning, though, the meandering path eventually disappeared, or we wandered off it, and we puzzled over our next steps. I resolved to keep the valley clearing in sight so we could maintain the correct heading. It seemed to work as we rediscovered a trail, which carried us along for another stretch before depositing us deeper in the woods with no obvious way forward. It was so overgrown. The pattern was getting frustrating, so we barged along, deciding on the fly which forest opening might lead to another trail connection or whether it would be worth bushwhacking through a ravine to find a trail upon the opposite hillside.

I stopped to dab beads of sweat from my forehead and glasses, squinting through the trees to spot Susie straining to climb the opposite slope. She'd picked up a sturdy branch for a walking stick, and she brought it down firmly into the forest duff to steady her step. We both faced rising walls of blackberry brambles, so we would need to circumnavigate the thicker patches to gain ground. Frustrating calls went back and forth, our voices distant among the tree cover. I lost sight of her as I plunged deeper into a valley and she rose up a sidehill, but I saw her descend again on a bit of a side trail. Placing her walking stick and taking a big stride, she called out in alarm as her foot plunged into a rotted downed log. Unsteady, her clothes caught on a thick vine, which flexed and released with a sharp slap across her forehead, the thorny cane drawing blood. I pivoted at the sound and flinched at seeing a trail of blood around one eye and down her cheek. Although she'd taken a painful slap, it looked worse than it was, and when she'd been freed from the entanglement and the blood dabbed away with a wet kerchief, we both calmed down and stood reassessing the situation. That blackberry vine to her face brought us to our senses. It was clear that the randomness of our method was not yielding forward progress, and the technique was certainly making the way unpleasant.

Susie sat and drank some water, the cut stopped oozing blood, and she said she was fine to continue. But I called an end to our bushwhacking technique. Using a map that showed contour lines and assessing our direction of travel, I charted a course that would keep us consistently at one elevation and continuing in one direction. I tracked the sun's position as we methodically moved forward.

Eventually, we emerged into a clearing. Stepping out of the woods into the chest-high grass filled my lungs with air. We stopped to rest, snack, and regain our good humor. We resumed our technique of circumnavigating the clearing and searching for a trail that led onward. More than two hours into our walk, I sensed that we had made scant headway. Much more hiking was ahead. But seeing glimpses of a road on my topo map, I also expected that the trail was nearby. We set off from the field in the direction of the road and soon came upon another fence, obscured and rambling through the trees, angling down into the valley. We kept it on our right, and soon we stumbled into another small clearing, out of which was an obvious trail opening.

After our determined resolution to soldier on, the trail connections began to reappear. The sun was sending beams sidelong through the upper tree branches, but we were no longer concerned. It was just time and steps to get us back to Artena. I began to consider what the terrain might have been like in 1944. It was impossible to imagine that the Force soldiers encountered anything similar to the forest in front of me, or the need to bushwhack as we had done. That would have been easy for them, their sheer numbers and full complement of gear no match for the underbrush. Time and weather would change a landscape, sometimes subtly but inevitably. The tallest trees could have been seedlings, or extreme weather could have carved new depths into the ravines and sent timber and rockfall sledding into the valleys. The Force could have skated across a nearly naked landscape or suffered through an old-growth density long since decayed.

Stepping finally onto the road that worked its way through farms and country homes back to Artena, we spotted real estate signs offering property for sale down a side road. Perhaps that gravel lane continued down into the valley, to that wide-open hayfield that I had kept in view as we struggled along the hillsides. But like those Force soldiers so many years previous, my destiny did not lie in that direction. The valley spread out before me, and around the bend Artena sat cemented to its rockpile, waiting for more Americans to trek up its stony stairs.

Chapter 32

May 1944

When the battle finally reached Artena in the last days of May 1944, the village became the pivotal point in the fight for Rome. The ancient settlement, hewn from the last rocky mass looming above the area's principal road, was so defensible it was once known as Montefortino. The hills gave way to a valley stretching thirty-five miles north to the Eternal City. To control access to Rome, it was necessary to take over the railroad passing Artena, one of the two lines going to the city from the south. Its station sat just below the village, within sight of the Borghese castle. Running parallel nearby was Highway 6. The Force had fought within sight of that road before, seventy miles south at the battle for Monte la Difensa, then again a dozen miles from that at Cassino. When they engaged in the Artena battle, they would be on top of the crucial point where the highway cut through the valley town of Valmontone. The road and rail were essential for any army to carry its matériel and supplies to battle. Take control of both, and the German grip would release. Together, Artena and Valmontone were the Nazis' last stronghold to be broken.

But first, the Allies had to get across the open ground flanked on the south by the German-held hill towns. The U.S. military newspaper *Stars & Stripes* reported that the Germans holding the high ground gave Allied infantry a "naked feeling" of exposure. "From the last mountains of the range causing trouble south to Cassino to the mountain mass of Colli Laziali, between highways 6 and 7, the Germans are still favored by excellent observation," reported the paper in "Flashes from the Anzio Front" on February 22, 1944. The Colli Laziali, also known as the Alban Hills, was a rising of small peaks northeast of the Anzio plains. "Even ships in the harbor of Anzio can be seen from the Ops on Colli Laziali," the article stated, "and with almost no defilade from the beach to the frontline, every tank, truck and jeep is a potential target on the main roads."

The Allies, with the Force as a primary spearhead, had chipped away at German positions in the first days of the breakout. The Germans had fled, or pulled back fighting, from the lofty towns along the front of the Lepinis all the way to Artena. As Force soldiers trod the cobbles of those villages in their leather boots, they kept expecting to have to take on the enemy in an uphill battle. But so swift was the Allied advance, the Force had charged along with nearly no resistance. They awoke from their night camp in the woods east of Rocca Massima to another fast advance. They were to guard the right flank of the Allies' Third Division as it pushed more deeply into the Velletri Gap, the narrow bottomland between the two sets of hills, through which ran that critical rail line. Allied infantry moved rapidly through the fields outside Giulianello. The Force was to continue to cover the infantry as they patrolled through the hills to Artena. Force soldiers assembled their Sardinian mule train on the wooded Il Muli trail while keeping an eye on the Third Division in the valley. By midday, the Force was at Artena's gates.

The face of Artena, the main way into the fortress-like town, opened east to Valmontone. Approaching from the southwest, as the Force was doing, meant engaging the town from below a series of sheer rock walls with strips of trees clinging to them. Artena was capped high above by its blocky church, twin towers rising from the west edge, its soot-covered white walls matching the jumble of buildings cemented to the rock. Just as the village was visible to the approaching Force soldiers, the commandos would be equally exposed to opposing troops defending their aerie. But once again, a mountainous firefight was not necessary. Infantry units from the Third Division had done the tough work of chasing the Germans from the village and, as the Force arrived, were busy ferreting out snipers. As they'd done in the previous hill towns, the commandos entered the town unopposed.

After making contact and relieving the Fifteenth Infantry of their defensive position, platoons of Force soldiers bivouacked in Artena's high buildings. The headquarters cadre and part of the Second Regiment took up quarters within the town, relieving the Seventh Infantry of command duty.

Headquarters chose a site at the top of the town that offered a sweeping view of Valmontone and the next Allied objectives in the valley. By nightfall of May 27, the strategic town and its high overlooks were under Force protection.

In the valleys below Artena, the battle raged, as the Germans held a front along the rail line north to the Alban Hills and east to Valmontone. From rear positions along those fronts, the enemy kept up a continuous, punishing barrage of artillery against the Force positions around Artena. The Nazis were marshaling all possible forces—including bringing to the fight the Hermann Goering Panzer and Parachute Division from its post behind the Winter Line—to hold the vital road as long as possible.

Force platoons advanced down the slopes of Artena on the morning of May 28 to engage the enemy from high ground nearer to the road and rail line. Overnight the Germans had moved a line of tanks into position in the woods next to the rail line, which Allied command intended to eliminate. Force troops were also directed to demolish nearby bridges on Highway 6. The First Regiment moved left toward the Valmontone road, attempting to intersect with the Seventh Infantry, which was mounting a simultaneous attack farther up the valley. The Third Regiment fanned out to the right toward Colleferro, a nearby valley town, to block any attack from the south. Both advanced against artillery pinpointed directly to the junction of the road. Erick's Second Regiment was held in reserve in the upper town with headquarters. Artillery and tank fire battered the Force, and casualties ran heavy. A smoke covering laid down by Allied artillery helped the commandos push forward, but with only incremental gains. "Enemy resistance to the attack from Artena to the railroad," wrote Force historian Burhans, "was probably the heaviest a Force attack ever faced." He recalled how tanks and looming, self-propelled eighty-eight-millimeter artillery guns set up a constant barrage at point-blank range, and snipers worked from every building. The Force advanced across open wheat fields, which were raked by high-volume twenty-millimeter flak wagons.

But by day's end, the troops had established a secure perimeter in a crescent shape around Artena. The First had dug in along the rail bed, while the Third had sandbagged a defensive line across the Colleferro road. The Germans faced them with a heavy complement of troops, artillery, and tanks in the lowland between the railroad and Highway 6. Overnight, the commandos reprised their Black Devil activities and infiltrated behind enemy lines to ascertain troop strength and movements, and a demolition patrol set out to blow bridges on the road and the railway. The demolition plans were thwarted by strong enemy defenses, but the reconnaissance patrol, returning after a full twenty-four-hour mission behind enemy lines, achieved a view of the extensive German presence massed against the Allied attack.

With the advance below, Force headquarters had also moved forward, deploying down to the middle of town and occupying the ancient castle, its command post secure behind the thick stone walls yet its overlook offering an even closer sweeping view of the battlefield to Valmontone. Perhaps the Second Regiment accompanied and defended the unit's leadership and assisted in setting up the Force's "collecting station" for wounded soldiers on the flat land of a church square below the castle.

The battle continued on May 29, with the Force taking heavy shelling, especially in its rear positions within Artena. The aid station was bombed. Any movement on the town's streets was countered with a deadly attack. The command post was rocked with shells exploding on the castle walls. General Frederick ordered the reserve battalion to evacuate the townspeople to the rear. During the mayhem it was discovered that a Fascist civilian in town was directing the attack with signals to German gunners "with a German telescope and a blinker light," recalled Burhans. The man also had been wreaking havoc by cutting phone lines as fast as the communications crew could lay them. The spy was swiftly dispatched, but the shelling continued and thwarted any further advance on the rail line.

By the afternoon, Allied commanders had bolstered the Force lines with two additional infantry divisions. A continuous barrage of fire from the Sixth Field Artillery Group, brought in to support the attack on the dug-in German rail defenses, began to have an effect. Overnight, the Germans mounted their most significant attack, advancing at many points along the line with the apparent objective, observed Burhans, of retaking Artena. The Allied lines held, and the German offensive eventually devolved into individual skirmishes that could not break through. But the battle had taken a deadly toll on the Force. The First Regiment sat at half strength, with three hundred men. The Second and Third each reported one-third of their members as casualties. Headquarters had lost many men as well.

The Allies continued to sweep in with more men and equipment to shore up the Force positions against further German attacks. The Nazis were expected to attempt to retake Artena again in a push to hold open Highway 6 for at least another two days until their retreating Tenth Army had passed through Valmontone. Meanwhile, Frederick was concerned about attacks on his right flank and from behind Artena. The First Regiment was holding a line nearly eight miles long, from the Colleferro road through the hills to Cori. French forces were working their way up from the south but were still many miles distant.

On the afternoon of May 30, the Germans mounted a battle toward the Artena train station, sending a battalion-strength phalanx of infantry and a cadre of tanks toward Force lines. Allied artillery and small-arms combat by Force fighters held the line. The four-hour battle repelled the infantry advance, but the German heavy tank weaponry remained in control of the station. Into the night, punishing artillery barrages concentrated on the German tanks. Allied commanders planned a TOT, shorthand for focusing all artillery into one area. This hailstorm was about to be unleashed when the Germans mounted an attack from the Artena rail station. Enemy tanks and swarms of infantry were seen through illumination flares as the barrage thundered down with deadly effect.

By May 31, the area was firmly under Allied control, but the Germans engaged in delaying actions along an arc that traced Highway 6 from Colleferro to Velletri, with Artena in the center of the bulge. The decision was made to push on to Valmontone and crush the German line still holding the railway, Highway 6, and the town. On the morning of June 1, Allied artillery flared into action and preceded the ground troops' advance, which began with the Force's Second Regiment "jumping off" their transports at 6 a.m. Within a half hour, the first wave of troops had crossed the high grasses of the open field and entered the woods that hugged the hills next to Artena's rocky mass. They saw little opposition. Soon, the entire regiment was through the flats and entering another area they called "the quarry," chased by mortar, artillery, and small-arms fire, at times an intense onslaught. They moved fast and lost track of their front line but by 7 a.m. approached the railroad tracks and encountered heavy German machine-gun resistance. On the open railroad bed, they overran the enemy troops and shortly had many prisoners. Their first objective of the day achieved, soldiers of the Second moved from the conquered flatlands and took over a ridge above the Artena rail station. By 9 a.m., the Nazis were fleeing.

Artillery barrages continued a rain of fire on the narrow valley between Artena and Valmontone through most of the day. Smoke curtained the battlefield. But at 4:18 p.m., American troops viewed a large white flag flying over Valmontone. The battle for the crucial edge of the valley—and its essential road and rail to Rome—had been taken.

Chapter 33

May 2011

Standing in Artena's Piazza della Vittoria in front of the castle, I imagined how it would have looked the morning Valmontone fell. Erick's unit had taken Artena with little incident days earlier, and they had been holed up in the old castle and a warren of homes. It took them a day to clear the village of concealed snipers. They continued taking artillery fire and engaging in skirmishes, and no doubt the rubble had piled up from artillery strikes in open spots like the piazza. I looked down to the valley and considered the historical accounts of the tornado of action that swirled along the front line in the valley. The Allies concentrated their blood, sweat, and firepower into shoving the enemy back beyond the tracks of the crucial north-south railroad and the towns along essential Highway 6, Valmontone and Colleferro.

Up in ancient Artena, rubble blasted from the stone walls and cobbled streets would have made it difficult to move along the steep, narrow lanes. Houses clinging to the rock high on the hill would have provided a clear vantage point of the situation below. From the piazza, the view across the valley would have shown other battles taking place. But the open valley also would expose any movement by the Allied army toward Valmontone and bring down a rain of German mortars from their strongholds east of the town. As the area's high spot, Artena was a strategic vantage point and thus a tempting German target. Clearly, that was the reason my father's unit had been chosen to defend it and why the Force had chosen the ancient fortress hulking off the plaza as its headquarters.

I winced and shifted my weight as I leaned in to shake hands with one of our hosts, who happened to be the fourth and most senior member of the famous Borghese family we had met. I quickly shifted back off my left foot and surreptitiously eased some of my weight onto Susie by putting my arm around her waist as I thought of the previous day's hike where I'd evidently injured my foot.

My hike into Artena had ended with a swollen foot, and I could not recall any particular moment when I'd done the damage to cause such a painful result. We had moved to a flatland hotel that sat on the road to Colleferro, just a kilometer from the castle where we now stood. When we entered the room, I had sunk onto the bed to cool off and rest, and I admitted to Susie that significant pain was throbbing in my right foot. It was visibly swollen, the stretched skin completely obscuring the ankle bone. I needed to rest, elevate, and medicate. The modern hotel, along a busy, noisy road, was square and lifeless. The airless rooms held little character. The sole window was covered with a security blind made of heavy metal panels, reminiscent of a blast door installed to shield the room from explosions. When the steel blinds were cranked up with a long wand, a glass doorway with a tiny, railed balcony was revealed. Beyond the hotel lay the verdant valley backed by the green Lepini Hills. The view looked directly at the forest that held the Il Muli. I had reclined on the bed and hoped relief would come to my foot before our local host, a family contact cultivated through email from an introduction by Camilla Borghese, would pick us up for dinner.

I had wrapped my foot with an Ace bandage, but it still throbbed as we made our way to the lobby to wait for Valerio Borghese. He was my age, the next generation of the family who was currently headed by his aunt Camilla and his father, Andreas, who had spent most of his life in Australia. Valerio—who had grown up in Australia and spoke both Italian and English with an endearing down-under accent—now lived in the family castle in Artena, and after an email from his aunt when we visited her, he had agreed to show us around. Finally, I was to get an insider's view of Artena and hoped to weigh the veracity of stories of where my father had been injured by revisiting the town.

Valerio stopped fast in the hotel driveway and jumped from his car to greet us, fashionably late. Admittedly, by Italian standards, it was still early to go out for the evening. We piled into his small car, wedged in with another couple, friends of Valerio's from Australia. They had an evening plane home, so they would join us for dinner before taking a train to the airport. We circled the nearby town of Valmontone before finding a pizzeria that would agree to serve us dinner at the shockingly early hour of 7 p.m. Over icy beers and lazy waiter service, we traded stories of our homelands and shared a Lazio regional specialty: arancini, a breaded, deep-fried rice ball with gooey cheese at its center. We followed that crispy treat with wafer-thin pizza topped by another regional treat, brick-red bresaola ham, a type of prosciutto without the marbling of fat. We had ended the evening early, with a promise from Valerio to pick us up first thing in the morning for sightseeing that would include a tour inside the family castle and a visit with his father. I had gladly rolled down the blast shutter and limped into bed in our tomb-like room.

Under a blazing morning sun, Borghese father and son stood with us in the castle courtyard, overlooking the valley. A stone arch over the snaking road below held the family crest, a muscular eagle with claws and wings flexed. I shook hands with Andreas Borghese and endured—no way was my aching foot going to keep me from the tour.

"Come in, come in!" said Andreas, who wore a red sweater, tinted glasses, and a friendly smile. He gestured for us to walk ahead through the castle's lower rooms. Valerio opened gates and doors as Andreas ushered us into a broad arched gallery. I glanced about for a good place to lean.

"These were the horse stables," he said, tucking his glasses by one bow into the collar of his sweater. It was evident that the doors and arches framed a reception hall for carriages. But the adjacent stables had been converted into a series of prison cells.

"The stables and this room had been used as an Allied command post," he told us, "and the rooms behind the stables had housed soldiers." In centuries past, those rooms were where the local constabulary locked up miscreants, and graffiti was scratched into the walls, with vertical lines marking the days, weeks, or months of an incarcerated life. Names, ages, and sentences were carved faintly into the cratered mortar walls, along with a phrase uttered throughout time by people in such situations and translated by Andreas that clinched the scene: "It says, 'I am innocent.'"

"I wonder what the soldiers bunking in those cells thought of that!" I said. Would they feel the same, even though they had lobbed hand grenades over the canal and flushed out the enemy hiding in farmhouses with a flurry of bullets or a flamethrower's flare? Would those soldiers, fighting for their lives against an enemy willing to use the same tactics on them, be able to understand the Cori elder's remembrance that not all German soldiers were bad? Were any of the forces at war ever able to claim innocence any more than a man incarcerated for a village crime?

"You can see evidence of the war," Andreas said, "everywhere here." He gestured to ragged fractures along the walls from mortar shelling and a series of smaller holes running in a rough line: machine-gun fire. The blasts had only penetrated the surface of the centuries-old fortress walls. The windows of the rooms looked out at a courtyard that faced the valley and would have had a direct view of the battle below.

Just inside the doorway to one of the larger rooms, our host pointed to a list of names scrawled in black, block lettering high on the wall. "Here is evidence of the Allied occupation," he said. It was a list of men billeted in the rooms. To my astonishment, I knew some of the names. There was Burhans, the intelligence officer for the Force who penned its history, and Finn Roll, the Norwegian.

"These men were part of the Force headquarters detachment!" I said, a chill gathering on my skin. "This must have been the Force command center."

We stepped into the garden, where Andreas wanted to show us a significant architectural feature. Above tangles of green vines and dense shrubbery, he pointed to a narrow balcony that bowed out from the castle's second floor. White marble columns defined a low wall in front of two narrow doors with many panels of glass. My mind flashed to Mussolini's famous exhortations from a high balcony of the palace in Rome, and I expected another detail of wartime significance, perhaps the location of a lookout or gun emplacement. But the story was much gentler.

"This was the 'Juliet balcony,'" said Andreas, "used by the famous director Franco Zeffirelli in his movie." The movie of Shakespeare's most storied romance, made in the late 1960s, was considered a classic. In the overgrown garden where we stood, he explained, was Romeo's spot to stand and call up to his lover.

Andreas asked his son to explain their plans for the castle to us. Valerio described how a setting so romantic would make the perfect place for a wedding, and the family was working on an idea for that section of the castle to hold such events and possibly even some B and B rooms. Gazing up at the empty balcony, I tried to picture myself standing in Romeo's shoes. But I couldn't shake the castle's more sober purpose.

Father and son Borghese ushered us out of the castle garden, and Andreas gestured across the plaza: "Let's have lunch." Gazing across the bustling village square, I recalled our first visit to Artena, when we discovered the plaque dedicated to the Force, its red arrowhead glowing amid the phrases of commemoration cut into white marble, the memorial dwarfing the adjacent sign identifying the spot as Piazza della Vittoria. To the right of the plaque was an arched doorway with two iron grates swung open to reveal a door. In front of the door, a scrum of young men lounged on blue plastic chairs. Evidently, it was a restaurant. We navigated through the crowd and into the trattoria. Called the Grotto, it embodied its name, with tables set beneath rough stone walls. Iron spikes held overhead lights to the cave-rock ceiling. Andreas quickly ordered lunch, and as we swirled red wine and twirled pasta in deep bowls, he told us another story of a famous family member, one who also had been a World War II commando, but on the other side of the fight. It was Andreas's father.

Junio Valerio Borghese, after whom our tablemate Valerio was named, was a prominent Fascist and a commander in the Italian navy. Well into his career by World War II, he helmed a crew who unleashed "the human torpedo," a two-man submarine that would approach an enemy ship and release its payload into the hull. While Junio was decorated and promoted for his work with the risky secret weapon, he also became somewhat of a pariah to many Italian people. When the country surrendered to the Allies and became occupied by the Nazis, Junio aligned with the Italian Social Republic, which continued to fight with the Germans. Valerio defended his grandfather's action as noble: "As long as it is believed and fought openly," he said, "it must be respected." The torpedo submarines and their commanders entered Italian lore, Andreas said. Junio himself wrote an account of the group's action, which echoed the nickname for my own father's unit. The book's title: *The Sea Devils*.

We walked back through the piazza in front of those former stables, and my eyes traveled across pockmarked walls. I leaned back on a railing that edged the plaza and lifted my aching foot off the cobbles. I heard Susie ask Valerio something, but the discussion was lost to me. The blue sky held no whistling missiles, not even clouds. The garden greenery gave no whiff of gunpowder. But the walls echoed the shouts of men who were being cut down by a spray of bullets, ducking for cover in the cacophony. Still, seven decades after the war, I sensed the battle churning in the air.

Chapter 34

June 1944

To finally conquer the crucial Artena area and move north toward Rome, the Force had one more battle to mount. Although the German troops could be seen retreating through the hills northward, they continued to engage the Allies approaching from the south. The enemy still held the town of Colleferro, the next town south of Artena on the rail line. It was rife with Nazi ammunition facilities and storage due to the town's abundance of minerals and mining industry.

Erick joined his Second Regiment comrades once again descending from Artena on June 2. They turned toward Colleferro. The Algerian Division of the French Expeditionary Forces was closing on the town from the south, having taken Segni, the next town down the line, at the same time as Valmontone fell. Force scouts were dispatched and discovered no concentration of troops in Colleferro but spotted heavy German activity on the highway to the east, probably Nazis on the retreat. As they were seeing repeatedly, the Germans would not be going quietly.

The flat terrain approaching Colleferro would provide scant cover for an army, and the members of 6-2 would have moved warily, rifles high, ears alert to incoming ordnance. They would be differentiating the sound of shelling in the distance from the particular whine of a rocket on a close trajectory. Perhaps the soldiers hit the ditch along the roadside multiple times as shell after shell tried to persuade the Americans that the Nazi ammunition depot was too costly a prize. At every explosion, men went down, and after the smoke would clear, some would not rise. That morning, Erick's platoon commander became one of that number, and calls for "Medic!" would get him bandaged and stretchered and on the road back to the triage point. Next in line of command was Erick, and he would step back onto the road with a reduced platoon behind him. Hand signals and eye contact would indicate high alert, so no more of the boys should be caught by the incoming fire.

Pretty busy for an abandoned town, Erick might have thought. He would peer into the roadside dust, waiting for it to settle between shellings. *Is it safe to move in? When will the next one hit?* There would be nothing heavier than the weight of leadership, of balancing life and death.

He would be looking for key signs that required reaction, studying every curve in the road, any building that blocked the view. And from that dusty view came not soldiers but townspeople, haggard and wary, perhaps some with white handkerchiefs, appearing around corners, stepping out from whatever shielded them. The company lead would freeze, and Erick would raise a hand high to indicate they hold fire. Cautiously, they would call out and get their interpreter to the front line. Suspecting a ruse, they would flank the group of civilians to make sure no German troops were lying in wait. Once certain of their purpose, the interpreter would tell them to speak.

"No Germans" was the nervous message. "They have left. The town is clear." But the soldiers could not risk their lives with trust.

Exposed on the road, needing to move lest another fusillade rain from the sky at any minute, Erick and the other Force commanders would give the signal to go ahead into Colleferro. Erick led his platoon into the village, each team fanning out from street to street to sweep thoroughly for Nazi resistance or traps. As sniper shots would ring out from pockmarked buildings, the structure would be surrounded and resistors neutralized, face down in the rubble or hands up with no weapons. They searched for the ammunition depot and found that the town was not completely clear. Methodically, they captured the entire garrison of men guarding the town, 425 Germans. The prisoners would be marched back along the road to join the corrals.

But as the town was taken, Force troops continued to face squalls of artillery raining through the blue sky and felt the ground shift every time another mortar cratered their paths. Although ground-level resistance was slim, the enemy still fought from afar.

Erick's platoon moved to secure yet another town square. Where neighbors would on a normal day have paused in their errands to greet one another, the soldiers walked through dust and smoke. *We'll get this done yet*, Erick perhaps thought. But through the air flew another missile barrage, discharging into a shatter of searing metal shards. As explosive earth erupted from a new bomb crater, shrapnel would be airborne in all directions, its hot payload slicing through anything not too solid, like uniforms and skin.

Erick was hit by artillery cratering behind him, an impact he never saw. For the second time that day, 6-2 would see its leader fall. He landed prone in the crossroads and lay facing the earth, his back and legs peppered with shrapnel.

The shock would knock him out. Time would pass before his nervous system would send out the alarm to wake up, to fight, to live. Regaining consciousness would mean facing a tidal wave of pain that would feel like fire across his back and legs. He could not move. Would the dirt have tasted of Colleferro's minerals, the raw materials of the bombs that would bring a soldier down? Would he pass out again from the pain, only to repeat the process of waking to a bodily nightmare?

He would not remember the trip back from the front. They say that after the missiles stopped, the townspeople came with mules and rescued the men left lying in the street. Erick took a second trip on an animal to the medical corps, and again, at least, he was one of the ones still breathing.

Western Union
Dz N 32 Govt

Wux Washington DC 335Pm June 21 1944

Mickel O Thorness
Epping N Dak.

Regret to inform you your son staff sergeant Erick G. Thorness was on two June slightly wounded in action in Italy period you will be advised as reports of condition are received

Ulio The Adjutant General
253 pm

Chapter 35

June 2011

Olive trees, a symbol of Italy, exude a quiet power, I thought from the vantage point of another countryside lodging. Their gnarled trunks grab at the sky, stretching in human proportions out from knobby burls at their base. The trees grow strong with single trunks but seem equally vigorous entwined as two trunks growing together, eventually merging their rough, chipped bark.

An olive's modest leaves are simple collections of spires, spiking along a curved young branch or sprouting tuft-like from the wizened trunk. Nearly hidden along the branches and an unassuming canopy, clusters of flowers sprout, each barely the size of an ant that might crawl across the leaf. From tiny white blooms, the future olives begin to form as swelling green nubs in quantities of a dozen or more per slim branchlet. The branch droops with the weight as they grow. When ripe, simply shaking the tree sends the fruit cascading to the ground.

I reclined in a well-used chaise lounger set among a grid of olive trees on the gentle hillside that gave our hosts—Ivano and Terhi—the name for their B and B: Colle Degli Ulivi, or Olive Tree Hill. Their two guest buildings sat at the bottom of the hill, with the family home overlooking it. A bumpy dirt lane on the edge of the hill town of Zagarolo, ten miles northeast of Artena, led to the quiet oasis. We had come there to rest my swollen ankle after our week of hiking the route of the Anzio battles. Rest and elevation of the foot were necessary before we finished our exploration of the Force's final route to Rome.

Surrounded by the olive trees, I felt I'd stumbled onto a metaphor for my quest. Forever the son of a farmer, I often sought lessons in nature, where contemplation was invited. I had seen plenty of olive trees growing along the Lazio region's hillsides. They seemed to prefer the rocky soil of a mountain glade as much as or more than the cultivated farm field, but I had come upon a sloping, grassy yard tended solely for the ancient-looking trees. Now June, the landscape was bathed in sunshine, but humidity had not yet congested the early summer air. Time slowed.

Human life should be as similarly rooted in gnarled history as the flaring trunks of those trees that clutched the soil, I thought. Lessons about growth and evolution, coming into your own as you age, were there to see. A person's value or unique abilities may not be evident early, as they slowly blossom into maturity, but you could look closely and perhaps see the future. I could only consider pictures of my father to read his thoughts, his aspirations, and his history, and there were precious few images, scattered across ten years of adulthood before the war and twenty-five after it. But stepping across the rocky hillsides of the war, I felt my father being formed, his character tested. War was an unfathomable storm, and battles could ravage the mind as deeply as they cratered the landscape. But if you endured past the hardship, grew scars over the wounds, you could soldier on into life past the whirlwind. I could not pretend to feel that storm on the warm spring breeze that settled the flower petals onto the lawn, but I could sense where it had been, how history had altered that person who was my father and, I thought, was transforming me.

At the base of the olive grove, I saw Susie walk from our room around the building to enter the common gathering place that was the B and B's reception area and communal dining hall. The ever-present Ivano Bruno was no doubt inside, standing over a steaming pot of something delicious, creating meals with homemade ingredients from oil to pasta to vegetables. As the evening's menu bubbled along, he would pop in and out to shuttle guests to and from the train station and provide direction about area tourism, always with a friendly "Ciao!" and an expressive arched eyebrow above his salt-and-pepper beard. Terhi, a slim Icelander with long flaxen hair, would tend to business behind the desk while looking after the couple's two children. The family would join guests at a large dinner table. We felt as comfortable at the Olive Tree Hill as at a friend's vacation cabin.

Arriving at Zagarolo, I had progressed farther than my father in his battle. The Allies had moved swiftly in the last leg of their Rome journey, clearing towns like Zagarolo to much gratefulness from weary townspeople. The soldiers would enter Rome on the second day after the Artena victory. My approach would be swift as well, an easy road and rail trip to the border of the Eternal City. That is, after my aching foot was once again functional.

It took only a day of recuperation for me to get antsy. We had explored so much area history, through caves and castles and mule trails, and I wanted to achieve the goal that had been on my mind since I conceived of the exploration: finish the trip for my father, cross the Rome gates like his Force compatriots did as he lay in a hospital bed, enduring the painful results of the raging Artena battle. Even if my own Artena battle resulted in a bit of pain (the parallel was not lost on me—was it sympathetic? Psychosomatic?), I felt the need to continue. I might not be able to strap on the pack and hit the road, but at least we could continue exploring the war's effects on the area. Zagarolo and its surrounding towns had been Nazi occupied and in the path of the retreating German forces. What scars and lessons lay beneath their surfaces?

Ivano was inspired by my quest and offered his services as a tour guide and taxi driver. Our first stop was above the sheer rock cliffs we could see from the Olive Tree Hill's valley neighborhood: old town Zagarolo. We had ventured from the Lepini Hills into the Apennine Mountains, and the village covered the flat top of a rocky peak. Walls and gates at each end restricted movement along its extended oval cap. Although home to less than one thousand people, we learned, it held four churches, a grand palace, and municipal buildings belying its size. One skinny road cut through the upper town's center. A narrow valley with steep, forested hillsides and a river at the base made the Zagarolo aerie all but impenetrable. Closer to Rome than Artena, it sat along another rail line whose next stop was the famous ancient royal city of Tivoli.

I learned, through an introduction to a local man by Ivano and his translation services, that the town owed its postwar existence to its shape and serendipitous location. Euginio Loreti, a Zagarolo elder who said he was "about 90," was contacted by Ivano and agreed to converse with me about the war. We met on Zagarolo's monastery square to talk, sitting under the umbrella of a closed pizzeria on the edge of the pedestrian plaza. I gratefully sank into a plastic chair across from the slight man, who wore layers of clothes even though the arc of the sun was about to banish the last shadows from the warming town square.

Because Zagarolo was easily defensible and situated behind the front lines but near enough for quick access by German troops, Signore Loreti explained, it was turned into a medical complex by the occupying forces. Their takeover was swift and severe.

"When they came," said Euginio, "they demanded that all able-bodied men of the town join the Italian army, which was then fighting with the Germans. 'Join up or be killed,' they told the young men." Euginio, who was twenty, did not want to go. The townspeople fled the invaders, like so many in other hill towns skirting the Anzio plains. Euginio went with his family into the fields below the town and hid in the valley farms and vineyards: "Many had a cellar or another hiding place." Because he did not take up arms, he said, "I am somehow still alive."

The Nazis turned the town's unused old castle into a large hospital. "It was the most important one for the area," said Euginio. "They painted a huge red cross on the roof." Soldiers injured in the Cassino or Anzio battles were taken to Zagarolo, patched up, and sent back to the front or sent home.

"The town was thick with Nazis, but mostly they left us alone," he said, through Ivano's translation. "In fact, the Germans ran the hospital with some compassion toward the locals. If locals needed medical help, they were taken care of."

But life was hard. "After the occupation, there was no food," he said, and people "started eating the grains from the field, the oats and barley." When that was gone, they ate what the cows fed on: hay. "People had little things, like eggs," he recalled, "and they traded the soldiers two eggs for a loaf of German black bread." In that way they survived "through the long winter and spring."

On June 2 or 3, 1944, the Allies began bombing the town. It seemed to Euginio that the artillery fire came from the Velletri area, which was almost directly across the valley. "But Zagarolo was hard to hit," he said, "on its high ridge, and flanked by two other high ridges with valleys in between. Picture three sine waves on an oscilloscope," he said, arcing a bony hand through the air and pointing with the other, "with the town in the center of three humps." The bombs overshot the town and landed on the hill behind it (the third hump), systematically destroying that hill. "If they had shot lower," he said, "Zagarolo would not exist today."

He told how the townspeople did not have specific knowledge of the battles raging around them. They did get radio transmissions from London, but the information was general, and they wondered what was happening. "One day the German soldiers started to move, and they left in a hurry," he recalled. All the Germans from Zagarolo and nearby Palestrina were heading northeast toward Tivoli. As they retreated, "they set mines at the entrances to the town and exploded them," he said. All the homes built close to the gates collapsed. "It was nearly impossible to enter the town."

Although the Allied bombing was sparing the town, the people of Zagarolo did suffer from the attacks. Allied planes would circle back after their raids, and "on the way back to their base they would drop their unused bombs on the fields outside the town, just where the townspeople were hiding," he said. "Many died because of that." Euginio remembered "incredible explosions" in the hills as well. The Germans had left their ammunition hidden, and the Allies attempted to find and destroy it. He recalled how the mountainsides would explode whenever their bombs hit the hidden German ammo.

"As soon as the Nazis were gone, the Allies were at the town gates," he said. They gathered at a destroyed bridge at the base of the town, "but they feared being ambushed and wouldn't enter. A group of young townspeople went down to the soldiers to tell them that the town was safe," he said, so the troops began to find a way through the rubble. They had to navigate a tank at an angle through the partially blocked archway entrance to get inside the city walls. Then they brought bulldozers and started to plow a road next to the town, through the valley to the east. "But it had not rained and was very dry," he said, "and the bulldozers raised so much dust that a black cloud hung over Zagarolo."

And the Zagaroleans suffered in another way—with the specter of marauding troops raising its ugly head—as again North African soldiers, attached to the American and British forces, struck fear and anger into Italian villagers.

I sat squinting as the sun blazed directly overhead, not really believing that I was hearing that story again. Signore Loreti, his eyes in shadow under a wide-brimmed hat to protect his mottled, papery skin, seemed as pained to tell the story as I was to hear it.

"The Moroccan troops were the first ones into Zagarolo," he said. "The townspeople had heard warnings of these wild soldiers from their neighbors," people from Cassino and other towns to the south where they had come through. The message was that "the African troops would rape the local women and act as though they were marauders," he said. "So the local women were gathered and hidden, and the townspeople raised their own guns to protect them. The Moroccans began to loot and steal, so the local people began to shoot at them." The soldiers were unorganized, he said, so "fifty or sixty of the soldiers fell." Finally, Allied leaders began arriving and swept out the "liberating" scourge.

The Allies continued moving toward Rome, but to Euginio it looked like the American troops occupying the area were trying to improve the situation for the locals. "The town had a Fascist mayor, which the Americans removed," he said. To the town's great relief, in the weeks after retaking Rome, "they made sure the hospital and the town services were safe, and they provided food for the townspeople."

Brutal hardship. Debilitating injuries. Death. Those were the grim outcomes of war that I learned about from the few surviving elders who crossed my path and the hill towns I visited around the edge of the Anzio plains. Such tragedies touched every family, whether it was someone sent to do battle, the worried family left behind, or others who were unluckily, disastrously, in the path of war. The ripples cascaded out in waves. Families were displaced, children were traumatized by events and actions they did not understand, and people suffered hunger and deprivation of comfort. In those ways and so many more, entire communities were devastated, and some people never returned home or had to rebuild elsewhere.

I pictured my grandparents sitting anxiously by their wooden box radio in the dim farmhouse parlor, hearing the latest news of each campaign, and imagining their son grimly moving forward under a hail of bombs. Multiply that by hundreds of thousands, a scene replicated by families across America, Canada, and many other countries. Even though ordnance was not exploding in their backyards, it was cascading through their thoughts and emotions.

Perhaps my father—walking through the rubble of those Italian communities, seeing the universal image of desperation in the eyes of local people who somehow survived the onslaught—also pictured his own land, imagining what such a conflagration would do to his dusty town or where the troops would hide and exchange volleys in the coulees of the rolling North Dakota prairie. At many turns and during the telling of those Italian stories, I pictured such a fate and wondered how my family would perform under those extreme conditions. I imagined that I saw the strength in my father's face and the determination in the matter-of-fact way in which my mother had raised a large family with few resources and a fractured husband.

The Allies liberated the villages, but the countryside's woods, ravines, and caves provided the hiding places for enemy troops on the defensive, so each had to be cleared to ensure that safety returned to the communities and that the Allied troops could securely continue marching north. In that process, the war flared again and again across the land. Visiting Zagarolo's neighboring towns of Genazzano, Cave, and Palestrina, it seemed that the luck of location would determine whether they found themselves in the crosshairs.

Genazzano, with its medieval castle nearly devoid of windows and its warren of narrow streets, was not destined to be a strategic location for the Germans in retreat, its village center far from the main escape route. Cave was nestled in a farming valley backed up against inhospitable hills. It, too, was served only by farm roads with tangential connections to Highway 6. But closer to the front sat Palestrina, a city of significant size and resources with an outlook from its Apennine slopes toward Valmontone.

Palestrina had a more auspicious history than its neighboring towns, I learned as I gingerly tried out my foot on a walk through the old town center. Built into a graduated hillside as so many of the towns were, it expanded to top the rocky peak, commanding a 360-degree view of the region. On a nearby hill, another ancient village, Castel San Pietro Romano, its cobblestones leading to a castle ruin, capped its own rock pile. Sparse woods separated the two. Three regional roads connected Palestrina with Highway 6, so

Nazis streamed through the town as the Allies conquered the road and rail to Rome. Refocusing their massive artillery from Valmontone to those hills, the Allies pursued. A barrage aimed at Palestrina sought to set the enemy on its heels and destroy its ability to respond so that the Allied ground troops could advance. Somewhat paradoxically, the destruction from that fusillade also uncovered hidden treasures.

We made our way to the center of Palestrina and came upon its boxy palace, the Palazzo Colonna Barberini, fronted by a semicircular lawn cut into the hillside. We could see the entire town below. Adjacent to the palace, the Chiesa of Santa Roselia, capped by a square tower of tan stone walls with marble corners, dominated the street above a stone archway that opened onto the lane from town. Together, the two structures commandeered the upper townscape. The rough exterior of the church masked its interior marble work, frescoes, and paintings. Ivano tipped us off that it also housed a treasure: a larger-than-life marble sculpture by Michelangelo called *The Pieta of Palestrina*. It served as the artist's pattern for the creation of his masterwork *Pieta*—depicting a bereft Virgin Mary cradling the lifeless body of her son Jesus Christ—which could be seen in a place of honor in St. Peter's Basilica in the Vatican in Rome.

But more impressive than the palace and even more astounding than the *Pieta* was an ancient temple that had been uncovered when the Allies bombed the city. Palestrina, which had been razed twice over the millennia in religious wars, had been built and rebuilt by stacking the relatively modern *palazzos* and *chiesas* and street after street of connected stone homes atop the truly massive temple of Fortuna, who in ancient Roman religion had been the goddess of fate or fortune. And until bombs rained from the sky in pursuit of Nazi invaders, the current residents had no idea the temple lay beneath their town.

After many blocks of houses had been flattened and the city was in Allied hands, clearing of the rubble began. Only then did the townspeople begin to discover archways and columns and ancient walls that were once dwellings. Rather than rebuild on top of these ruins, the modern Palestrinans continued to clear and investigate and found a temple calculated to be 3,500 years old that stretched from the palace that crowned the town far down into the city. The temple stairstepped down the hillside block after block, covering a space as wide as the town's long shopping street. Incredibly, there were no records or stories of its existence.

We hiked up from the lower town to the palace, with me leaning heavily on a scavenged walking stick. Across from the grassy plaza that looked over the town and within steps of the church door, the palace hosted an archeological museum. Below street level, the plaza had been cleared so visitors could get a sense of the extent of the ancient temple. Stone walls built against the hillside made of many types of rock cascaded from the edge of the lawns. The walls, which ingeniously had been built two layers thick to account for moisture coming through the hillside, stretched at some points three to four stories high. Multiple renovations over the centuries could be seen in the excavated ruins, where temple arches had been walled in and new buildings added on. By the twentieth century, those had all disappeared. Stones and pillars had been reused in different configurations, and many of the structures showed evidence that pieces had been brought from other temples. One excavated section showed a floor covered in an ancient mosaic style, with multicolored rock tiles depicting a scene of fish swimming in a bright blue river.

Cutting through the hillside along the edges of the temple could be seen massive white stones that would have formed its exterior protective walls. Those partial walls, surrounded by homes from later eras, gave clues as to how much larger the temple might have been. Locals said the giant homage to Fortuna that proceeded down that long, sloping hillside would have been visible from the ocean and from Rome, more than twenty miles away. Its ultimate size and shape will never be revealed—barring the fate of another bombardment.

I sat in Palestrina's lower town square under a shade tree, waiting for Ivano to end my misery by bringing around the car. The climb and exploration sent spikes through my ankle and frustration coursing through my mind. I should be walking the next leg of the soldiers' path to Rome, I thought, rather than hobbling around an ancient temple. Exploring by car felt like a failure, a betrayal of an oath to Erick. I was inadequate, not up to the task, a poor legacy for my father. Was that to be my flicker of education, the intergenerational truth I had been seeking, expecting? The events of the battlefield travel lay inside my head like a stack of file folders bursting with information, and I had cascaded them all to a pile of paper on the floor in search of a final, most important dossier. When I parted my hands to open it, I found it empty. I tried, but failed, to convince myself that the failure, too, was only in my head and only cast there by me, not some attitude from my father's ghost. Fortune seemed buried beneath too many layers of life and death.

But that was the impression of a farm boy visiting seventy years after the war. To Adele d'Uffizi, whom Susie and I met in the lobby of Palestrina's palace museum, the memories seemed fresh, and she sat in the quiet gallery for a few minutes to relate her experiences in broken English.

At the start of the war, she was eighteen and operating a shop in Littoria, now known as Latina, a town in the middle of the Anzio beachhead. Her father, who had a large property in the hills beyond Palestrina, told her to close the shop and come home. "Papa took all the kids up on the mountain" to their estate, said Signora d'Uffizi. There, they found a young American soldier, whom she called "mulatto," a term of the time for mixed race, whom they would shelter in their home. "We found him sleeping under a tree with rose hips and chestnuts in his pockets," she said. He and other soldiers who came through "were escaping, starving, from the Cassino campaign." They would burn their uniforms to deceive the Germans.

From the hilltop property, she could see the bombing when the Allies came ashore. "It was like New Year's Eve," Adele said, "but a bad one." Compared to the Cassino campaign, "which was never successful," she said, "Anzio was very fast."

When the Americans began bombing Palestrina, the Germans fled, but they left behind a ruse: "One tank and one soldier that could go from one end of town to the other and shoot to make it seem like many."

Her father's property housed 105 people during the Anzio campaign. They tunneled from the house into the hills and sheltered many people in the caves. They built bunk beds into the stone shelters. They hid food, battled Italian partisans who were still working with the Nazis, and sheltered wounded men. The property had multiple places to take refuge, and her father "made the family split up so if the bombs hit, it would not kill them all." She proudly stated that "the family stayed together, did their jobs." Still, the horror of the bombs was in her mind. "If you could hear it," she said, "it would pass you by."

When the Americans came, "Liberade!" Open arms. "It was joy. Boogie!" They handed out candy and delivered, finally, a feeling of freedom. "War," Adele d'Uffizi told us, "is the worst thing that can happen in your life."

Beyond Palestrina, we continued to explore the hill towns and seek war stories as my swollen ankle returned to its normal size, but mostly we discovered a gift wrapped in traditions: small-town Italian life. An evening celebration in Genazzano's plaza set a glow on old plaster walls as lights wired to festive shapes like flowers and stars were strung over the street.

Although we experienced only a handful of villages in the path of the Allied campaign, I could feel the impact echoing through the towns as loudly as my boots on cobblestone streets. Zagarolo, held hostage by invaders, or Palestrina, where centuries of buildings were reduced to rubble, or Cori, with its destroyed churches and legacy of young women pregnant from rape: all this from one campaign, taking place in a fateful year of occupation followed by four months of battle. Such destructiveness echoing off the stone walls of those villages was multiplied and amplified by the breadth of the war into a cry of anguish that would rise up from thousands of communities and millions of voices across many countries. What would my father have made of such sights and stories, surely evident in every place he went? He was brought up religious and a few months earlier had written to his parents that a person should count their blessings. I hoped that he would have been able to access those feelings in the face of such horrors. My vision of the war, which had been formed from the dry leaves of words on paper, evolved into scenes of pulsing blood and gritted teeth. How could anyone, from farm kid to soldier, escape without permanent scars?

Back in the olive grove, I nursed disappointment along with my aching foot. I had come just as far as my father and was now failing him at my stated purpose of finishing the job and walking into Rome on his behalf. Or perhaps I was failing myself, an old sentiment that resurfaced from time to time.

I had always been a big kid, with early indications of being on my way to size thirteen feet and six-foot-two height. But when faced with a family broken in a way that I didn't understand, a great hunger seized me, and I filled a hole in my life by retreating into myself. Instead of filling that hole with resolve to understand and move forward, I just added layers of defense by eating more and being less active. In the years after my father's death, I became bigger and bigger, perhaps feeling that the weight would insulate me from emotional vulnerability. Of course, it did not, and instead I nursed a deep sadness. It would take years of social unhappiness into young adult life before I began to face the causes, through therapy and regularly repeating embarrassing episodes, to drive myself toward change. Finally, as my professional writing career took hold, I began to look past the youthful turmoil and take better care of myself, mentally and physically. My health and happiness inched up as my waistline inched down.

Sitting in that olive grove, I knew I had come a long way emotionally and in the understanding of my father's plight. But there I was, my swollen foot betraying my goal, as had happened so often with my body. And I would take the figurative steps that also were my regular fallback: I would adjust my expectations, swallow the regret. And then move on.

No voice over my shoulder told me it was okay to fail. But I looked up into the olive trees and felt forgiven. It wasn't necessary to carry my father on my back to his goal. But maybe the memory of how he faced his challenges could carry me to mine instead. My foot had failed, but my resolve to understand was unbroken.

Chapter 36

June 1944

I thought the battle of Artena would have been the end of it. Next stop, Rome. In my father's case, the next stop from a Colleferro street was to a hospital tent. But his mates, and so many other regiments of determined men in Allied uniforms, had broken the German lines, silenced their giant guns, and sent them on the run. Then they continued the chase.

On the day Erick was cut down by the flak of shrapnel and the Force was tracking the enemy from Colleferro, the Allies pushed northwest to a final battle along Highway 6. Throughout the day, German mortars harassed the troops as the Nazi army continued their retreat through the hills east of Rome. The resistance of the Germans was broken, and they knew they would lose Rome. Hitler had declared Rome an open city, meaning that it would not be the location of battles. He would not destroy the treasures of the Eternal City, and the Allies would not be forced to respond. But of course, that was not assumed by the troops on the ground. There were still many Germans in the city and in the nearby hills. Fellow Force soldiers could have regaled my father with stories of mopping-up activities that kept them on high alert as they moved from burg to burg, as was happening along a broad front that stretched west across the Alban Hills and to the Appian Way. All along, enemy forces streamed north, resisting as long as possible the inevitable liberation of the entire country of Italy.

At 3 p.m. on June 2, the French Algerian forces entered Colleferro, finally linking the Allies' southern campaign with the Anzio front. The Force turned Colleferro over to the Algerians and returned to Artena to prepare for the next push.

By June 3, companies of Forcemen were on transports that flowed up Highway 6. As usual, they were the spearhead, among the first troops to surge forward on that battle-scarred road. An advance team from the service battalion entered the town of San Cesareo and began to set up a Force command post but signaled to the passing troops to continue toward the city. At the train station at Finocchio, one of the last stops before entering Rome's suburbs, small-arms fire triggered a swift response, and the resistance was addressed with no Force casualties. As they moved, they swept up lagging or disoriented German soldiers and dispatched them to a growing prisoner of war corral.

Erick surely would have heard about his unit's final honor for the campaign: the FSSF and other special forces units under the Fifth Army were given the task of occupying and protecting the city. They would become the Rome Area Allied Command. And they were competing to see who would receive the honors of being first to set foot in the city itself. I imagined the excited recounting of a good-natured race by another Forceman in a hasty note to my father: "We got there, Pops!" he'd write. "Second and Third moved up the road all night, and they were all set to be first in!" Those regiments were on pace to reach the suburb of Tor Sapienza—the unit's new digs—by dawn. Meanwhile, at exactly 1:06 a.m., General Frederick received a radio message from General Keyes. It read, "Secure bridges over the Tiber River above 68 Northing within the City of Rome." The Force was to capture and guard Rome's bridges, all the ones north of the map coordinates marked 68.

"When the old man got that message, everybody knew it was time to go," Erick's friend might have written. With those orders in hand, the race could be won. Frederick dispatched two companies of the First to join the tanks of Task Force Howze and head into Rome. They waited until dawn to ensure safe tank movement, then traveled the final miles of Highway 6, passing a sign marking the city limits at 6:20 a.m.: "They got to a big blue sign with an arrow that said Rome, so everybody took a turn mugging for the cameras!" Soldiers overcame bone-weariness to stop for pictures by the sign. But they weren't out of the woods yet, and again came upon Nazi troops that had been left behind and started shooting from their flak wagons, even lobbing artillery. They quickly returned fire, scouted the situation, and determined how to shut down that last-ditch German effort. They moved on toward the stretch of ancient stone wall with a massive arched gate: Porta Maggiore.

"But they moved forward all night, they took fire, and still they weren't first in!" The end of the story would require another push. "Good thing we split up and headed for two 'Portas'!"

As the Force was skirmishing at the end of Highway 6, a separate patrol from the Allies fighting in the Alban Hills had been tasked with scouting Highway 7 into the city. A unit of sixty men in jeeps, led by Force officers and others from the Ellis Task Force, moved into the city through the Porta San Giovanni gate at 6 a.m. With this move, they laid claim to the title of first in. They too were met with defensive fire from Germans guarding the route, and more firefights ensued. The path up both roads into Rome would require fighting well into the day before the Allies broke the German defenses. Smoking hulls of disabled tanks sat roadside, and small-arms skirmishes echoed from retreating Nazi units as the Force and compatriots moved toward the Tiber River bridges.

Scouting reports revealed that the only German troops left in Rome were guarding the bridges to aid the retreat of their comrades. By the end of the day on June 4, Force patrols were guarding eight of Rome's sixteen bridges that spanned the Tiber, with the other bridges being held by other Allied units. "We got here, Sarge! I'm looking at the river right now, with that big dome of St. Peter's behind," Erick's scribe friend might have written. "The sun's going down, and the river is blazing orange and red. Never seen anything so beautiful."

The spires of St. Peter's Basilica hovered over lanes stretching west from Force-protected bridges, while the warren of tiny streets housing the Pantheon and composing the birthplace of the ancient city honeycombed out from the Tiber's eastern bank. Allied forces pushed north and east out of the city in pursuit of the retreating enemy. The bulk of the Force fighters, finally relieved of duty, retired to a camp at Tor Sapienza to rest.

The next day, the last of the Force troops on bridge duty were relieved. The front line was already well north of the city, with the Germans still on the retreat. The Force pulled back from Tor Sapienza to a much more comfortable bivouac at Lake Albano, where they could rest in the sun, swim, and heal. Although the unit would write another chapter in their tales of battle action by joining the war again in the south of France, the Anzio campaign would enter the history books and the minds of many as the apex of the Force's brief, storied career.

Chapter 37

June 2011

As we exited the comfort of Olive Tree Hill and headed to the city, we picked up old Highway 6, still a significant road, at the town limits of Zagarolo. But the road soon became overshadowed by express highways. To the west a half kilometer sat San Cesareo, a compact grid of streets overshadowed by those branching concrete rivers that split and wove into Rome. Highway 6, known there as Via Casalina, narrowed and hosted a series of roadside shops and cafés backed by modest agricultural operations. The pizzerias and bodegas became more frequent at Finocchio, which began to feel like a Roman suburb. We found that town's section of the old road bordered by a commuter rail line, so the once mighty, and mightily fought-over, highway became an access lane adjacent to train tracks and provided a rather inglorious, industrial way to enter the city.

Tor Sapienza, the old Force bivouac spot, sat five kilometers northeast of the diminished highway. It also was just beyond another looming border, Il Racordo. Locals called it "the Junction," Rome's mammoth ring road, officially the A90—or the Grande Racordo Anulare, the "Grand Junction." Of course, it was not in place during the war. Presently, it heralded the beginning of the city proper, which I could see meant an increase in building density at every road juncture, where the shops became shoulder to shoulder. Like everyone else, we were passing through the suburbs on wheels. I was distracted by train traffic and disappointed by the uninspired landscape. Even if I can't hike it, I can still explore, I thought. But what there was to see could essentially be framed by the windshield of another diminutive rental car. I was missing no revelations, leaving no valuable historical stones unturned. Behind the wheel of the Lancia, buoyed on a set of tires like the Force team headed to their triumphant entry, Susie and I pushed on toward the city.

Inside Il Racordo, we entered Municipio V, Rome's fifth municipal district. However, passing under the A90 on Highway 6, we were not yet in the city of World War II. That would not come until entering Municipio I, the first district of Rome. Via Casalina, the vaunted old Highway 6 whose essential pavement triggered the grandest clash of armies ever seen on Italian soil, ended ingloriously at a small piazza unremarkable except for a few stone benches under small trees where a person could walk their dog. The modest park could have used a thorough cleaning. But beyond the apartment blocks and local tram stop, across a road buzzing with traffic, loomed the Porta Maggiore, one of the grand gates into the old city. Dating to the first century BCE, it carried a storied history.

The ancient gate appeared not as one entrance but as many. The crumbling red stone and brick city wall, which rose as part of the third-century Aurelian construction of the city's defenses, rambled into view through weedy grass that flanked the gate. The wall split at a series of narrow, arched entrances. The archways were half the height of the wall, which, though decrepit, remains at nearly thirty feet high. One-lane, one-way roads or wide sidewalks provide entry to Rome under the archways. Voluminous trains clattered by constantly on their way to nearby Termini, the city's central train station and an area that, considering its value to German movement, was the victim of one of the few significant Rome bombing attacks by the Allies. Considering Maggiore's distinctive stacked arches, I realized that the gate was visible to us when arriving in the city via the Leonardo Express train from Fiumicino Airport.

Sadly, the main gate, the official ancient porta, seemed forlorn behind a mess of weeds and fences, derelict and unused. But from where we sat in the piazza across the street, you could still feel its faded grandeur. Crumbling white travertine marble abutted the red wall and rose another story above the wall's height. Its two large portals, whose archways nearly matched the height of the adjacent walls, represented the convergence of two roads that met at the gate: Via Casalina and Via Prenestina. The second road connected Rome with Palestrina. Incongruously, those grand arches were topped by another layer of marble, one that was not just an ornament. The structure was originally an aqueduct, or rather two aqueducts, stacked one upon the other. From the side, the two water channels were visible above the gate. In ancient times, they rushed fresh water into the city high above the roads—surely an awe-inspiring achievement to travelers entering Rome.

I traced the great arches to three smaller arches on their flanks that sat within their own decorated niches, edged by Corinthian columns and capped with triangular gables. The base of those arches would be well above a visitor's head. The center one held yet another arched opening, that one at ground level. I imagined Roman soldiers guarding the gate from the elevated archways, always of course maintaining the crucial high ground over potential adversaries and able to gaze over the scene. It illustrated a precept of defense as old as civilization.

I pictured the soldiers of my father's unit on their predawn march through the gate, the red spearhead shoulder insignia tagging them as the leading commando force. Just over a kilometer to the south, I imagined the other scene, where twenty minutes earlier, Porta San Giovanni had been stormed by the Allies, which included the other Force contingent.

The plentiful fragments of the ancient city walls could be traced on a walk between the two ports. Much of the way, in fact, tracked the edge of a narrow park along Viale Carlo Felice, a busy thoroughfare cooled by a canopy of pollarded trees. We arrived at a gate set in a much finer piazza than Maggiore's, centered with a statue of St. Francis of Assisi, his arms raised as if to offer absolution. His praying figure faced the Basilica of San Giovanni in Laterno, a massive cathedral and the official seat of the pope as the bishop of Rome.

The gate reflected the grandeur of its setting, with multiple soaring archways through which heaving traffic ricocheted across the plaza's stones and clattered over crisscrossing train tracks. Brick walls and arches led the eye to the central arch, again white marble but with much less mass or ornament than the Maggiore gate. Again atop the gate could be seen the ruin of the aqueduct. Walking through the gate and encountering the expansive church plaza and the statue, dating from 1925, I tried to picture the scene as Force soldiers would have found it at dawn on June 4, 1944. The early morning sun would have cast the face of St. Francis into shadow but sent silhouettes of his raised arms across the road. The cathedral's ornate white marble would have gleamed. Coming under the two-century-old wall into that scene would impress even the most battle-hardened soldier of the value of the historic city.

For me, however, the imposing plaza and the grand cathedral's impact were outdone by a modest historical spot a few blocks north. Before the war, the Germans kept their embassy in the neighborhood, in a building on Via Tasso that had been a small palace. During the war, the building, simply called Via Tasso, became a prison. When the Nazis prepared to occupy Rome in September 1943, they met a valiant, if ineffective, resistance by the Roman people. The former embassy became the site where the Germans would incarcerate, interrogate, and torture Italians who were part of the resistance.

The prison was not the only atrocity perpetrated by the Nazis against Roman citizens. Persecution of the city's Jewish population took place a few neighborhoods west of the museum, in the Roman Ghetto. It was a crime committed throughout German-occupied cities and countries across Europe during the war, and it was intended to enact the Holocaust, or the extermination of the Jews. The Ghetto neighborhood, which had been an enclave for Jews longer than any place outside of the Middle East, was sealed off in a raid by German soldiers on October 16, 1943. Two days later, more than one thousand Jewish residents of the Ghetto were shipped off by train to the Auschwitz concentration camp. Only sixteen of them survived.

For the next eight months, the Germans operated their embassy prison. When the German secret service fled, executing fourteen prisoners by machine gun just hours before the Allies stormed into the city, the people raided and occupied the building, freeing the remaining prisoners. Repurposed as a museum, it has been maintained as it was in the war years. Exhibits and artifacts showed the atrocities of the place. My imagination played echoing shouts against the rattle of cage doors and the distant rapping of gunfire. Touring the second floor, home to the prison cells, rooms appeared as they were during the war, with heartbreaking graffiti scrawled on the walls by the prisoners and grates on the doors and windows of the cells. Historians estimated that two thousand people passed through the prison in the nine months of occupation, most brought up before a Nazi war court and sent off to a camp or held for brutal interrogation. The building that became Museo

Storico della Liberazione, just two minutes from where the Force and other Allied soldiers entered Rome to finally free it, quietly bore one of the most anguishing stories of the war's effect on the people and the grand city.

The liberation of Rome was symbolic but also cathartic. It represented the dam breaking on a stalemate on the plains of Anzio, one that took many thousands of lives; uprooted countless innocent civilians; expended the firepower rarely, if ever, seen in any previous clash across the world; and contributed greatly to changing the course of the war as it set a marauding, ruthless enemy onto its heels. As I stood on a Tiber River bridge, its dark water swirling below a glowing sunset, I had a sense of my father's thoughts. Lying prone beneath a fog of pain and finally getting word of the achievement, he would have reminded himself that he never doubted they could do it.

PART 4

Postwar

Chapter 38

June 1944

"I finally made the white sheets, as we say when we make the hospital," Erick wrote to his parents on June 6, 1944. "It was kind of a relief too, as we have had quite a siege of it on the front lines. My wound wasn't so very bad, just shrapnel in my left leg, so I am getting along pretty good now."

Erick's first post-injury letter, sent on the army's V-mail stationery with the censor's stamp and signature as prominent as the address at the top of the page, went out only four days after he was cut down by shattering ordnance. And it was dated on D-Day at Normandy, which would be lionized as one of history's greatest days. The letter was sent from the Ninety-Third Evacuation Hospital, where he was transferred on June 2 after being taken to the Eleventh Field Hospital, where the medics triaged injured soldiers less than two miles south of Valmontone. The Ninety-Third was a "motorized" hospital, meaning semimobile, with forty doctors, an equal number of nurses, and four hundred beds. In June 1944, it moved through the Caserta area between Rome and Naples. Erick's letter from the hospital was the standard way soldiers got news home. Communication during the war was largely through letters, routed to service members around the world by the U.S. Postal Service using an intricate system of customized collection drops. Letters, packages, and such official documentation as absentee voting ballots would be routed through major cities and shipped to the army's delivery system at "base detachments" around the globe.

A letter from home, though, held much more than the day's news; the emotions of an anguished nation and its stalwart fighters were bound up in Air Mail envelopes that were rimmed in blue and red chevrons. Brown butcher paper and sisal twine held together not only care packages but also as much love as could be infused into photographs, tins of cookies, and monogrammed underwear. In those days, a telephone was a rare appliance in many rural households—nonexistent in Erick's farm home—and a telegram, costly to send and difficult to deliver, was reserved only for extreme situations, as when the army would inform a soldier's family of his injury or death. Letters from the front assuaged a worried family, and letters from home, whether delayed or mangled or censored, were as satisfying as eating your mother's home cooking.

The battle was still fresh in Erick's mind, but he couldn't share much detail. "We had the Jerries on the run quite a while before I was hit and I guess they are still going," he wrote. "We've been hearing news of the front opening today so it may not be too long now before the war is over in Europe." Images of home must have swirled in his head, not just for himself but also for all the young men who had been at his side and who had sweated blood together on the battlefield. Immobile in an army hospital bed, Erick would read every battle's news account with an expert eye, perhaps reading between the lines as he understood what could not be said about campaign strategies or Allied casualties. As with his censored letters home, the news reports needed to be viewed for unintentional slips that could reveal plans to the enemy. Fleeing or not, the German army was a deadly killing machine. The urge to put an end to the horror must have raised the blood in all who served, whether or not they still held a gun in their hands.

As with all his letters, Erick closed with questions about family and the weather—thinly disguised prompts for the folks to write back with news of home. It would surely be the most comforting information, however mundane, to any soldier in the white sheets, thoughts tearing among pain and medication fog and tragic news of their comrades—layered onto their vivid memories. "This will have to be all for now," he wrote, with no explanation of the necessity. Whether it was his inability to focus any further, an emotional breakdown, or an appointment with the surgeon, Erick did not say. But he had reached the bottom of his one page of stationery, so perhaps it was simply the end of the paper and not the terror behind his eyes that he could not bear to let seep through in ink.

By June 14, the army had moved Erick again to the Thirty-Sixth General Hospital, a sprawling complex near the Force's old headquarters at Santa

Maria Capua. Situated in the ancient royal city of Caserta, where a thousand-room palace marked the town's previous grandeur, the Thirty-Sixth was one of the many military medical facilities in the area through which Erick would tour. "Dear folks," he wrote on American Red Cross stationery from the 2628th Hospital Section, "I'll drop you a line again today and let you know that I'm getting along fine, just eating, sleeping and reading." As time passed, he seemed to realize the privilege and the duty of communication: "I have quite a few visitors too as there are other fellows from my company here. Yesterday one of the boys of my platoon was in and wheeled me outside for a while as I can't walk now as long as I have this cast on my leg. I got a shrapnel wound and a bone fracture out of the deal." As before, hints of the battle crept in: "We lost our platoon officer before this drive started so I was acting in that capacity when I was hit." It seemed to signal the turning point in the letter, which ended with questions about family and instructions on the hospital address to use when writing back: "Well I hope to hear from you soon and often as soon as you get my new address." As a temporary release from boredom and night terrors, the news from home could not come too soon or too frequently.

His Force comrades evacuated to other medical facilities would occasionally write back as well. A fellow staff sergeant from 6-2, Lawrence D. "Andy" Andrews, sent a note from Lawson General Hospital in Atlanta on July 5, 1944:

Dear Thorness,

I was really glad to receive your letter yesterday, but sorry to hear about your injury and hope it's not too serious. Also hope Chapman, Stubbs and McCarthy are not wounded too bad either. By what you say about your foot being paralyzed, you must have a nerve injury similar to mine, as my foot is paralyzed too. And still no feeling in it. I'm also still in bed, and no telling how much longer I'll be [in] bed yet.

Let me know about some of the battles you've been in, maybe the censors will let a little by. Capt. Barnard was up to see me, and he is being discharged from the Army on account of stomach ulcers I think.

I haven't heard from Rosetti lately but at least I heard he was doing OK. Well Thorness, I hope you're feeling fine when you receive this and the best of luck always.

Andy

By early August, Erick counted his bed rest in months and recorded on the back page of a slim leather notebook his fourth transfer to the facilities around Caserta and nearby Naples. He had, by then, been processed out of the Thirty-Sixth on June 28 and sent to the Sixty-Fourth General Hospital at Maddaloni, south of Caserta. It, in turn, had passed him on to the Third General Hospital on July 14, so he traveled back across town to its location two miles north of the old royal city. Finally, just days after he wrote his brother Ed on August 3, he would arrive at his last hospital in Italy, the Thirty-Seventh General Hospital, a medical center set up on the Mostra Fairgrounds in Naples.

"I am starting my third month in the hospital today," said his letter to Ed, "and much as I dislike lying in bed for so long, it is still better than dodging shells and bullets. We practically lived in foxholes or caves since we came to this country." That would pass the censors. He went on: "I just received the letter that you wrote July 11th," he wrote. "The reason my mail has taken so long getting to me is that I've been transferred to so many different hospitals." He mentioned their brother Melvin, in the navy and evidently still in the Pacific battle theater: "I wonder just what island they are on." He closed another brief letter with comments about the harvest and the weather, then tasked Ed with putting a little pressure on his best friend for some communication: "Tell Rueben that it's quite a while since I had a letter from him now." To his parents and his younger sister Helen, he ended each letter with "Love," but the virtual hug for his brother had to be read between the lines: "As ever, Erick."

Chapter 39

August 1944

Erick walked out of the army hospital on three legs, one of his own and two crutches. His left foot hung limply, back and leg pain dampened by pills. It was to be his last day in Italy, after two months in hospitals around Naples, suffering through the heat and humidity of a south Italy summer. He would hobble into an endless parade of wounded soldiers, most gritting their teeth and heading for trains, ships, and planes to make the long, painful journey home. If they didn't know they were going home, the trip might have been unbearable.

I thought of my father's limping departure from Italy as Susie and I joined a throng of tourists on a narrow side street that linked one Roman piazza to another. My foot had become only an occasional annoyance, something that Erick probably never could say after the war. I imagined the Force soldiers tramping through the streets of Rome in their combat boots, rifles slung over their shoulders after the Nazi threat had been excised from the city. The intricate stone fountains of Piazza Navona had aged more than a half century since the war, but the marble gods and fish and detailed scrollwork had been completed hundreds of years earlier, and my eyes traced their lines in the same way a soldier's would have done. Pangs of sadness and guilt struck me as I pictured Erick's mates enthralled by the ancient sites, a view that my father would never hold.

Erick's road would not lead to the Eternal City as he readied to return to the States, and he'd never see the wonders of Rome. He would hoist himself into a truck for transport to Naples, returning to where his Italian campaign had started. On August 8, 1944, he would act on orders from his latest commanding officer, Captain Rubbin at the Thirty-Seventh General

Hospital: report to headquarters and then evacuate to a transport flight, which would leave for the United States via North Africa. The journey was to be a reverse trip from the previous winter. It had been ten months since his unit of battle-ready commandos had steamed into that harbor, uniforms fresh and jaws set for a fight. His troop ship had docked in a Naples harbor that looked more like an army depot, albeit one set up in sooty, crumbling ancient buildings. The Force had proceeded into the fray down roads that had seen centuries of traffic but were shattered by months of bombing, then set up camp in a similarly ruined location.

On revisiting Naples in the summer, Erick found that the FSSF had settled into a base detachment headquarters in a squat, cement building in the cleaned-up city. Its unit name soared above the front doors, and the red spearhead logo flanked the lettering. It was vastly more visible and centrally located than the vacant, bombed college outside of the city where the Force first stayed and more accessible than the half-destroyed Italian Artillery School twenty miles north at Santa Maria Capua where the Force had operated its field headquarters and recuperated between battles.

The rough stone under the truck's wheels would have been cause enough to take more of the pain medication Erick had in hand for the trip. The doctors had pulled a lot of shrapnel from his back and legs. The surgeries had left him bandaged, and he knew something else was wrong because the numbness in his leg remained. Some of the shell fragments had severed veins and nerves, which meant a lot of patching up and sewing back together. They said he'd need more surgeries to recover, and they were keeping quiet about whether he'd see a full recovery. One thing was certain: his wounds were bad enough that he was not going back on the line. As he moved south, the Force moved north, storming an island off the coast of France and preparing for a push toward the center of the waning war.

I looked down at my own feet, once again in hiking boots after my undiagnosed condition had tapered off with rest and ibuprofen. The uneven cobbles sent reminders to my brain that all was not completely well. I knew the lingering jolts meant a doctor visit when I got home, and my muscles tightened involuntarily as I thought of our own impending trip back across the ocean. It would be a direct flight in a modern plane, and I longed to get it over with, but the distances those jets could travel meant marathon sitting sessions, which would be uncomfortable and possibly cause my foot problem to flare. Still, thoughts of my father's return stifled those concerns with a dose of comparative reality.

Erick's flight would take off from Naples for Oran, Algeria, where the Force had bivouacked the previous November before gathering their gear and crossing the sea by transport ship on the way into battle. As the plane would rise over the city, Erick's view would have been through a portal framing a line of military ships entering and leaving the harbor, filled with soldiers on their decks and mountains of gear in their holds.

Then would come Casablanca, once again a return to another port city, Erick's first sight of Africa from the deck of a ship. But heading home on a reverse trek, he was to be not on the waves but in the sky. A brief layover in the famed Moroccan city would end with a flight bound for New York. His airplane landed for refueling in the Azores, an archipelago of tiny islands in the North Atlantic. From there, another leg delivered him to the U.S. air base in Stephensville, on Newfoundland's western shore. His orders indicated a final stop at New York Municipal Airport (which recently had been christened La Guardia Field and later would be renamed LaGuardia Airport), but instead his plane landed at Michel Air Force Base on Long Island. The series of flights that had begun on August 8 ended on August 9. It was Erick's first trip on an airplane, other than a few short parachute training flights low over the Montana prairie, and the long transocean experience would have been as similar to those as Naples was to Epping, North Dakota.

The air transports were crowded, mostly with wounded military men sporting white tape and gauze or missing limbs, their hesitant movements hinting at endured pain. If being stuck in an airplane seat for a long flight would be tough on able-bodied men, it would be hell on wounded soldiers. The flights could turn rough in turbulent air, with jolts coming up through the airplane's flooring like a truck hitting deep ruts on a muddy farm road. The only recourse would be pain medication and the war-enhanced ability to endure nearly anything.

I knew from my own brushes with the medical world that painkillers could turn your head into a carnival and make your eyes unfocus. You might get some distance on the pain, like the receding sound a rumbling tractor would make when heading away toward the field to drop its plow. But slowly, as the hours wore on, your senses would creep back toward that throbbing ache—and the tractor would reach full throttle right over your shoulder, its blades digging into the unturned prairie inside your head. When the growl overtook you and you faced the roaring head-on, you had no choice but to get on board and ride it out.

Ultimately, the pain would not matter to my father. His stoic Norwegian heritage had prepared him for it, and he had seen many men and boys who'd had it worse and so many who never got off the battlefield. Just to get back to American soil would be a miracle for any soldier. Summer in bed in the temporary hospitals and commandeered facilities had been a blur of heat and dust and noise all compressed into two months that could have been two years, but a sigh of relief must have escaped from my father as he stepped stiffly off the plane at Mitchel Field, following the directions of orderlies to load onto old school buses, painted gray with a white cross on the side and hoods over the top of their headlights. They would drive off the airstrip to nearby Santini Hospital, a large complex with spiffy buildings and lots of grass. Before the war, the patients learned, it had been a golf course.

Erick had never been to New York before either, except to pass through on trains from Vermont to Virginia. He was delivered to the doors of a hospital complex called Cantonment, where he was settled into a bed on a ward where every man had similar injuries so common to the explosive style of warfare in use: nerve damage caused by shrapnel.

But he would not be treated at that Long Island hospital—they kept the wounded soldiers moving. After a few days, orders came, and he boarded another transport bus back to Mitchel. Again he settled into a crowded airplane. This time, the scene below was not desert or endless ocean waves but a stunning parade of city blocks, seeming to stretch forever outward from the flat roofs of New York City's high-rise office towers. And then they were over farmland, the regular tan lines of country roads separating field after field of lush green growth. To returning soldiers, America would seem, far from battles and safe from marauding bombers, an innocent place. As the plane rose into hazy summer cloud banks, if Erick could relax and drift into sleep, the calm countryside would be replaced in his dreams by visions of scarred Italian farmland, cratered and smoking, with soldiers moving fast and searching for cover. Such scenes would play out in his mind whenever he slept for the rest of his life.

"I can hardly believe I am back in the states, it went so fast," Erick wrote to his folks on Red Cross stationery on August 16. He had arrived in Clinton, Iowa, just across the Mississippi River from Illinois and one hundred miles from Chicago on Monday, August 14. It was exactly two years since he had stepped off the train in Helena, Montana, to begin training for the Force. More astounding, though, was his reintroduction to America after three months of foreign convalescence. Schick General Hospital was an impressive new army facility, with dozens of blocky buildings erected just to serve wounded men coming home from the war. It had been open just since March 1943. Of the men lining the corridors when he hobbled to his first appointments, many of them were missing an arm or a leg, and he felt grateful to at least have all his limbs, even one that wasn't working at the moment. He told his folks that he felt Schick would finally be the landing spot where he could recuperate. "Yesterday was quite a long day," he wrote. "I guess I saw just about everybody in the hospital here. The doctor told me that they were going to get me a furlough so it shouldn't be too long before I get home."

A reunion on the farm with parents and siblings would mean big smiles as everyone crowded around the car when he stepped out into North Dakota's hot harvest winds. It would be quite a contrast to his long months in hospitals overseas and the exotic ports that brought him back to American land. And then he pictured their faces when he emerged, clutching crutches, and limped over for his mother's embrace. They would need to know about his condition. "I don't know what they are going to do with my leg, if they operate or just let time take care of it," he said in the letter. "There isn't so much wrong, I have some paralyzed nerves in my leg so I have no control of my foot." Judging, though, by all those doctor visits, he expected surgery was coming. But that hospital, like the others along the way, was overcrowded with wounded soldiers, many suffering from more immediate conditions. Sure enough, it would be more than a month before they could tackle it, so they sent him home.

Erick's first furlough came five days after arriving at Schick. On Saturday, August 19, he boarded a bus to take him to Davenport a few miles southwest, then a train to Chicago. It was the start of a long trip, at the hottest point in the summer, that he would make many times throughout his convalescence. The Empire Builder departed daily from Chicago's Union Station, chugging northwest to Minneapolis and then eventually into North Dakota, where it traveled north from Fargo to Grand Forks before turning due west across the flat farmland. When he stepped out of the depot at the end of Main Street in Williston, he would be twenty miles west of the family farm near tiny Epping. At its best, the train trip was a twenty-four-hour ride, but more often breakdowns and stops made the trip longer and made it feel interminable. His furlough ended during a blazing hot Labor Day weekend, and he returned to Clinton during a welcome cooling trend.

On the commuter train from Rome back out to Zagarolo for a final night at Ivano and Terhi's, I thought of his long Empire Builder ride. I'd taken it many times myself, but from the other direction, east from Seattle to Williston, also a twenty-four-hour ride. But my ride on Amtrak's silver-and-blue airconditioned "streamliner" cars, which included comfortable sleeper rooms if you could afford them, was a wholly different experience than Erick's. Then, great clouds of steam would erupt from the giant engines as the train gained speed. It was operated then by the Great Northern Railway and cut an orange-and-black figure chugging through the countryside. A train ride for me signified that I had the luxury of time, whereas for him it would have been the only logical choice. At least on the train, you could get up, swaying with the rhythm of the wheels in contact with rails, and stretch your legs. Even though the leisurely attitude and civilized pace of train travel always beckoned me back, I recalled many visits that ended with a bit of dread over the potential tediousness of the return trip.

But Erick was to make that trip many times, and once back at the hospital after his first furlough, he found some familiar faces. I could almost hear my father's voice rising in surprise: "Russ, what the heck are you doing here?" Another man from Epping, Russell Ellingson, was also recuperating at Schick, and it made the great world so much smaller for them both. Russ's family also had been area pioneers, his grandfather operating the town's first general store. When Russ went down to Erick's ward and surprised him, they talked the day away. Perhaps Erick's meeting with Russ and his furlough home took his mind away from the war, but it would return mightily with a visit from another man, Gerald Whitmore from Cedar Rapids, Iowa. Gerald was a member of his Force platoon, but the two had not seen each other since the breakout from the Anzio beachhead in May. Their reunion, mentioned only briefly in Erick's next letter home, was undoubtedly a more sober, if also joyful, one.

"I got back here all right and found everything about the same," Erick stated drily to Helen in his September 6 letter. The weather and his visitors composed most of the letter, with a note that he'd also received a stack of delayed mail that had been sent to Italy, "so that was interesting reading." And he told her of an article on the Force in *Time* magazine: "It starts on page 62, if you happen to see that issue." Finally, he noted a rumor that he would be moved yet again, which would turn out to be true. One last transfer would land him at the medical facility where he would spend the next eighteen months as doctors tried to repair his extensive nerve damage.

Back home, his younger sister unsuccessfully combed the nearby town for the Force article. "At the news stands they said that they sold all the Time magazines as they came in," she reported in a September 12 letter. "I certainly think it would have been interesting to read that article." A good part of her letter told of the fun times of youth, going to town to a movie, stopping by "the Zigzag" and "the barn," and seeing so many of her early twenties friends, engaging in endless rivers of talk. Of course, she wrote of the harvest activities, saying the weather was "just right for combining, and tomorrow they'll finish, I think Ed said. Then it'll be the threshing left." In those days, getting the wheat out of the field required two separate operations, cutting the stalks and then threshing the kernels, long since consolidated by one modern machine. Meanwhile, their mother was in canning mode, having bought boxes of peaches, pears, and plums, and intending to put up jars of sweet corn as well. That harvest-time activity would remain largely unchanged by time or technology.

Helen was about to begin her first year teaching school, and their older sister Cora had driven her down to the school to look it over. "It hadn't been dusted or washed, but had been painted inside and out," she reported. She was nervous for the school year to begin. "I really think I'll like it when I get started," she said about one of the few professions open to women in those days. "I'll be glad when the first day is over though." She closed the letter by saying she needed to turn to her ironing.

Just a week after returning from that first furlough, Erick got orders to again move out. The rumor was true. He was headed to another hospital, this one in a location that seemed even hotter and more humid than the army field hospitals in Italy. He was moving one state west but four hundred miles south to Illinois's capital city in the dead center of the state, Springfield, the birthplace of Abraham Lincoln.

O'Reilly General Hospital sprawled over its grounds with whitewashed siding—and not a canvas tent in sight. When he arrived at O'Reilly on September 15, 1944, the white paint everywhere was so fresh it seemed the place had just opened, but in fact it had received its first patient a month before Pearl Harbor. Still, it was another of the army's expanding facilities needed to handle the tsunami of wounded soldiers flowing back across the oceans that flanked the country. Army engineers had been continually expanding and refining the facility. Rows of rooflines topped long, single-story wings that fanned out behind the admissions building like formations on a parade ground. Long corridors ran perpendicular to the ends of the buildings. Formerly covered walkways across the campus, they had been enclosed and connected to form one continuous facility on a massive grid. The shade trees flanking the hospital's front doors were tall but dwarfed by the flagpole flying the Stars and Stripes.

Erick made his way to his ward, a long room with a polished floor and rows of beds under the windows along each side. The steel beds sat high on wheels, and everything was white, from the tubular bed frames to the blankets and nurses' uniforms. It was shipshape and serious and reputedly had the best medical staff available. At that last hospital stop, where he could finally get down to the business of getting healthy, the echo of the war was becoming a more distant report in Erick's ears. There would be no exploding mortar rounds to interrupt his sleep, just nurses and nightmares.

When he entered the Illinois army hospital that September, Erick didn't know how long he'd be there or when he would be released to go home. As it happened, he would only see North Dakota sporadically on brief furloughs during the next two years of hospital convalescence. He would recall to his wardmates—the fellow patients suffering through war wounds significant enough to send them away from the front—his memories of the prairie and stories of family and farming life. If those fellows ever talked about their war, he never mentioned that to his family. Like so many soldiers who'd fought in those battles and returned with haunting mental images, physical scars, and "shell shock"—the term of that era for a syndrome that would come to be called post-traumatic stress disorder—he doubtless would avoid those subjects. Society in that era did not encourage men to share their feelings. And his training as a farmer on the solitary Dakota plains, where nothing was said because generally there was nobody to talk to, would serve him well.

Erick's response to his sister that fall spoke of the arrival of cold weather and the hope that his doctor would return from New York in time to do his surgery so that he could get a furlough and be home in time for Christmas. The idea of a family Christmas must have towered over his thoughts, especially after the previous year, when he wrote of longing to be home for the holidays on the day his unit memorialized the largest loss of men they'd experienced to date, in that first brutal battle at Monte la Difensa.

The surgery would take place in time, and he would indeed get home for that holiday, but in closing his letter, Erick warned about something that sat heavily on his mind: "Helen, I hope when you kids go out on Saturday nights that you never do any drinking. That would be an awful habit to get into. I was surprised when I was home to see everybody doing it, and I've worried some about it too, because I know what it is." Such sober worries predated an affliction that the now-worldly wounded soldier would battle for the rest of his life.

Had my father survived long enough to see me to adulthood, he also might have issued that admonishment about alcohol to me. Perhaps by the time he wrote his sister, he felt the numbing tug of drink that he couldn't control. He hinted at it when the doctors had been administering medications in advance of one of his surgeries and he felt the stew of painkillers taking over: "Thorness, you better stop this," he recounted in a letter to Shirley, "you know how disastrous the results are when you imbibe too much." Had he been waiting there during my late-night returns home in high school, rather than my quietly concerned mother, surely my weekend carousing would have unfolded differently.

Even though he was gone long before my high school years, at some level I received his tortured message. Although it would be decades before I'd read his admissions and admonitions in the letters, the warning of his example lingered in me constantly. Even if, as a boy, I'd never truly understood what had happened to my father, I feared the disease would be passed down. I would consider, in the glow of happy hour drinks with friends or wine over dinner, whether my alcohol use presaged a turn toward abuse. Was I susceptible? Could it damage my health and ripple out destructively to my family and life? As I came into adulthood, I resolved to keep clear-eyed about my own relationship with alcohol, and his lesson has been a significant influence, as I've never felt that it gripped me as it did my father after his marathon of hospital stays and disabled life.

Erick would endure two surgeries, six weeks apart, in the fall of 1944 before being furloughed again for the holiday trip home. But in 1945, two more operations in January and August, bookended by two-month furloughs, would continue his medical odyssey.

Life must have been tedious for Erick at that hospital, I thought, recalling that small pack of family letters that I combed through for clues to his war and life. Movies shown in the evening, marathon card games, or the occasional USO show could distract them, but the nights out to go "downtown" disgusted him. The boys (or "the cripples," as he once called them) would get drunk and "fight the battle of Springfield" or meet up with girls, and his girl was waiting at home, so he wanted none of that.

Meanwhile, life was moving on for family and friends. On his Christmas furlough in 1944 when he met Shirley, he had "stood up" for his best friend Rueben when he married his sweetheart, Arlene Snydal. "Yes, Erick, I am sort of settled down and even feel kind of married now," the bridegroom wrote in February 1945. He lamented that his biggest problem with the new situation was "to have to get up the next day," surely intended to give his bachelor friend a chuckle. "I am convinced now that for the first 2 or 3 months a guy shouldn't ever get out of bed except maybe to eat some eggs now and then." But then his buddy got more direct, going for the belly laugh. "I've got a sad story to tell you. You see I always figured I was good enough a man to produce at least 2 or 3 kids, but about 3 weeks ago I had to admit defeat, as hard as we tried it turned out [to] be only an overgrown BOIL on Arlene's hind end. I thought it would be a 15-pound boy." He demurred on providing more insights into married life, saying, "I am afraid this letter might have to endure censorship before I get it into the envelope."

By spring Erick was anticipating another furlough but wrote to Helen about hearing the news of President Franklin D. Roosevelt's death: "That was quite a shock but it makes us realize that life is pretty uncertain. The high as well as the rest must take that last trip." As such, "Army life" continued for Erick during his medical stays. His scant journal entries recorded the names of his commanding officer at every hospital "posting." Returning to Springfield in 1945, he was reassigned to a bed at the State Teachers College, which had been commandeered for use by rehabilitating soldiers due to the continuous influx of the injured. The school was "a pretty good deal," he told Helen, "except that we have reveille at 6:30 and then we have to stand retreat in the evening." The days evidently began and ended too early.

"Coming back to Army life now," he wrote to his folks in July 1945, "after being home so long is almost worse than when I first went into the Army. I sure hope I get out but they don't seem to be in a hurry about releasing any of these boys, so I may be stuck here for a while too." He received what would be his final operation on August 21, 1945, and wrote to Helen the next day that his leg was in a splint and he was "feeling fine." The surgery had been delayed first because he'd had an infection in his leg that had to clear and then because "everybody was celebrating Victory so they didn't have enough help to do it then." The Germans had surrendered on May 8, 1945, but it wasn't until August 14 that the Japanese accepted the terms of the Potsdam Agreement and unconditionally surrendered, bringing an end to further challenges from any of the Axis powers. The commotion in the hospital on "V-J Day," he wrote to his folks, was a din akin to the sound of the Anzio battle. Finally, it was time to bring the troops home.

Erick was released, with an honorable discharge and a steel brace for a "drop foot" from severed nerves that did not respond to surgeries or therapies, on February 15, 1946. He was about a month shy of his thirty-fourth birthday.

Chapter 40

June 2011

I thought about Dakota as we walked Rome's ancient cobbles for one last visit before our return home. I shouldered through a crowd, wondering what commemorations were really all about. Spectators would line the curbs to watch for something special coming down the center of the street, people marched in step, bands played, and smiling dignitaries would wave from atop shined-up vehicles. The impetus seemed to come from a deep desire for ceremony.

We had reached the end of our road from Anzio to Rome, visiting historic sites with Force families, trekking through ancient hill towns, and hiking along the highways and byways of the Anzio farmland, an invisible battlefield. As an auspicious anniversary of Rome's liberation—June 4—approached, I heard of a commemorative parade to be held in the city and resolved to attend the Sunday morning event. Our Zagarolo host, Ivano, enthusiastically offered to take us on the outing. I suggested to him that Susie and I could just take the train to Rome for the day, surely a light day on the commuter rail. Also, that was his traditional day of rest, and he'd commented that Terhi had wanted him to take some time off. He was visibly drained from burning the candle at both ends to run the B and B. But his other guests had moved on, so we were the only ones in residence, and accompanying us on my war explorations had whetted his appetite for history. So I happily accepted, and he was waiting behind the wheel of his car when we came out of our room.

He was concerned about the traffic near the Vittoriano, the national monument named after King Vittorio Emmanuele II, the ruler who had unified Italy. That would be the prime viewing spot for the parade—if there was indeed to be a parade with the commemorative event. Details were sketchy, but we did know that, whatever was happening, the Force's Italian historian, Gianni Blasi, was to give a speech, and there would be a general from the Italian military speaking as well. So we entered the city on a circuitous route, getting off Il Racordo well before hitting the inner circle, skimming along side streets and passing by the Porto Maggiore until we got to the neighborhood south of Termini.

As we skirted the train station, twin dark statues appeared in the distance, and I recognized them as the sculptures atop the Vittoriano—identical images of the winged goddess Victoria riding in a chariot pulled by four horses. Ivano slowed the car, seeing the street ahead was blocked. Sure enough, roads had been closed for the event. He lucked into a parking spot, and not wanting to miss anything, we started a fast walk toward the proceedings. Ivano was concerned that our casual preparation had made us late and that the trip would be a waste if we missed the speeches. As we approached, I could see the Colosseum's crumbling archways filling the cross street ahead of us like a smile full of broken teeth. In front of the quintessential Roman ruin ran Via Labianca, a wide thoroughfare that became the Via dei Fori Imperiali—and that significant arterial was the parade route that would pass the Vittoriano.

We reached the piazza outside the Vittoriano. The cleared street was lined with spectators. Gazing up the banks of broad marble steps, I looked over the Tomb of the Unknown Soldier, with its flickering eternal flame that sat dead center on the monument's front wall. The street was normally so rife with traffic that tourists stuck to the crosswalks at stoplights and even shied away from the sidewalk near the curb so as not to get too close to the onrushing vehicles. For the event, however, onlookers crowded onto the lanes. Over my left shoulder the road curved gently toward the glorious ruin of the Colosseum, whose graceful curves defined the arc of the street. Looking over the gladiatorial amphitheater, my eyes traveled quickly from the sweep of its intact wall through its hollow rows of arches to the crumbled outer wall that stairstepped down in a jagged line to the ground. The grand, decrepit Colosseum—which one American soldier, upon first seeing it during the liberating march into Rome, was heard to have said something like "Oh, no, they got this too!"—was far from the only piece of ancient history visible along the boulevard. Directly across from the Vittoriano sat Trajan's Column and the ruins of Trajan's Forum, one of Rome's original marketplaces. The column, one hundred feet of intricately carved marble erected to commemorate a war triumph, still towered over its plaza, topped by a statue of St. Peter. The market buildings, though now in ruin, must have been a fine gathering place. So just as I mused on the value of commemorative events, I realized that we stood on land once ruled by a world-conquering warrior empire, in the shadow of a battle zone created so that deadly "games" could be enjoyed by spectators, and in view of monuments to previous wars and fallen soldiers. All of it topped, as are so many historical artifacts, by religious iconography. And there we stood to commemorate yet another conflagration, the most terrible conflict of the modern era, fueled not in the name of religion but due to the xenophobic visions of a madman. My attitudes toward government, conflicts, religion, and memorials all swirled above my curiosity about the auspicious day.

As we waited for the speech of a military man and the rolling display of armaments, I took my mind off the day's events to appreciate the city's other nearby treasures. On the near side of the Colosseum sat the facade of an even older civic treasure, the Roman Forum, the center of ancient city life and site of Rome's earliest buildings. Prominent among the excavated ruins, sitting two stories below street level, was the crumbled front of an ancient temple, facing away from the street and invisible to the throngs on the sidewalk above. But climb a bit on the Via dei Fori Imperiali, which made its way to Capitoline Hill, and the grandeur of the Forum became visible. Massive blocks strewn about implied the presence of toppled temples, and one could compare architectural styles through the ages by taking a sweeping gaze across the site.

Capitoline Hill above Piazza Vittorio Emmanuele also held the utmost significance to the city, both old and new. City administrative agencies and a generous plaza, often the location of ceremonial events, were to be found there. Two museums dedicated to the history of the city could be visited, as could some of the most impressive statuary in Rome, from emperors to pantheistic gods. Stately white marble buildings ringed a red-tiled plaza, and between the buildings were some of the best city vistas. The Vatican filled one view between giant statues anchoring the Michelangelo-designed steps and plaza, a broad promenade connecting the municipal seat of power with the most ancient neighborhoods of Rome.

Surrounded by two thousand years of history, we waited on the piazza to take part in the commemoration of the liberation of Rome, the most recent conflict commenced to preserve all that grandeur. We stepped onto the street and amazed ourselves by walking down its broad traffic lanes, a feat that on any other day would have resulted in a hospital visit, if you were lucky. Vendors offered cold drinks to ward off the already hot sun, and people clustered along the fringes under bits of shade cast by trees or buildings.

In front of the Vittoriano, a boxy platform had been erected, with rows of red padded chairs facing the street. The structure was covered to shield dignitaries from the sun, and a red and gold fringe edged the angled awning. Spectators were sitting on the broad steps to one side of the square, under a smattering of shade trees. A military band, perhaps a dozen musicians, stood near the platform, in front of which people were milling, some in uniforms, others in suits. Gianni, in a blue blazer and tie, stood among them. We stepped up and said hello to him, introducing Ivano. He expressed resigned disgust at the lackadaisical pace of the event, which he told us was, amazingly, the first public commemoration of Rome's liberation that had ever been held. It seemed incredible, as it had been nearly seven decades since the Allies walked those worn cobbles.

On the sidewalk in front of the Vittoriano, whose white marble blazed so harshly against the sun that we were forced to squint and shade our eyes, was a photo exhibit, large prints on easels. Scenes from the liberation were on display, with soldiers in jeeps being kissed by women, handing out food, or marching decisively up the steps to the ancient city hall. One telling image showed soldiers on the "Mussolini balcony" across this square, where Il Duce had stepped out many times from a room high in the marble monument to address crowds of Fascist supporters. In another picture, a soldier held his arm high, initially calling to mind the Nazi or Fascist salute, except that his fist was closed and his elbow had a slight bend, indicating that he was caught in midgesture; it was an Allied fist pump of victory.

While we discussed the photos and waited for the event to begin, Gianni asked us about our plans after the event. Since we had none, he invited us to join him for the afternoon down in his home region near Cassino. We would ride with him and spend the day examining the history of the area, and he would send us back to Zagarolo by train. We agreed, happy to have more direction beyond our idea of wandering Rome for the day. Ivano was relieved, as he could leave us after the parade and enjoy the remains of his rest day.

Finally, the event got underway. The featured speaker, resplendent in uniform and ribbons, droned exhaustively about the battle from Sicily and Naples to Anzio that set the stage for the freeing of Rome. I heard enough place-names to recognize the recounting of significant military actions, and Ivano contributed the occasional translation. Looking around, it seemed that most of the growing throng of attendees were tourists (which no doubt could be said about any gathering in the old city), so it was curious that this event was presented only in Italian, especially given the focus of the celebration: the Americans entering Rome. Perhaps that contributed to Ivano's visible indifference and Gianni's frustration. Clearly our Italian history professor was also agitated because, due to the general's exhaustive oratory, he was not able to speak at all. I imagined his talk would have been in English and no doubt would have mentioned his particular interest, the FSSF.

Then the parade came at us in waves: a series of military vehicles and people dressed as troops of the day. The military band continued to play, interspersing Italian and American marching songs (heavy on John Phillips Sousa) with popular swing music of the era (heavy on Glenn Miller). The result was festive marching and parading, and the crowd of spectators swelled to see the olive-drab jeeps, trucks, and DUKWs of the U.S. Army, interspersed with high-stepping companies of soldiers or, more likely, civilian war buffs dressed in their period costumes. Gianni explained that all the vehicles were privately owned and maintained by people with a strong interest in the war. A jeep idled by with the distinctive red arrowhead emblem of the Force stenciled on its olive green door. Then I began to notice that emblem of the Braves on more than a few uniforms. Erick's unit was well represented.

After the parade, we walked among the vehicles, snapping pictures as Gianni spoke to some of the collectors and also to dignitaries, like Her Majesty's military attaché from the British government, bedecked in his ceremonial dress uniform. As the jeeps and spectators trailed away, we motored south toward Cassino, reclining in Gianni's air-conditioned sedan, the verdant countryside flying by beneath a blue sky. The purple hills of the Lepinis creased the landscape between the road and the coast. We drove past and crossed over many of the areas where we had just walked, which caused a bit of frisson in my brain.

Gianni led us on a stroll through his small hometown, sharing his love of history and architecture, pointing out clues to each era in the stone. As the shadows lengthened, we relaxed in a plaza while he stepped away to, of all things, cast his vote. It was coincidentally the day of municipal elections in the village. Enjoying one more pistachio gelato and eyeing the flow of life that filled the square, Rome's intensity faded, as did the commemoration, and my thoughts strayed from my father's war. I commented to Susie that the people shopping and chatting and voting, hand in hand with their ice cream cones, surely retained only a glimmer of what had happened there two generations before. Those who had lived through it would perhaps be thankful for memories that had dimmed with the decades. If you grew up hearing about it endlessly from teachers and elders, you too might be ready to file those events into a closed drawer in the back of your mind. Paradoxically, the closer I got to the physical war—on the ground, in the chambers where the troops bunked, or next to a restored jeep and a uniform emblazoned with the red arrowhead—the more I felt it recede in my mind. Revisiting had populated the details of history, but the inevitable chasm of time passage distanced me from seeing life as it must have been lived. How do you bring closer a fading memory when overwhelmed by the immediacy of ongoing life?

Changing demographics also joined with time in removing war from our daily lives. Fewer sons of the current generation search military history for the actions of their parents. In World War II, 8.6 percent of the U.S. population served in the armed forces. That number has shrunk to just one-half of 1 percent. Fewer Americans will experience the sadness of a lost loved one or a life changed forever by a permanent disability. At the same time, a greater percentage of soldiers seeing action—an awful turn of phrase—are coming back injured rather than dying on the battlefield due to the ways of modern warfare and its weaponry.

I thought of the sons of today's soldiers, who I imagined to be much more conflicted about their fathers' roles in the inevitable current war. Those soldiers wouldn't be talking either, cast mute by . . . horror? Trauma? Shame? What one word could convey a psychological condition that encompasses all three?

Back in my armchair in Seattle, I considered my connection to war as I read the war account of another North Dakotan who also coincidentally shared my father's name, the journalist Eric Sevareid. He waded through the European theater observing and reporting for CBS News beginning in 1939. In his broadcasts and then in the memoir *Not So Wild a Dream*, published shortly after the war, he brought the distant battles home.

> War happens inside a man. It happens to one man alone. It can never be communicated. That is the tragedy—and perhaps the blessing. A thousand ghastly wounds are really only one. A million martyred lives leave an empty place at only one family table. That is why, at bottom, people can let wars happen, and that is why nations survive them and carry on. And, I am sorry to say, that is also why in a certain sense you and your sons from the war will be forever strangers.

A tightness formed in my throat. I imagined my grandfather listening to that Dakota boy's grim proclamations come through the mesh-covered speaker on his big radio, knowing that man was the same age as his soldier son and also born to Norwegian immigrants such as himself. In those words, I could picture my father: *Things will never be the same, and you will never understand.* I saw the empty place at our dinner table, recalled the distance between us. I remembered it through a boy's eyes, thinking that my age prevented me from connecting with adults. But because Sevareid's accounts sprang from firsthand observations and a direct understanding of the attitudes and actions of the American soldier, I considered I had misinterpreted the reason for that distance.

The war had become his very life; these men were all his world. Here with them under the dark moon, in the middle of the hellish noise, in this moment when his comrades prepared to challenge the unknown, he was intensely alive. Elsewhere, he was half-dead. And, I thought, there will be many like this man, many who will remain but half-alive when all this is ended.

How do you define "half-alive"? How does it manifest in everyday actions? Perhaps in the going about of work without conviction or the inability to aspire beyond the basic necessities. I saw my father in that concept, working menial jobs around our hometown, helping out on the family farm but never gaining ownership of it. Perhaps in succumbing to the limitations that serious war wounds laid upon you, leaving you crippled physically as well as mentally. That would be a powerful limiting factor, combining a loss of confidence with the reduced expectations of others who see the limp and the long face. Perhaps in the desire to escape from day-to-day reality through the dark, destructive force of alcohol served up in a dusty, neon-lit room populated with similar lost souls.

> I suspect many soldiers, too, felt what I now felt: a kind of dull satisfaction, a weary incapacity for further stimulation, a desire to go home and not have to think about it any more—and a vague wondering whether I could ever cease thinking about it as long as I lived.

How often was the war not on my father's mind? I imagined that I could have seen it behind his distant gaze when he sat at the wheel of the farm truck. I suspected the cause when he cried out in his sleep as he napped midday on the sagging couch, one arm thrown over his eyes. I sensed it went with him when he left the house and came back in with the slamming of the door. Only Erick knew, as he went about his solitary duties on the farm or drove the dusty roads looking across the flat orange horizon.

> I thought: "Your life has so conditioned you that you can function only in the achieving and are unfitted for the achievement. In your own way you bear the curse of the Commando major: you live only in struggle, and the triumph leaves you bored. You are capable only of the motions of life and not of its substance. Either private seeds or your times have left you rootless, as unfitted for stability as a fish for dry land."

Did triumph, or the idea of it, leave my father bored with the fluttering of life? Was it the limitations of a postwar economy that did not ripple abundance onto the northern prairie that prevented him from finding a calling or a vocation where he could prosper? What thoughts would go through his mind as he served the motorists behind the pump at the gas station he briefly owned or as he talked to a county roads administrator about the job of keeping the ditches mowed and cleared?

> I was thirty-two. Yet I had a curious feeling of age, as though I had lived through a lifetime, not merely through my youth. In a special but true sense, I had. For the age of man is reckoned in eras as well as in years, and what I had vaguely sensed as a student was true: history had been moving in geometric proportions. History is speeding up, telescoping upon itself, so that the time of one man in life is no longer confined within one era.

Born in the same year, tested through international travels and violent war, the perspective of age had come early to both of those men named for a redheaded Viking. Folded in was a certain type of wisdom, certainly a weariness, and very probably a feeling that nothing to come in their lives would ever match the horribleness and grandeur of what they had been through. Truly, both had set foot in two eras: the prairie upbringing, where events of great cities or other countries were as foreign as an ocean view, followed by the cacophonous, deadly march to set the world straight when it had gone terribly wrong and all the feelings and experiences one lone speck of a person would have when set down in the middle of such a roaring conflagration.

> In Velva and everywhere the folks are the same, except for this: that a boy from Velva, who also swam in the brown river and saw the rim of the world along the horizon of the prairie, now lies buried in a place called Anzio of which his sixth-grade geography book showed no pictures.

I became certain that part of my father remained in Anzio, crushed among the scrabbled slit trenches along the Mussolini Canal, cast echoing like a call to a dying comrade through the stunted trees clinging to Monte la Difensa, or smeared red beneath a donkey's hoof in the town square of bomb-ravaged

Colleferro. He would have to leave it there, because carrying it home would have been madness. Of course, he was not successful in leaving it on the battlefield, either the horrible memories or indelible images of war. Passing through the quiet arenas of the war, I could only conjecture and surmise the feelings of the ghosts of those soldiers when seeing where they walked and knowing how they fought. Some of them were still there, and not just under the clipped grass and blazing white crosses in the American cemetery. There's a bit of Epping, North Dakota, out in the fields there too.

Once, I came across a quote from the Roman philosopher Cicero, inscribed above the door of a university library: "He who knows only his own generation remains always a child." Perhaps my father and uncountable numbers of other young men had been thrust out of their generation too fast in the course of such world-changing events brought by the war. Perhaps his son, no matter how far the journey in the imprints of his father's boots, could never escape childhood.

For a farmer, events are few, and excitement only occasionally interrupts the predictable routine. In my parents' youth, world affairs entered the atmosphere around them on twice-daily radio news reports and in the smudged typeset column of a weekly newspaper. The world of the weather and the chickens and the rusty tractor gears was much more immediate than the workings of government or ravings of madmen. I could not deny an allure to that simple existence—or its perceived simplicity—while living through another warp of cultural change. It's no doubt a generational feeling, often after attaining a certain age, that society was changing too fast, and things were better in simpler times. I am my stoic father's son and could see myself facing the prairie wind, happily unspeaking, not feeling the need to profess a conclusion.

I realized that sometimes I wanted the world to slow down, come to its senses, society just fading into the background. Or rather, I wanted to slip away, let others handle the pressing issues or feel the urgency of coming challenges. I had lived beyond the age attained by my father, and I wondered if he also had reached that point of perspective. The everlasting demons of war surely caused him to withdraw from a problematic society. But it's likely that, in his day, most men were not as predisposed to the inward gaze as today. You might deserve a hero's welcome, but you received your lot in life, no thanks beyond a moment's applause.

When I finished my Italy trip on the banks of the Tiber in Rome, I realized that my search for a better understanding of my father had been percolating for nearly a decade. Although I did not believe that ten years of sliding into middle age had significantly altered my worldview, I did feel that the pathway toward guiding principles for living had become clearer, due in part to my quest to rediscover my father and honor my mother's life after her passing. From him came the conundrum of courage and resignation, while from her came loyalty and perseverance. All those traits and more coexisted in me. They gave what they had to bring me up, and I owed a debt to that effort. Perhaps with another decade, or five, I would come to understand how their actions had played out in my approach to life.

Inevitably, Sevareid's reporting brought to mind American armed forces currently in the news, at the time battling multiple foes in Afghanistan and Iraq. The justification for those wars ranged from a vow for revenge over the 9/11 terrorist attacks to a set of political motivations that were as murky as the swirling waters of the river in the darkness beneath that Tiber bridge. What would Erick have made of those wars? Would he have deemed it worth the risk to create another generation of shattered soldiers and broken families? Did I learn enough from him to apply his ethics? I pictured him restless on the sagging couch, eyes shielded by his forearm, in the grip of memory. At that realization, my decade-long effort seemed as pointless as a letter to the president demanding a stop to war. But perhaps the quest to find guidance from a long-lost father was itself the lesson. My questions were about not who he was but rather what he would teach me, and I hoped for peace for future children of those current soldiers feeling the need to set out upon a path like mine.

The biggest parade in my hometown was not held to honor veterans. Early winters would often result in weather unfriendly to outdoor celebrations, so even Halloween trick-or-treating required me to wear a parka over my costume. Veteran's Day was honored in the newspaper and at the VFW hall—and in a weekend of retail sales. Neither did Independence Day claim the biggest parade. On July 4, cars formed conga lines out to a park on the edge of town for a fireworks display at dusk. But the town would come out in droves for Band Day, a celebration of spring featuring high school bands marching down Main Street. It vied with New York's post-Thanksgiving parade for greatest acclaim, but with the latest farm implements instead of balloon animals and a beauty pageant winner replacing Santa Claus. The VFW would have a convertible idling along the parade route with a couple of vets waving from the back seat and a few more, in their dress uniforms, marching alongside. Erick never sat in that car or even walked next to it.

My exploration of Dad's war and his history had instilled in me a yearning for recognition and commemoration of his efforts, and yet I could not conjure an image of him being saluted or applauded in public. I had stood in the crowd of tourists in Rome and watched the red arrowhead pass by on uniforms and jeeps, but I had not seen my father. Rather, I felt him standing next to me, our shoulders touching, a deep inhalation coming as he contemplated the results of his efforts, of the Force's accomplishments. And in me, pride swelled, not for their feats and accolades, but for the character of a man who would step into line with that group, set about his tasks, and endure the life-altering results of that determination, that bravery. Most Americans are not asked by their country to step up and put their lives on the line. My life had been free of such a challenge. No parades or salutes for me. But my father's example had guided my life in unseen ways, in everyday decisions. He had been there, I realized, a shadow cast along the path in front of me that I would step toward over and over, trying to show that I had learned how to stand up straight, working to keep up the pace.

FURTHER READING

Adleman, Robert H., and George Walton. *The Devil's Brigade.* Annapolis MD: Naval Institute Press, 1966.
Allen, William L. *Anzio: Edge of Disaster.* New York: E. P. Dutton, 1978.
Atkinson, Rick. *The Day of Battle: The War in Sicily and Italy, 1943–1944.* New York: Henry Holt, 2007.
Burhans, Robert D. (lt. col.). *The First Special Service Force: A War History of the North Americans, 1942–1944.* Washington DC: Infantry Journal Press, 1947.
Clark, Lloyd. *Anzio: Italy and the Battle for Rome—1944.* New York: Grove, 2006.
David, Saul. *The Force: The Legendary Special Ops Unit and WWII's Mission Impossible.* New York: Hachette, 2019.
Joyce, Ken. *Crimson Spearhead: First Special Service Force History, Uniforms, Insignia.* Ottawa ON: Service Publications, 2010.
Joyce, Kenneth H. *Snow Plough and the Jupiter Deception.* St. Catharines ON: Vanwell, 2006.
Pyle, Ernie. *Brave Men.* New York: Henry Holt, 1944.
Ross, Robert Todd. *The Supercommandos, First Special Service Force, 1942–1944: An Illustrated History.* Atglen PA: Schiffer Military History, 2000.
Sevareid, Eric. *Not So Wild a Dream.* New York: Atheneum, 1976.
Springer, Joseph A. *The Black Devil Brigade: The True Story of the First Special Service Force.* Pacifica CA: Pacific Military History, 2001.
Underhill, Adna H. (col., ret.). *The Force.* Tucson: Arizona Monographs, 1994.